Advance Praise for
GO GLOBAL

"Oh, if only my children were young again! This curriculum is exactly what I was looking for so many years ago and would have saved me hours of time spent planning my own literature-based, hands-on geography lessons. Its gentle approach to teaching serious geography concepts through meaningful work is perfect. Children will find geography to be such a joyful subject as they journey through good books and complete worthwhile activities. Parents will be thankful for the ease of use and how it can seamlessly draw multiple ages of children together for learning."

—**Cindy West**, speaker, author of *Homeschooling Gifted Kids*, and writer at OurJourneyWestward.com

"*GO GLOBAL* is just the kind of curriculum we love for young boys—literature-heavy and movement-rich. Heather and Colene understand children and they've created a geography curriculum that kids will love and that will help them to love learning. You'll enjoy it as much as your children, too!"

—**Hal & Melanie Young**, award-winning authors of *Raising Real Men*

"I have been spatially and geographically challenged for as long as I can remember—*GO GLOBAL* looks like just the thing that may have given me 'hooks' on which to hang my learning about the world around me and the cultures we studied! Colene and Heather have compiled a vast selection of quality books for perusal and read-alouds, as well as activities to make cultural and geographical literacy come alive for various levels of learners. What a gift to have all these great book lists and hands-on suggestions all in one place, lesson-planned out by the week for the busy parent who wants the structure, or simply as a buffet of choices for the more adventurous teacher."

—**Vicki Bentley**, mom of many, HSLDA Educational Consultant, author of *Home Education 101: A Mentoring Program for New Homeschoolers*, EverydayHomemaking.com

"What Heather Haupt and Colene Lewis have created in *GO GLOBAL* is a comprehensive, well-paced, and winsome guide to learning about geography and culture together with your young student. The complementary keys to primary learning—story and hands-on experience—are the foundation of this excellent curriculum. Utilizing both classic and recent literature, you and your child will enjoy stories that engage the imagination and feed the voracious appetite that youngsters have for learning, especially for whatever is novel, adventurous, and exotic! (Frankly, I would purchase this curriculum solely for the excellent listing of Christmas and holiday books they have curated!) Haupt and Lewis pay careful attention to the brain-body connection, as well, incorporating a wide variety of activities that enlist the child's senses and involve movement and physicality. This is not a 'simply insert and press play' curriculum; *GO GLOBAL* will get you and your child cuddling on the couch, extending learning beyond the school table, and experiencing wonder together at the exciting world we live in!"

—**Cindy Duell**, AZ Families for Home Education Board of Directors, homeschool mom since 2000

"Moms and children cannot help but be excited as they actively learn (and retain!) knowledge of the wonders of God's good world. This cultural and physical geography adventure will captivate every child and the clear, minimal prep will relieve busy moms."

—Dr. Brian and Betsy Ray, homeschool pioneers and researchers at NHERI.org

"If anyone understands the fine art of how to teach young children in an effective and engaging way, it is Heather Haupt and Colene Lewis. With *GO GLOBAL*, they gently introduce geographical awareness by engaging children in activities that are both fun and rich in learning. Geography is everywhere and learning about it is a part of faith-building. *GO GLOBAL* sets a strong foundation not only for children to understand where people, continents and oceans are in the world, it will help them understand their own place in it as designed by their Creator."

—Marcy Crabtree, homeschool mom, owner of the popular homeschool blog, BenandMe.com

"One of the many benefits of homeschooling is being able to teach more than one subject at a time. *GO GLOBAL* is IDEAL for this! Not only do our 5–8-year-olds learn about the world they live in, they are exposed to literature rich books and plenty of movement/hands on activities which open up their minds to absorb so much more of what they are learning. *GO GLOBAL* includes prompting questions that will help engage our kids in conversations that are far beyond informational. They invite us to into the process of teaching our kids how to think for themselves. The preparation is minimal. The format is simple, yet the possibilities are wide open for going whatever direction our children find interesting!"

—Durenda Wilson, author of *The Unhurried Homeschooler*, speaker, podcaster, and writer at DurendaWilson.com

"Rarely can I find a curriculum that combines my desire to inspire learning through well-written, language-rich literature and my kids' desire to wiggle. *GO GLOBAL* masterfully pairs them both. Packed with mom-tested lessons and kid-approved activities, this curriculum is an incredible gift to the homeschooling community and will, no doubt, help moms cultivate a sense of curiosity and lead their children to a deeper understanding and appreciation for other countries and their cultures."

—Jamie Erickson, homeschooling mom of 5 and author of
Homeschool Bravely: How to Squash Doubt, Trust God, and Teach Your Child With Confidence

GO GLOBAL

A LITERATURE-HEAVY, MOVEMENT-RICH
LEARNING ADVENTURE

HEATHER HAUPT & COLENE LEWIS

Copyright © 2019

Go Global
A Literature-Heavy, Movement-Rich Learning Adventure
Heather Haupt and Colene Lewis

All rights reserved. No part of this publication may be reproduced, distributed, or transmitted in any form or by any means, including photocopying, recording, or other electronic or mechanical methods, without the prior written permission of the publisher, except in the case of brief quotations embodied in reviews and certain other non-commercial uses permitted by copyright law.

CL Publishing
P.O. Box 292284
Lewisville, TX 75067-9998
CultivatedLearning.org

ISBN: 978-0-9903442-1-6 (print)

Ordering Information:

Special discounts are available on quantity purchases by corporations, retailers, co-ops, and schools.

For details, contact

info@cultivatedlearning.org

Publishing and Design Services: MartinPublishingServices.com
Illustrator: Katie Beth Krueger, katiecreates@gmail.com, Instagram @azkatiebee

GO GLOBAL

Introduction

Week 1   Overview—Maps and Globe 11

Week 2   Overview—Continents and Oceans 17

Week 3   North America—The United States of America 24

Week 4   North America—Your State 32

Week 5   North America—Canada 35

Week 6   North America—Mexico 45

Week 7   *Catch Up or Take a Break*

Week 8   South America—General and Andes Mountains 54

Week 9   South America—Amazon Rainforest, Part I 60

Week 10   South America—Amazon Rainforest, Part II 70

Week 11   South America—Pampas and People 79

Week 12   *Catch Up or Take a Break*

Week 13   Antarctica—Part I 84

Week 14   Antarctica—Part II 90

Week 15   Christmas Around the World 95

Week 16   Africa—Sahara Desert, Nile River, and Ancient Egypt 102

Week 17   Africa—Savanna and East Rift 114

Week 18   Africa—Savanna and Coastal Bulge..121

Week 19   Africa—Jungle and South Africa 127

Week 20   *Catch Up or Take a Break*

Week 21	Europe—General and France	134
Week 22	Europe—Spain	142
Week 23	Europe—British Isles	149
Week 24	Europe—Italy	155
Week 25	Europe—Germany	163
Week 26	*Catch Up or Take a Break*	
Week 27	Asia—Russia	172
Week 28	Asia—The Middle East	181
Week 29	Asia—India	190
Week 30	Asia—China	199
Week 31	Asia—Japan	207
Week 32	*Catch Up or Take a Break*	
Week 33	Australia—Animals	214
Week 34	Australia—Coral Reef and Culture	223
Week 35	The World—Wrap-up, Part I	230
Week 36	The World—Wrap-up, Part II	235
Appendix	How to Co-op	237
Acknowledgements		239

INTRODUCTION

GETTING THE BIG PICTURE

You and your child(ren) are about to embark on an amazing journey of discovery and delight as they learn about their place in this great big world. From there you will explore the peoples, cultures, animals, and geography found around the globe.

Learning one's place in this world and having a strong geographical awareness is foundational to future learning because it provides context to so much that happens in history. Everyone is affected by geography, culture, weather. For instance, studying the pioneers and westward expansion comes alive when one has a greater understanding of the vast undertaking these pioneers took up to make the trek across a continent.

Learning is laid down in layers. Over time we build understanding and appreciation of the world around us across both time and space. The aim of *GO GLOBAL* is to facilitate the laying down of this layer of understanding in powerful, developmentally appropriate ways—utilizing the power of narrative and the effectiveness of involving the whole body in the learning process. Having a literature-heavy, movement-rich approach maximizes learning potential at this age because it inspires a play-based approach to learning. Children remember stories far more than isolated facts because they engage the imagination. Their minds are wired to absorb narrative. When children's whole bodies get up and actively participate in the learning process their enjoyment and retention of what they are learning sky rockets. This combination of good books and movement makes learning stick.

A PHILOSOPHY OF EDUCATION, A PHILOSOPHY OF PARENTING

As parents, it is helpful to know *why* you do what you do. Knowing the why's and developing a philosophy of education provides a clear idea of where you want to go and how to direct your children.

Heather's parental goals are to raise kids who

1. Love God with their heart, soul, mind, and strength.
2. Love others.
3. Love learning and make it a life-long endeavor.
4. Are prepared for whatever they are called to do in life (a commitment to academic excellence).

Do you share these goals? If so, you will want to circle back to these goals as a parent and use them as a framework for making decisions in life. Will this help or hinder these goals? *GO GLOBAL* was written with this framework in mind.

Childhood is brief and yet full of many unique seasons. You have an opportunity to spend time with your children as you point out God's beautiful and diverse creation. Learning about this big world we live in provides an opportunity to learn about and appreciate other cultures. You have an opportunity to help your children understand that not only are THEY created in the image of God and worthy of love, care, and respect, but that ALL people are worthy of this kind of dignity.

GO GLOBAL was built upon a philosophy of education and parenting that recognizes that children are born with an innate desire to explore, discover, and learn about the world around them. The goal is to foster this love of learning and curiosity in order to equip children with the tools they will need to enjoy this life-long process of learning. Learning is not only for children, but for everyone. As you actively participate in the learning process your lives become characterized by a lifestyle of learning. It is truly a family affair!

Making learning a lifestyle means discarding the notion that learning takes place only at a desk or between the traditional school hours of 8am-2pm. There is time for seat work—though for younger children this should be kept to a minimum. For instance, children 4-5 years-of-age do not need more than one 10 to 15-minute segment of seatwork per day. By the time the child is 6 she can probably handle two 15 to 20-minute segments per day. But this doesn't mean that those are the only periods of learning. Powerful things happen when one embraces the idea of learning that is not limited to sitting at a desk with a writing implement in hand.

GO GLOBAL inspires and equips you and your children to learn as you are living life. Simple cultural dishes (like tacos for Mexico; rice with stir-fried vegetables for China; bananas, mangoes, papaya for South America) paired with conversation about the food and countries will heighten learning and build family relationships. Games (some played with the parent and some with siblings or alone) solidify learning. Dramatizing what they are learning happens with some encouragement, and then continues naturally. And of course, good books are crucial! Reading in the morning for "school", in the afternoon rest time, and at bed time will also increase both learning and the pleasure in learning.

You can transform into the family that learns all the time and everywhere—in the kitchen, on the sofa, outside. You can teach your children when you sit at home, when you walk along the way, when you lie down, and when you rise up! (Duet. 11:19)

RELATIONSHIPS ARE FOUNDATIONAL

Relationships are crucial. Children and adults thrive when they relate in healthy ways to those around them. But this kind of relating does not happen automatically. We live in a fallen world and must learn how to relate to one another. The job of parents is to lovingly help children learn what it means to live in community.

Homeschooling provides a beautiful opportunity to extend our family relationships into the learning sphere. It provides the flexibility to slow down and work on relationships, knowing that this relationship work prepares them for everything else. *GO GLOBAL* fosters a coming together daily, to huddle close, and enjoy great books together. It provides memory making moments playing and creating together in ways that both solidify learning and strengthen relationships. Powerful things happen when we learn alongside our children—both for them and for us. *GO GLOBAL* provides the inspiration and direction for making this a natural part of your life and will lay the foundation for the life-long learning adventure.

WHAT MAKES *GO GLOBAL* UNIQUE?

There is certainly no shortage of curriculum choices available to homeschool families today. *GO GLOBAL* is marked by key distinctives that together set it apart. It is a unit study type approach that incorporates the following four elements—literature-heavy, movement-rich, multi-level, and easy-to-use.

Each of these elements are utilized to provide a developmentally appropriate approach to learning. While everyone is wired to learn, young children's brains are wired differently than an older child or adult brain. Jean Piaget, Maria Montessori, Charlotte Mason, Rudolf Steiner, Raymond Moore, in addition to countless modern developmental psychologists are all in agreement that how a child learns in the first seven or so years is fundamentally different. They learn best primarily through play and in a more holistic, experience-based way.

The modern culture is focused on producing 'super-kids' and there is incredible pressure to introduce formal academics in the hopes of giving your child an edge. Not only is there no research to back up this focus on formal academics in the early years, there is considerable evidence that it can indeed harm a child and crush their ability and interest in learning. That is why the learning in *GO GLOBAL* is story-based, activity-rich, and play-full.

Children, especially young ones, are CURIOUS. This curiosity can propel learning forward. Rather than covering a lot of detailed information that the child will probably quickly forget, delve deeply and really learn something of interest. That is why *GO GLOBAL* will not cover every country—even ones that are important. An overview of the continent and a deeper look into just a few countries and/or cultures is more effective. If we skip a country or culture that is personally important to you, feel free to add or exchange. For instance, we cover China, but not Korea, or the Southeast Asia countries. If one of these other cultures is personally important to you, gather some books and draw your children into the richness of that culture. But resist the urge to skim over *all* of them. Don't lose the benefit that is found delving into one or two. Aim for a rich, deep learning experience, rather than a shallow, but expansive exposure. This is especially critical at this stage in a child's development!

With this concept of deep vs. wide in mind, let's explore the four major distinctives of *GO GLOBAL*.

1. LITERATURE-HEAVY

Narrative has a powerful influence in our lives—it can inspire us, inform us, and change our lives in seemingly effortless ways. There are few things more enjoyable than curling up on the couch to read good books with our children.

A good book is a delight to any age and can be read over and over again. The great educator Charlotte Mason, referred to these kinds of narrative-focused books as *living books*. Living books draw you in, causing you to want to read further because they are written in an engaging way. A living book can be either fiction or non-fiction. The passion comes through in the writing as a book draws you into the excitement by providing interesting information in an invigorating and engaging way.

GO GLOBAL equips you as the parent to provide great books, which prompts delightful and deep conversations, and leads to hours of play. The provided list of well-written books will draw your children into learning. Rather than dull, dry text books, read captivating stories that cause the people, places, and events to come alive! Rather than vocabulary-restricted, dumbed-down books, read rich stories that feed the heart and mind.

Thousands of books were read and vetted for *GO GLOBAL*. Each book that is recommended has been vetted for the following qualities:

- **Literary quality** (well-constructed sentences, vibrant images, rich vocabulary)
- **Academic content quality** (facts and information about the people and places in our world)
- **Artistic quality** (aesthetically pleasing and culturally enriching)
- **Spiritually true** (generally affirming truth as understood in the Judeo-Christian perspective).

Each week, three to five primary books are listed. An additional list of supplementary books is provided to include if desired and if you are able to find them. We suggest that you buy some of these books, but hopefully, most of the primary books will be available in the public library. Be prepared to read these books over and over again—perhaps not in one sitting, or even on the same day. Remember, there is power in reading a story multiple times and then playing with it.

A brief word on studying other religions. During your trip around the world, your children are going to "visit" lands that are different than theirs—perhaps hotter, colder, wetter, drier, hillier, flatter. And they will "meet" people who are different as well. Perhaps they will be richer or poorer, they will have different foods, different clothing, different homes, different skin colors, and different religions. Teach in such a way that will engender compassion, interest, and appreciation for different peoples. Children and adults should be respectful of people who believe differently. However, one needs to be careful to present information to children in an age-appropriate way. Young children should be taught the truth of their faith before they are taught the doctrines of other faiths. Books that broach religion-specific information are clearly indicated in *GO GLOBAL*. While the books listed do not encourage the worship of other gods, each family needs to decide what to present to their children. We suggest that if you choose to use these specific resources that you include a gracious and short discussion with your child about these religions.

A NOTE on library use. Before using the curriculum, look to see if your library has the primary books in their collection. If they do not, ask your librarian to order them. You should do this respectfully, letting them know that these are exceptional books, and that you believe their fine collection will be enhanced with these high-quality books. Do not have an entitlement attitude! And only ask for a handful at a time. Many libraries love to receive good book suggestions from their patrons. Asking for high quality books benefits not only yourselves, but also others.

Explore interlibrary loan to get some of these books if your library is not able to purchase them for you, or not able to purchase them quickly enough. Some libraries offer this as a free service.

2. MOVEMENT-RICH

Something powerful happens when our children move and interact with what they are learning about. They remember it. Movement wires the brain to learn. When we make learning truly multi-sensory and movement-rich, children understand and retain so much more.[1] Everyone benefits, children especially, from adding a little more movement into their day. While movement is beneficial for all children, there are some kids who absolutely MUST move to learn.

> *"Without experiences, there are no concepts.*
> *Without concepts there is no attention.*
> *Without attention, they don't know what you are talking about."*

This is the crux of what Dr. Jane Healy wrote about in *Endangered Minds: Why Children Don't Think and What We Can Do About It*. Children need learning to be concrete and relatable. This means they need to interact with and then touch real objects. They need time to play with these concrete facts so that they can make sense of them and cement learning into long-term memory. Play is the primary engine for learning in the first seven to eight years of a child's life, which is why *GO GLOBAL* grounds everything the child explores and learns about within the realm of play and activity. This should be more than simply adding a flat coloring sheet. In *GO GLOBAL*, each week has a number of activities to do with your children. While there are some art activities (especially three-dimensional ones) each week, the bulk of the activities involve play without added supplies. Reading great books to your children and providing a few prompts to get them "playing," lays the groundwork for learning and helps them make this kind of solidying play a regular part of their lives. Dramatization is one secret go-to way to make learning active. *GO GLOBAL* will help train you as the parent to recognize opportunities when you can incorporate this kind of play that makes such a big impact on long-term learning.

3. MULTI-LEVEL

Multi-level teaching means teaching more than one age at the same time. There are a few subjects that are grade specific because of their sequential and/or developmentally appropriate nature. Math and phonics would both fall into that category. But everything else is far more fluid. There are no hard and fast rules stating that world geography, for instance, must be covered during the 1st grade or the 5th grade year. This means that you as the parent/teacher have the flexibility to include all your kids in learning adventures such as this one.

For the homeschool family, multi-level teaching has its benefits when you have more than one school-aged child because it decreases the number of subjects you need to teach, oversee, grade, etc. In addition to making it easier on the parent, embracing a multi-level model of learning beautifully fosters a natural learning environment because the entire family is participating.

Embracing a multi-level model of education also benefits younger, non-school aged children as well. *GO GLOBAL* was written with the idea of laying a foundation of geographical awareness for future learning, but it is not something that must be covered at a specific age, making it perfect for your five to eight-year-old as well as any younger siblings. Because *GO GLOBAL* is built around the ideas of utilizing a literature-heavy (aka narrative-driven picture books) and a movement-rich (play-full) approach, it is easy to bring younger siblings along on the journey!

Anyone with a toddler or eager preschooler understands the perks of being able to include them in what-

---

[1] The Ultimate Guide to Brain Breaks explains *why* if you want more of a scientific explanation.

ever you are doing. Of course, their attention span is shorter and sometimes they "choose" to go off and play, but usually younger ones wants to be in on the action. The key for this age is welcoming them, but not requiring them to participate. You will be surprised by how much they will learn, simply by being in a rich home-learning environment where they are allowed and encouraged, but not required, to participate.

Those of you with younger children will want to experiment with what this looks like for your specific family dynamic. When there is the occasional messy project, you might see that you don't have the bandwidth and patience to help everyone at the same time and opt to do this during naptime so you can focus on your older children. If you have a nursing baby, you might opt to center much of the read-aloud time around your nursing schedule. Heather referred to this season in her life as "couch-schooling" since she spent so much of her day there with a hungry newborn! The key is to be flexible and look at what is working for you in this given season and then be willing and ready to adjust as the seasons of parenting continually change.

4. EASY-TO-USE

A hallmark of *GO GLOBAL* is the fact that it is easy-to-use. Many parents aspire to make learning fun, interactive, and impactful. You would not have bought this curriculum if you didn't love the idea of delving into great books and engaging in meaningful play with your children. But crafting these opportunities can be a lot of work. Our desire is to walk you through how to teach and how to make natural learning an everyday reality in your homes!

GO GLOBAL is designed to make this kind of learning as easy as possible with its open and go format with clear directions, carefully curated book selections, and fun, short, interactive lessons.

Each week follows the same easy to follow format, so you know what to expect. Extra activities and books are provided for those of you who want to go deeper and explore more.

Discussion questions are provided, so you can have ready-to-use ideas for making your reading more interactive. Directions are designed to be detailed enough so that you don't have to be distracted by the internet in search of tutorials or better instructions on how to accomplish things.

You will have access to the *GO GLOBAL* Resource pages where you will find embedded and linked videos specific to the content of *GO GLOBAL,* linked booklists to make for easy ordering, and step-by-step tutorials with full-color pictures of many of the projects.

Since each child is unique, *GO GLOBAL* is flexible. What works for one child, might not work for another. Taking an individualistic approach to education can really go a long way to engaging them in the learning process and helping them to succeed!

HOW *GO GLOBAL* WORKS

In the following pages you will find 36 weeks of lesson plans, with four days of lessons per week laid out. Between each continent studied, there is a built-in catch-up week. Each day is designed to last approximately two hours. Frequently, you will find that when children are immersed in good books and given ample time for unstructured play that they will take some of what they are reading and learning about into their spontaneous play times. When this happens, treasure it!

Each week will include the following four elements:

1. BIG PICTURE

Here is the content rich introduction to what you will be exploring with your children that week. Included will be an overview of the physical and/or cultural geography of that week's particular region. Concepts that your children should understand/learn are underlined. Other concepts are included for you to present if applicable, but do not need to be mastered by this age of children.

2. MATERIALS

We understand how busy you are as both a mom *and* homeschool parent. Our goal is to make life easier for you by giving you a heads up on what resources you will need to collect for that week.

Books that will be used that week will be listed here and divided into two categories—primary and secondary book recommendations. The primary books are strongly suggested and are usually specifically used in the curriculum. A larger list of secondary books is provided for those who want to delve deeper. You can read some of these extra books as you have time and the inclination.

The supplies needed for each week's activities are listed after the books. If you would like a list of all supplies for the entire year in one spot, be sure to go to the resource page on the website. (www.CultivatedLearning.org/GoResources)

3. FOUR DAILY LESSON PLANS

There are four days of lesson plans per week giving you a bonus day for other responsibilities and outings. Each day will include reading at least one outstanding book and one or more activities to explore the information presented.

The "everyone" activities are for all ages where foundational information is imparted. Some days have additional activities for older children. Many activities are simply reading and discussing what is read. This includes many open-ended questions to develop your child's reasoning and imagination.

Other activities are dramatization and play based—providing an easy and powerful way to foster understanding and promote long-term retention of what they are learning.

In addition, each week has one art/craft activity. Occasionally there will be more than one art/craft activity. You do not have to do *all* of these.

Everyone loves to eat! Many weeks also include some food from the area, making this a truly multisensory curriculum. We see and we listen to wonderful living books. We touch and move as we explore the countries, regions, and concepts. We speak about what we have learned. And we even smell and taste the food of the region.

The *GO GLOBAL* Resource page (**www.CultivatedLearning.org/GoResources**) To make everything easy for you we have collected any online resources you will need—including additional map downloads, step-by-step picture tutorials of the art projects, videos of the cultural dances your kids will be learning, etc.

We understand the frustration of wasting time looking for that supplemental video on You Tube or searching Pinterest for more detailed directions for projects. While it is impossible to anticipate everything that someone might need, we have pooled our collective busy mama brains to gather any needed additional resources here, so you have curated and "child-safe" resources that you can share with your kids to maximize learning this year!

The *GO GLOBAL* Resource page also will have links for additional printables, templates, and links for purchasing additional games such as Penguin Bingo and Australian Concentration.

You can also find all the books listed out for each section of *GO GLOBAL* here to make it easy to gather at the beginning of the year or send out as gift ideas for birthdays or Christmas. (We are firm believers in giving the gift of reading to our kids!)

4. *GO GLOBAL* GAME

You will want to be sure to purchase the *GO GLOBAL* Game. This game will be utilized throughout the year to reinforce both a big-picture understanding of the world's continents and oceans as well as provide an opportunity to add reviewing of your knowledge of the continents as you study them.

This is played "Twister" style. It starts out with placing right or left hands and feet on various continents but expands as they learn more to include the oceans, and then trivia questions about the various continents to change things up! Heather created this game for her kids when she first started pulling together what would become the curriculum you are holding now. It has remained a much loved and often played game over the years as well as a world map resource that gets pulled out when needed. The kids have mapped the Pilgrims' progress across the Atlantic, Ferdinand Magellan's first circumnavigation of the globe, and the map even helped answer a child's random question of why the family couldn't drive to Hawaii!

A WORD ON ACADEMIC VS. INTELLECTUAL DEVELOPMENT

In the early years learning doesn't have to be complicated. Children need some math instruction, a phonics/spelling program, and then something interesting to learn.

The phonics/spelling and math instruction encompass academic development. They focus on skill acquisition. This is important. But children at this age are also intensely curious about the world around them and feeding this desire by learning about interesting things helps to foster intellectual development. The intellect is developed as children are introduced to the world of ideas through stories and as they interact with what they are learning.

GO GLOBAL provides everything you need for the "interesting things to learn part" with its literature-heavy, movement-rich approach. This curriculum does not include phonics instruction or systematic math instruction. You will want to research and purchase those subjects separately. While the instruction in early skills is important, do not wipe yourself out doing the "basics" and skip the important content presented here. *GO GLOBAL* provides the opportunity for intellectual development as you learn about interesting things and discuss the world around you. Your children need to pursue the academic goals of learning how to read, but they also need exposure to books they will *want* to read and they need to have interesting things to think about! Yes, teach them the basics, but also light the fire that will be the catalyst to life-long learning.

GETTING STARTED...

GO GLOBAL is designed to be fairly open and go. It consists of 36 weeks of lesson plans. To get the most out of it and you will want to take a look at your schedule and map out when you want to start and when you need to take breaks for things like vacations or the birth of a new baby.

Set a time each month to reserve your books and look over the supplies for the following few weeks of learning. It is easier to request books for a couple of weeks in a row. That way if a book is checked out, you still have an opportunity to get it in time for that week's topic.

Set a time weekly, to read through that week's lesson so you know what to expect and you can decide what will work for your week.

Decide, in general, when will be the best times to explore and learn together. Each day's activities and initial reading of some of the books is designed to take two to three hours. If you are anything like us, you will spend additional time enjoying these great books with your kids during spontaneous reading times. And ideally, they will be taking what they are learning into their free play time. But having a general routine often helps both mom and kids slide into a daily rhythm in a way that reduces conflict because everyone knows what to expect. The beauty of homeschooling is that YOU get to decide how this will look for you and your family. Which brings us to this final point…

DON'T MISS THIS—THE POWER OF PERSONALIZATION

There are principles in life—including parenting and education—that are uniform. But there is so much to life that is art. The power of homeschooling is that it allows you as the parent to personalize education to fit the needs and style of your unique family dynamic and each of your one-of-kind children.

Our desire was to lay out something that would walk anyone through the process of developing a life-style of learning in their home. But this works best when you personalize it and make it your own.

You do not have to do EVERY activity, and probably should not! There are many choices and options. If you see an activity that you or your children would not find interesting—SKIP it. It's ok. No one is looking over your shoulder. No one is going to give you grief. Your kids will be just fine if you don't do it all. We promise.

Have you had a crazy week where life upends itself? Give yourself permission to cut back or simply move on. You should never feel like you are a slave to your curriculum. Curriculum is intended to be a guide, a starting point for you as the parent/teacher.

READ and TALK with your kids, making time for PLAY. This is what matters. You don't have to do every activity. Remember the goals—develop a lifestyle and love of learning and build relationships with your kids.

Enjoy the adventure.

WEEK 1
OVERVIEW
MAPS AND GLOBE

BIG PICTURE

We live on a marvelous blue ball spinning in space. Our children love to learn about their home and the people, plants, animals, and landforms that fill this wonderful creation. Learning about the world will give them a foundation for all their future learning. Understanding place and location is necessary to start to categorize and make sense of history, plant and animal biology, and life!

> Underlined words indicate what your child
> should be familiar with by the end of the week.

Your family will learn that the earth is a <u>sphere</u>, spinning like a top with a pole poked through it. By observing a <u>globe</u>, your child will begin to understand that the spinning earth is slightly tilted. Your child will become familiar with the location of the <u>North and South Poles</u> and the imagined line around the waist of the earth called the <u>Equator</u>. The cardinal directions of North, South, East and West will be explored on maps and in your own yards. Your child will experience how a compass is used to find directions.

You will learn that <u>most of the earth is covered with water, which we call oceans, seas, and lakes</u>. The major oceans are the <u>Atlantic</u>, the <u>Pacific</u>, the <u>Indian</u>, the <u>Arctic</u>, and the <u>Southern</u>. The seven large bodies of land called <u>continents</u> will be introduced: <u>North America</u>, <u>South America</u>, <u>Antarctica</u>, <u>Africa</u>, <u>Europe</u>, <u>Asia</u>, and <u>Australia</u>.

MATERIALS

Books

1. ***Beginner's World Atlas 3rd Edition***, National Geographic. 2011. Ages 5–10. We recommend you purchase as we will use all year. This book is the spine for whole course as it is filled with the latest data, large maps, and bright, bold images. Organized by continent, each section has a physical and political map, with information on the land, culture, and people.
2. ***Me on the Map***, Joan Sweeney, Ages 3–8. A girl shows herself on a map of her room, her room on the map of her house, her house on the map of her street, all the way to her country on a map of the world. The best introduction to maps and geography available!

Secondary Books: Find *some* of these excellent books to read aloud and make available to your children for their quiet times. The * means especially recommended.

1. ****As the Crow Flies: A First Book of Maps***, Gail Hartman. Ages 3–7. Simple story of where individual animals go and the maps of their travels.
2. ****The Whole World in Your Hands: Looking at Maps***, Melvin & Gilda Berger. Ages 5–7. Easy reader introducing maps starting with a home, and going to town, state, country, and world.
3. ****Maps & Globes***, Jack Knowlton. Ages 6–10. Comprehensive (lots of information and many concepts), so would be good for the child who has already learned about maps and wants to know a bit more.
4. ***The Way to Captain Yankee's***, Anne Rockwell. Ages 3–6. Charming story of using a neighborhood map to go visiting.
5. ***Mapping Penny's World***, Loreen Leedy. Ages 6–8. As Lisa's class is learning how to make maps, she goes on an imaginary trip around the world with her pet bull terrier.
6. ***Somewhere in the World Right Now***, Stacey Schuett. Ages 7–9. Time zone information if you want to explore more with an older child.

SUPPLIES

1. My Map Book printable, available on the *GO GLOBAL* Resource page (http://www.cultivatedlearning.org/GoResources)
2. Globe
3. Compass
4. Chalk
5. Orange
6. Cardstock

DAY 1 — ME ON THE MAP

EVERYONE

1. Read ***Me on the Map***. This book is the perfect introduction to our study. Even preschoolers and kindergarteners will have a grasp of location and maps after reading this book, from maps of their rooms to their place in their home, on their street, in their town, in their state, in their country, and in their world.

2. Have your child make his own map book. Each child needs nine pages of card stock—you can use four pages cut in half to 8.5" by 5.5". If your child does not write yet, print out the labels and let him cut and paste them on the appropriate pages. Cutting, pasting, and working with printed words are prewriting skills. They develop hand-eye coordination, and build the hand strength needed before children hold pencils for an extended time. Printed words and some images are available on the *GO GLOBAL* Resource page.

    a) Card 1/Cover: Let your child paste a picture of himself on the cover and write his name: i.e., Tom's Map Book. Print for him if he does not write yet, or use provided printable.

    b) Card 2/Page 1: A map of his room from the view of the ceiling. Have him draw the walls, the doors, the windows, and the prominent furniture. He can draw himself in his room if he would like. Label this "My Room."

c) Card 3/Page 2: Have your child draw his street and his house. He can add details — his friends' houses, any parks, etc. Label "My House and Street." Add your street address and have him learn it this week.

d) Card 4/Page 3: Print a street map of your town small enough to fit on the small page. Let your child cut it out and glue onto the page. Let your child mark where your house is! Label "Town of <name of your town>". Add a north arrow: "↑" with an "N" below.

e) Card 5/Page 4: Print a map of your state. Let your child cut it out and glue onto the next page. Find your town on the map. Label "<Name of State>." Add a north arrow. There are links to sites with free printable maps of each state in the United States available on the *GO GLOBAL* Resource page.

f) Card 6/Page 5: Print a map of your country (a political map with the states/provinces showing). Printable is available. Let your child cut it out and glue onto the next page. Have your child locate his state on the map. Label "My Country: <Name of Country>." Add a north arrow.

g) Card 7/Page 6: Print a map of your continent. Printable is available. Let your child cut it out and glue onto next page. Have your child locate his country on the map. Label "My Continent: North America." Add a north arrow.

h) Card 8/Page 7: Print a map of the world. Let your child cut it out and glue onto the next page. Have your child locate his continent on the map. Label "My Planet: Earth." Add a north arrow.

i) Card 8/ Back Cover: Write your child's name, the date, and his age. Hole punch two or three holes on left margin. Tie with yarn or fasten with brads.

ADD FOR SEVEN-YEAR-OLDS AND UP

3. For your seven-year-old, or advanced six-year-old, you can measure for the map of his room. Let them walk the length and then width of their room; record the number of steps. Each step equal one square on a sheet of graph paper. Draw the outline of the room. Using their footsteps measure the length and width of each piece of furniture and add all to the map in the proper location. Add doors, closets, and windows. And, of course, add a picture of them!

DAY 2 — ME ON THE GLOBE

EVERYONE

1. Find your place on a globe. Explore your location by asking him what he knows about it. Does he know the name and shape of your state? He should know this since you did the activity yesterday,

though it will seem different on the round surface of the globe. What other states or bodies of water are close?

> DO NOT lecture or instruct. Let him tell you what he knows and answer questions he might have.

axis is an invisible line around which an object rotates/spins.

2. Read **Beginner's World Atlas,** pages 4–5, which will be a review of what you learned yesterday.

3. Using the globe, show how the world spins on its axis and point out the North Pole and South Pole. Also, point out the equator. Explain that there are no actual poles, and there is NOT a line on the ground at the equator. These are imagined (and calculated) points and line. You could look at and discuss property lines (e.g., how the edge of your front yard may not have a fence or physical line between your property and your neighbors.)

4. Ask your child if he knows his address. Then take him outside to find the number on his house and the name of his street. Make sure your child knows his complete street address, as well as his name, his parents' names, and a family phone number. *write on back of map book.*

ADD FOR SIX-YEAR-OLDS AND UP

5. Using a mapping software (such as Google maps) on your computer show your child a map that shows your house, your street, your neighborhood, your city, and your state. Slowly scan out so he sees that he is looking at the same location, but at a different scale.

DAY 3 — MAPS AND DIRECTIONS

EVERYONE

1. Have your child spin like the globe/earth. Older children can learn that the earth spins clockwise. Use a clock to teach clockwise and counterclockwise. Spin correctly.

   Ask him to point to his "North Pole" (at the top of his head), his "South Pole" (at his feet), and his "equator" (his waist).

   Does he get dizzy and fall down? Rejoice that the earth never gets dizzy!

2. Talk to your child about the water and the land. Many globes and maps show the "political world" which means they emphasize where people live by highlighting countries and cities. There are also globes and maps that emphasize the physical world by highlighting mountains, rivers, forests, and deserts. Just introduce these concepts. We will discuss this more next week.

ADD FOR SIX-YEAR-OLDS AND UP

3. Ask your child if the earth seems round to him. Of course, the answer is no: it seems flat. You can explain that the earth is HUGE and so the part we live on seems flat. Find where you live on the

globe. Also, find a place that you have traveled to (by car or train) that would seem a great distance to your child. He might be surprised to see how close it is on the globe.

4. Learn about the cardinal directions of north, south, east, and west. *Compass*

   a) Go outside and teach your child what direction is north by having him stand to face north.

   b) Then, have him turn 90 degrees to the right and tell them he is now facing east, where the sun rises;

   c) Then, have him turn another 90 degrees to the right and tell him he is facing south;

   d) Then, have him turn another 90 degrees to the right and tell him he is facing west, where the sun sets.

   e) Finally, turn one more 90 degrees so he is facing north again. Ask him if he remembers what direction he is facing.

   f) Call out directions and let him turn to face that direction.

   g) Teach that the sun rises in the east and sets in the west. Play the game of calling out directions in the morning and evening. Try this in other locations as well. If you do it at sunrise or sunset, he should be able to at least find that direction! And then perhaps deduce the other directions.

DAY 4 EXPLORING DIRECTIONS

EVERYONE

1. Play with a compass. Children LOVE real tools. Look at the compass and review what N, E, S and W mean. Show them how to hold the compass in front of them, completely flat. Explain that the arrow always points north. If they want to go north, they just follow the arrow. If they want to go south, they keep the arrow pointing at themselves. Younger children will only be able to find north, but they will love it!

2. Find and discuss a compass rose. Almost all maps have one. Ask your child, "Why is it called a rose?" [Answer: It is called a rose because the figure's compass points resemble the petals of the well-known flower. In the 14th century, cartographers (mapmakers) started drawing ornate roses on their charts and maps.] The rose will always have a written N for north. Some roses will have the other directions as well. North is "up" on the map almost all of the time. Add a compass rose to the map of your room.

3. Draw a compass rose outside of your house with chalk on the sidewalk or porch. Make sure to point to the north!

ADD FOR SIX-YEAR-OLDS AND UP

4. If your child is very clear on the cardinal directions, you MIGHT explain the intermediate directions, known as ordinal directions of NE, SE, SW, and NW.

ADD FOR SEVEN-YEAR-OLDS AND UP

5. How can we make the round globe flat? Take an orange (or grapefruit, tangerine, etc.) peel half and have your child make it flat. What happens? You can explain that making a flat map means the picture is a bit distorted. Read ***Beginner's World Atlas***, pages 6–7.

> When your child is MUCH older he will learn about different map projections. Now it is enough to know that the world is actually round and we make flat maps which are not perfect representations. This information will help you explain if he asks why Greenland is not a continent when it seems larger that South America and Africa. Or, if they have questions about how HUGE Antarctica or Alaska is. Do not give them this information unless they ask.

6. With the globe, explain that the equator divides the world into two hemispheres. The Northern Hemisphere and the Southern Hemisphere. Have your child repeat these words and show you where they are. Turn the globe upside down and see if they can still do it correctly. An older child might also be interested in hearing about the Western Hemisphere (North America and South America) and the Eastern Hemisphere (Europe, Africa, Asia, and Australia). The concept of the International Date Line and the Prime Meridian is too difficult for this age.

WEEK 2
OVERVIEW
CONTINENTS AND OCEANS

BIG PICTURE

The seven large bodies of land are called continents and we will be introducing them this week: North America, South America, Antarctica, Africa, Europe, Asia, and Australia.

The earth has different kinds of habitats. We will cover these habitats: mountain, grassland, deciduous forest, coniferous forest, rainforest, desert, tundra, and icecap. Different animals and plants live in these different regions. In addition to these natural divisions, we will briefly introduce the political divisions of nations or countries.

The naming of these habitats or biomes can be confusing because there are different names for very similar areas. For instance, deciduous forests are also called temperate forests, coniferous forests are also called boreal or fir forests, and rainforests can also be called tropical forests or jungles. You do NOT need to teach this kind of detail to your young children, but parents should be aware as different books use different terms.

You will learn that most of the earth is covered with water, which we call oceans, seas, and lakes. The major oceans are the Atlantic, the Pacific, the Indian, the Southern, and the Arctic. If you went to school in the 20th century, you learned that there are four world oceans. In 2000, the International Hydrographic Organization created a new world ocean—the Southern Ocean from the southern portions of the Atlantic, Pacific, and Indian Oceans. This new ocean is defined as the ocean from the Antarctica coast to 60 degrees south latitude.

You will learn about the giant of the oceans, the blue whale, and experiment with salt water. In future weeks, you will learn about penguins in the Antarctica section, polar bears during the week on Canada, and the coral reef animals in the Australia section.

In addition, you will introduce the *GO GLOBAL* Game—a large floor map game that will be used throughout the year.

MATERIALS

Books

1. ***Beginner's World Atlas 3rd Edition***, National Geographic. 2011. Ages 5–10.
2. ***How to Make an Apple Pie and See the World***, Marjorie Priceman. Ages 4–8. A whimsical trip around the world to find the ingredients to make an apple pie.
3. ***Over on a Mountain: Somewhere in the World***, Marianne Berkes. Ages 4–8. Discover 20 animals on 10 mountain ranges on all 7 continents. Counting, singing, animals, and maps!

4. A nonfiction book about forests: **About Habitats: Forests**, Cathryn Sill. Ages 4–9. A guide to different kinds of forests with lovely pictures and simple text describing forests around the world. Wonderful end notes will help parent to discuss the book with the child. Or **Over in the Forest: Come and Take a Peek**, Marianne Berkes, Ages 4–8. Follow the tracks of ten animals from deciduous forests. Counting, singing, animals, behavior and hidden bonus animals. Use both books if you can find them.
5. **About Habitats: Oceans,** Cathryn Sill. Ages 3–8. Great first glimpse into the oceans of the world. Lovely art, easy to understand, with significant additional information about the animals in the back.
6. **The Blue Whale**, Jenni Desmond. Ages 5–8. This nonfiction living book is a story that will pull in even young readers, and clearly and entertainingly communicates so much information.

Secondary Books: Find *some* of these excellent books to read aloud and make available to your children for their quiet times. The * means especially recommended.

1. *****People**, Peter Spier. All ages. Classic picture book of people all around the world. Though we all start from Adam and Eve (pictured on first page), we celebrate the ethnic and cultural variety in our wonderful world.
2. *****Listen to Our World**, Bill Martin, Jr. Ages 4–8. Simple celebration of some of the animals and habitats of the world. A great introduction to habitats and some of the animals we will learn about during this course.
3. *****Eye Wonder: Oceans**, DK. Ages 5–8. Dramatic, atmospheric photography with great age-appropriate information.
4. *****The Four Oceans,** Wil Mara. Ages 4–7. Easy Reader. Very simple text, nice photographs. You will need to add the Southern Ocean to the information provided.
5. **The Eye of the Whale: A Rescue Story**, Jennifer O'Connell. Ages 5–8. Story of humpback whale freed from fishing line.
6. **Discovery Science: Oceans and Seas**, Nicola Davies. Ages 5–8. Chock-full of colorful photographs and simple large text with more detailed information in smaller text. Parental Warning: evolutionary bias on pages 16–17.

SUPPLIES

1. Globe
2. *GO GLOBAL* Game, available for purchase on CultivatedLearning.org
3. Apple pie ingredients
4. Whale art: long measuring tape, and sidewalk chalk
5. Salt water experiment supplies: three cups, salt, sand, and light-weight dollar store jewels

DAY 1   CONTINENTS

EVERYONE

1. Read **Beginner's World Atlas**, pages 6–7. This will be a review of what you learned last week with some simple information on the difference between a globe and flat map.

Then read pages 8–9. Discuss that we will be learning about the physical world (landforms and animals that we can touch, see, and feel) and the political world (countries and cultures). Ask her which area she is most excited to learn about.

Now explore the information on pages 10–11. This map shows the physical world—the kinds of land regions. We are going to learn about the land, climate, plants, and animals. Ask your child what she can tell you about each of the land regions: mountain, grassland, deciduous forest, coniferous forest, rainforest, desert, tundra, and icecap. This is just to whet the appetite. After you have discussed, read pages 12–13.

2. Name each of the seven continents. Find on the *GO GLOBAL* Game mat. Explain that each continent has several countries in it (except for Antarctica). Explore **Beginner's World Atlas**, pages 14–15. Ask your child if she knows of any of these countries. Does she know anyone in these other countries? Where is your family from?

DAY 2 CONTINENTS

EVERYONE

1. Review the names of the continents. Call out the name of a continent and see if your child can go and stand on it on the *GO GLOBAL* Game mat. After she does, point to a continent and have her tell you the name. Keep it light and fun. This might take a few days to master! We will continue to drill with the *GO GLOBAL* Game.

2. Read **Over on a Mountain** to learn about some of the famous mountain regions and the animals that inhabit them. Do NOT require memorization at this point. We will learn about many of these mountains when we study the individual continents.

3. Read **Over in the Forest** to learn about the forest ecosystem and the animals that live there. This series of books has delightful illustrations, and many things to learn—they are made to be read over and over again. This particular book is a based on a temperate forest with mostly deciduous trees. We will learn about the tropical rainforest when we study South America.

4. Play the *GO GLOBAL* Game with continent cards. Start by just having your child stand on the continent. Once the child knows the continents consistently you can add the right/left hand/foot portion of the game.

ADD FOR SIX-YEAR-OLDS AND UP

5. Read **How to Make an Apple Pie and See the World**. Find all the countries she visits on your globe. And make the apple pie!

DAY 3 — OCEANS

EVERYONE

1. Ask your child to find the largest ocean on a globe. Tell her the name—the Pacific Ocean. Ask her if she knows anyone who lives near this ocean. Discuss any time she has seen this ocean, if applicable. Now have your child find and stand on the Pacific Ocean on the *GO GLOBAL* Game mat. Because the map is flat, the Pacific Ocean is both on the far right and far left.

2. Find the second largest ocean, the Atlantic Ocean, on your globe. Ask her if she knows anyone who lives near this ocean. Discuss any time she has seen this ocean, if applicable. Now have your child find and stand on the Atlantic Ocean on the *GO GLOBAL* Game mat.

3. Find the third largest ocean, the Indian Ocean. Ask her if she knows anyone who lives near this ocean. Discuss any time she has seen this ocean, if applicable. This might be a good time to discuss that there is a country of India that this ocean is named after, and that it has nothing to do with American Indians (Native Americans). Now have your child find and stand on the Indian Ocean on the *GO GLOBAL* Game mat.

4. The Arctic Ocean is an ocean, though much of it is frozen solid for most of the year. Find it on your globe. Now have your child find and stand on the Arctic Ocean on the *GO GLOBAL* Game mat.

5. The Southern Ocean is the ocean in the southern portion of the earth surrounding Antarctica. Find it on your globe. Now have your child find and walk along the Southern Ocean on the *GO GLOBAL* Game mat.

6. Play the *GO GLOBAL* Game with ocean cards. Stop at this point if your child is struggling.

    Play with the continent cards to see if she remembers the continents. STOP at this point if the child is struggling.

    If it is still a fun game to your child, play with both sets of cards.

ADD FOR SIX-YEAR-OLDS AND UP, IF THEY ARE INTERESTED:

7. Other important large bodies of water to discuss and locate are the Gulf of Mexico, the Mediterranean Sea, the Caribbean Sea, the Red Sea, etc. If any of these are relevant to your child NOW, discuss and locate. DO NOT give her too much information. We want her to understand the big picture first.

DAY 4 — OCEANS AND THE BLUE WHALE

EVERYONE

1. Read **About Habitats: Oceans**. Take some time to look at the map opposite the title page. See if your child can name the five oceans. Read through once. Then on the second read discuss the oceans. If you do not have this book, use what books you do have to discuss the first four concepts listed below.

a) The ocean is salty. You might ask your child if she remembers tasting the salty ocean. You can mention that we will be doing a salt water experiment later in the week. Discuss while looking at Plate 1 in the book.

b) The various oceans are interconnected—the water intermixes between them. On a globe or Plate 2 in the book, have your child trace with her finger from the Pacific Ocean over to the Indian Ocean, then down to the Southern Ocean, then back up into the Atlantic Ocean and all the way north to the Arctic Ocean. In this way, your child can "experience" and see that all the oceans are joined together.

c) Some parts of the oceans are warmer than other parts. Ask your child where he would guess that the water in the ocean would be warm? [Answer: Near the equator.] Plate 6 in the book.

d) Some parts of the ocean are colder than other parts. Ask your child where he would guess that the water in the ocean would be cold? [Answer: Near the North and South Poles.] Plate 7 in the book.

e) While looking at Plates 14 and 15 which show some of the animals that live in the ocean, you might mention that meat eaters are carnivores and plant eaters are herbivores. Most children like big fun words like these.

f) The afterword has additional information that you might want to read and impart to the children…. if they are interested.

2. Read *The Blue Whale*.

   a) Some vocabulary words you and your child might learn effortlessly while reading this magnificent book include: mammal, mottled, microorganisms, dorsal, buoyant, baleen, krill, blowholes, fluke, logging, and consciousness. At a second or third read, see if she can tell you what some of these words mean. See if she can define the word by the context in the book. I bet she can, at least to some extent. Try to work some of these words into your conversations about the book and this unit.

   > Do NOT make this a test, but keep it a light, fun conversation. You might just choose one word to talk about.

   b) Measure the size of the blue whale. One person could stand at the starting point and another march out 100 feet to see the size of a whale.

   For even more fun, take some blue chalk and draw this huge animal on your sidewalk.

- The whale's eye is about six inches long. This is small for the size of the animal—which makes sense because they do not rely on their sight much.

- The blowhole is 20 inches across! Ask your child why it is so big. [Answer: He breathes through it, and not through his mouth.] How big is your child's "blowhole", i.e., nostril?

- The tail fin is 25 feet wide. You may not be able to add this unless you live on a very quiet street.

- The whale's heart is the same size as a small car, like a VW Beetle. See if there is a small car in your neighborhood to see the size.

3. Play the *GO GLOBAL* Game with ocean cards, continent cards, and then both!

ADD FOR SIX-YEAR-OLDS AND UP

4. The oceans and seas are salty, unlike rivers and most lakes. And salt water not only tastes different, but it has different properties that make it a hospitable place for the huge whale to live. The salt water buoys up the massive animal. Try this salt water experiment.

   Materials
   - Three clear cups full of water
   - Salt, 1 Tbsp
   - Sand, 1 Tbsp
   - Light-weight pretend jewels (from dollar or craft store)

Process

- a) Label each cup either: Salty, Sandy, Plain
- b) Dissolve 1 tablespoons of salt in one cup, 1 tablespoons of sand in the second cup, and leave third cup as plain, fresh water.
- c) Make a hypothesis: ask the child to guess what will happen to the jewels when she puts them in the water.
- d) Drop in a few of the same sized jewels in each cup.
- e) Observe—what happened?

Conclusion

Mom can then explain. Salt makes water denser and so causes things to be more buoyant. Salt molecules interact and bond with the water molecules, rather than just existing next to the water. Mom can hold her fists next to each other and let her kids see if they can pull on her arms and pull her hands apart. That is water next to water, or water next to sand. But salt bonds with the water—mom now interlaces her fingers in both hands. Now can your child pull mom's hands apart? No. And this is how bonded salt water holds up the objects.

> For the parent: more technically the salts sodium (Na) and chloride (Cl) split apart and the oxygen of the water molecules connect to the Na, while the two hydrogens of the water molecules connect to the Cl. This clustering makes the solution denser, and therefore it buoys up the jewels, or the whale.

WEEK 3
NORTH AMERICA
GENERAL AND USA

BIG PICTURE

North America is framed by the Pacific Ocean to the west, the Atlantic Ocean to the east, the Arctic Ocean to the north, and the Gulf of Mexico to the south. The major landforms are the lofty Rocky Mountains in the west, the more rolling Appalachian Mountains in the east, and the Great Plains between. The mighty Mississippi River is flowing north to south through the middle of the United States. In the far north of the continent is the tundra region, and in the southwest is a large portion of desert. You will learn this general physical geography as well as the specific geography of your home state.

North America is made up primarily of three countries—Canada, the United States, and Mexico. You will learn just a bit of each of these distinct cultures. Technically North America includes Central America, but this area will not be covered in this study.

Rather than just a traditional look at boundaries, flags, capital cities, exports, etc., you are going to look at the larger picture of the land forms and the cultures in the area. Everything will not be covered! It is normal to finish a study with even more questions and curiosity than when one starts. Tell your child that there is so much more to study, and that she will be able to return to this continent, country, state, or region in the future to learn more. As was famously said, "Education is not filling a bucket, but lighting a fire." This study is a taste and a framework for future learning.

Studying the United States is so broad and deep, and you will revisit it many times in the coming years. This year you will do an overview of the country using a picture book of **America the Beautiful**. Do not get caught up in presenting (or expecting your young child to memorize) detailed information such as all the states and capitals. The goal here is to understand that the USA is a big, diverse country that spreads from sea to sea, has majestic mountains, fruitful plains, a wide variety of wildlife, and a mighty river called the Mississippi. Next week we will provide you time to focus on your local state to be able to talk and learn about your home—something all people (big and little) want to do!

> Remember to review and make sure your child knows, or at least is familiar with, the information underlined in the Big Picture section. Do NOT get caught up in the minutia. Let the fire be lit! Let the learning begin!

MATERIALS

Books

1. *Beginner's World Atlas 3rd Edition*, National Geographic. 2011.

2. ***America the Beautiful***, Katharine Lee Bates, Wendell Minor. All ages. Using all four verses of "America the Beautiful," this book celebrates the American landscape from NYC to the Oregon Coast. It includes information on the poem and song, and a description with a map on each of the locations of the paintings.
3. ***Over in a River: Flowing Out to the Sea***, Marianne Berkes. Ages 4–8. Discover animals in North American rivers. Counting, singing, animals, maps, activities, and extra information in the end notes!
4. ***River Boy: The Story of Mark Twain***, William Anderson. Ages 4–9. Beautifully illustrated biography of Samuel Clemens in a pleasing story format with an emphasis on his childhood on the Mississippi River. It is chock full of interesting tidbits of history and anecdotes of a mischievous young boy who became one of the most famous Americans.
5. ***Mountain Town***, Bonnie and Arthur Geisert. Ages 4–8. One year in the life of a small mining town in the Rockies.
6. ***Prairie Town***, Bonnie and Arthur Geisert. Ages 4–8. The railroad is coming to a 1900's town in the Midwest. Great overview of the social and economic lives of this farming community through the four seasons. Detailed, map type pictures to explore over and over.
7. A nonfiction book about prairie dogs such as ***Prairie Dogs in Danger***, A.J. Grucella. Ages 4–8. Or, ***Prairie Dog's Hideaway***, Dee Phillips. Ages 4–8.
8. ***The Three Little Javelinas***, Susan Lowell. Ages 3–8. Humorous retelling in the American Southwest.

Secondary Books: Find *some* of these excellent books to read aloud and make available to your children for their quiet times. * means especially recommended.

1. *****We Came to America***, Faith Ringgold. Ages 4–8. Reminder of Americans' diverse heritage encouraging unity and mutual appreciation.
2. *****Adèle & Simon in America***, Barbara McClintock. Ages 4–8. Siblings from France crisscross the USA, losing items along the way, which your child can hunt for. Maps and additional information on locations and historic figures are on the back pages.
3. *****Lady Liberty's Holiday***, Jen Arena. Ages 4–8. The Statue of Liberty goes on a vacation across the USA, from Cape Cod and Niagara Falls to the Golden Gate Bridge and the Grand Canyon. Delightful!
4. *****River Town***, Bonnie and Arthur Geisert. Ages 4–7. A year in the life of a historical small US river town. Detailed, map-type pictures to explore over and over.
5. ***LaRue Across America***, Mark Teague. Ages 6–10. Older kids and adults will find this book hilarious; younger kids know they should laugh, but the jokes are a bit subtle.
6. ***America the Beautiful; Together We Stand***, Katharine Lee Bates. Ages: 4–9. Modern multicultural picture book features illustrations from different contemporary artists, quotes from US Presidents, and US National Landmarks and symbols infused throughout. If you use this book, find the location of the landmarks on your map of the US. Note there is a mistake on the last few pages. The USA is not a democracy; it is a republic.
7. ***Anno's U.S.A.***, Mitsumasa Anno. All ages. Anno travels across the USA from West to East in this cross-cultural book that includes events from different eras in the same picture.
8. ***America the Beautiful***, Robert Sabuda. All ages. Beautiful pop-up book, but really for older children/adults as it is fragile.

9. ***The Hallelujah Flight***, Phil Bildner. Ages 5–8. Story of the first transcontinental flight by an African-American pilot. James Banning flew during the Great Depression and saw much of the US. Book includes a map of his flight path.
10. ***Cactus Hotel***, Brenda Guiberson. Ages 4–10. Wonderful story of the animals that inhabit the giant saguaro.
11. ***The Runaway Tortilla***, Eric Kimmel. Ages 4–8. Southwestern retelling of the Gingerbread Man with desert animals, counting, and some Spanish. Or, ***The Gingerbread Cowboy***, Janet Squires and Holly Berry. Ages 4–8. Another Southwestern retelling of the Gingerbread Man with a Wild West flair.

SUPPLIES

1. Map of North America (available on the *GO GLOBAL* Resource page) printed on cardstock
2. Map Legend (available on the *GO GLOBAL* Resource page) printed on cardstock
3. Colored pencils
4. Diorama materials: large plastic bin, blue foam sheet, tape, lentils, sandpaper, small sticks and materials collected from outside; Safari TOOB River, North America, or Nature animals. Link for purchase available on the *GO GLOBAL* Resource page.
5. Homemade fruit salad makings or homemade soup ingredients
6. A dollar bill and various coins
7. *GO GLOBAL* Game

DAY 1 — OVERVIEW AND USA

EVERYONE

1. Read ***Beginner's World Atlas***, pages 16–21. Discuss the map of North America. Mention that there are three main countries in North America—Canada, the United States of America, and Mexico. While Central America, the Caribbean Islands, and Greenland are also part of North America we will not be talking about those countries in depth and it is enough for them to know there are additional countries they will learn about when they are older.
2. Using the North America map and the map legend provided on the *GO GLOBAL* Resource page:

    a) Trace the Rocky Mountains and the Appalachian Mountains with a brown colored pencil. Make sure to point out that the Rocky Mountains extend up into Canada and Alaska. Label the Rocky Mountains and the Appalachian Mountains. You might point out the Sierra Nevada Mountains to older children, but do not label them. Extend the Sierra Madres and Rocky Mountains (that are renamed Sierra Madre Occidental) into Mexico.

    b) Color the deciduous and fir trees in the forested areas in the US and Canada. We will do Mexico's vegetation when we study that country.

    c) Color the green grass tufts of the grasslands, which are called prairies or the Great Plains in North America. Point out that they extend into Canada. Label the Great Plains.

d) Glue some sandpaper on the desert region, marked with a "d". Make sure to extend into Mexico.

e) Color the moss symbol in the tundra area, and snowflakes in the icecap.

f) Color the Mississippi River blue and make sure they learn the name. Count, name, and then color the Great Lakes. Do NOT make your young child print all these names. Older children will revisit the Great Lakes tomorrow.

g) Label the oceans and color them blue: Pacific Ocean, Atlantic Ocean, and Arctic Ocean. IF your child already knows these oceans, Add Gulf of Mexico and Hudson Bay.

3. Play the *GO GLOBAL* Game to review oceans and continents.

DAY 2 — USA

EVERYONE

1. Read ***Beginner's World Atlas***, pages 22–23.

2. Review your map of North America. Have your child trace the outline of the United States of America with his finger.

   a) Add a star on the map and label Washington, DC.

   b) Add where you live to the map.

   c) OPTIONAL: Add one or two cities where you have extended family and have visited.

3. Read (and sing) ***America the Beautiful***. This lovely book will give an overview of the United States of America. Second time through the book you should talk about the pictures—where they are and what they represent. Then you can look at the map in the back of the book and discuss where they are located. Which have you seen? Which one or two do you want to see the most?

4. Read ***Over in a River***. Read again and count the babies. Read/ sing again and talk about the rivers and maps. Read again and look for the hidden animals. Read again and act out the animals.

> We can never overestimate the power of reading a book over and over again. Young children want it, and they learn significantly more each time you read the same book to them.

5. Make a diorama of a river scene. Art tutorial available on the *GO GLOBAL* Resource page.

   ### Materials
   - Plastic bin
   - Blue foam sheet (for river), scissors and double-sided tape
   - Safari TOOB North American Wildlife animals (or the River or Nature TOOB) links for purchase available on the *GO GLOBAL* Resource page

WEEK 3 | 27

- Lentil beans for the ground
- Materials collected outside to make the forest: pinecones, seeds, acorns, leaves, small rocks, and tiny plants
- Small sticks to make beaver dam

Process

a) Go on a nature walk to collect materials for your diorama. It can be in your neighborhood or a local park/wildlife area where you can take materials home.

b) Cut blue foam to make river. Using double stick tape, affix to bottom of bin.

c) Add lentils for ground.

d) Add materials from your nature walk.

e) Add animals. Build dam.

f) Play!

ADD FOR SIX-YEAR-OLDS AND UP

6. Add a major river that is close to where you live such as the Colorado River, the Rio Grande, the Missouri River, the Ohio River, the St. Lawrence River, or the Colombia River.

7. Add one or two major cities near you: New York, Philadelphia, Atlanta, Chicago, Dallas, Phoenix, Los Angeles, San Francisco, or Seattle. You will add your state capital on another day.

ADD FOR SEVEN-YEAR-OLDS AND UP

8. Mark on your map and learn the names of the Great Lakes and the St. Lawrence River.

DAY 3 — MISSISSIPPI RIVER AND THE GREAT PLAINS/ PRAIRIE

EVERYONE

1. Read ***River Boy, The Story of Mark Twain***. See if your child can tell you the story with some prompts. Or you could have the child look at the pictures and share what he remembers.

> Some of these prompts are for older children. Do NOT make this a test, but a time to talk about the story.

Prompts could include:

a) Where was Sam born? [Answer: Florida, MO.] If he just knows Missouri, don't make a big deal. If he is aware of the state of Florida, you might want to talk about how there can be cities and states that have the same name.

b) Then where did the family move next? [Answer: Hannibal, MO.] Note that it is on the Mississippi River. At this point your child might remember some of the adventures that Sam had during his childhood.

c) What was Sam's first job? [Answer: A printer's assistant at the newspaper.] What did he want to do next? [Answer: Explore the Amazon River in South America.] Find South America and the Amazon River. Mention to your child that you will explore and learn about that soon!

d) What happened on the steamboat? [Answer: He decided not to go to South America, but learned to be a steamboat pilot instead.] Locate the places on the Mississippi mentioned in the book: New Orleans, St. Louis.

e) Where did Samuel Clemens go next? [Answer: To the west in order to mine for gold and silver.] Locate Nevada and California on your map. Next, he went to Europe (find on map/globe). He got married and moved his family to New York and then Connecticut. Find all these locations.

f) Read the story to your child again and have him point to the places on the globe when you mention them.

2. Learn about life in a small town on the prairie by reading **Prairie Town**. Take time to read the book multiple times. This book will give you a peek into small town culture which will be especially helpful if you live in a big city or suburbia.

Read through the first time to get the flow and story, as small as it seems. Pause after you read the brief text to look at the picture. Discuss briefly the big picture of the story. These illustrations are so perfect for our study because they are map-like. The second time read slower and discuss.

a) Ask your child to describe the land after reading page 4–5. [Answer: It is flat, has patchwork fields, is farmland, etc.]

b) Allow your child to explore the picture of the town on page 6–7. What is he interested in? Does he think the skyscraper of the prairie is a funny metaphor? Does he notice the firetruck going to the house fire? This is not a test. Just talk to him about what piques his interest.

> A metaphor is a term or phrase that compares two unlike things. You do not teach the term metaphor until they are much older. But even young children can grasp the concept of a metaphor, in this case comparing a silo to a skyscraper.

c) Continue through the book. Does he notice on page 10 the house being rebuilt after the fire?

d) Another thing I love about this series of books is the final page with clues of other things to find… and for you to talk about. So, go back, and read again…. And I bet you will find them looking for more and more, and comparing various pictures to see the progression of change.

ADD FOR SIX-YEAR-OLDS AND UP

3. Learn about the prairie dogs by reading one or more books about them. Then have your child dramatize the prairie dogs. Link to video about prairie dogs is available on the *GO GLOBAL* Resource page.

    a) They can peek out of their burrow (a box or laundry basket).

    b) Dig a burrow.

    c) Stand up on their two back legs and watch for danger.

    d) Sound the alarm with a "chirk, chirk" sound if a predator (i.e., coyotes, bobcats, snakes, falcons, eagles) comes. All the other prairie dogs dive for cover!

    e) When the danger is gone, the lookout can make a "wee oooh" noise to let the others know they can come back out. When he makes this noise, he holds his paws up in the air and jumps!

    f) Prairie dogs, like young children, enjoy wrestling.

    g) Prairie dogs also greet one another with what looks to us like a kiss. In reality, they touch their teeth!

DAY 4 — ROCKY MOUNTAINS AND DESERT

EVERYONE

1. Learn about life in a small town in the Rocky Mountains by reading **Mountain Town** in a similar way to what you did with **Prairie Town**. First, read to get the story. This town book has more "story" and so don't go so slow you do not follow it. Then go back and read slowly, allowing and encouraging your child to interact with the story and pictures. Make sure you are enjoying the book together, not drilling or lecturing him. Don't forget to reread after looking at the details in the back. Another time read through looking for the blue car; telling the blue car's story will be great fun.

2. Learn a bit about the southwestern desert by reading *The Three Little Javelinas.* Read first for fun, and then go back and explore. Conversation prompts could include:

    a) What did the first Javelina use to make his house? What did the pig use in the traditional story? The second Javelina and the traditional story? The third Javelina and the traditional story?

    b) What other animals do you see in this story? The mouse reappears several times; where is he always living?

    c) If your child has never seen tumbleweeds, she might like to see a video of tumbleweeds. The link is available on the *GO GLOBAL* Resource page.

d) Check out **Cactus Hotel** for more information (in a fun, living book) on the saguaro.

e) Adobe are sun dried mud bricks that are very durable in dry climates. Typically, some organic material (straw or dung) is added to help bind the mud brick together and keep it from shrinking and cracking. Consider letting your child play in mud. Let her experiment making mud blocks with and without grass. Beware—my brother used to make mud balls to make war in the southwest where we had no snow balls!

3. Play Simon Says with desert animal movements. Printable available on the *GO GLOBAL* Resource page.

Howl like a coyote.	Pinch like a scorpion.	Stand tall like an eagle.
Hop like a kangaroo rat.	Creep like a tarantula.	Run like a roadrunner.
Scurry like a desert mouse.	Roll up like an armadillo.	Dart like a hummingbird
Pounce like a fox.	Strike like a snake.	Peck like a woodpecker.
Run like a desert cottontail.	Shake like a rattlesnake.	Flap your wings like a bat.
Clack your teeth like a javelina.	Slither sideways like a sidewinder.	Creep slowly like a Gila monster.

4. America is called a melting pot because there are people from everywhere around the world who have come here to make the US their home. While they have different cultures and customs, the USA is, for the most part, a land of immigrants. Even the Native Americans probably immigrated to the New World across the Bering Strait thousands of years ago. While no one is really melting together, those who live in the US interact in numerous ways that produce a commonality out of our different backgrounds. Talk to your child about where you grew up, where their grandparents grew up, and the land of your ancestor's origin, if you know it. When and where did your ancestors come to America? If your ancestors came from another continent, you will want to take some extra time when we study that continent to go more in depth with your child about your roots.

An even better analogy might be a salad or soup. While there are different ingredients that make up the dish, each ingredient keeps some of its characteristics, and together they make a better dish. Make a salad or soup for dinner and let the kids tell dad about what they learned today.

Read **We Came to America**, if you have it.

ADD FOR SIX-YEAR-OLDS AND UP

5. *E Pluribus Unum* is one of America's national mottos. This Latin phrase means "out of many, one." This motto appears on all US coins. It refers to the fact that we are a cohesive single nation formed out of the unification of the thirteen original colonies into one nation. In 1956, the honor of being the official motto was given to "In God We Trust" by an act of Congress. Find both mottos on our bills and coins.

WEEK 4
NORTH AMERICA
USA: YOUR STATE/REGION

BIG PICTURE

You, the parent, are going to have to step up this week, since there is no way to include plans for each state in the Union. But your child will love this week, perhaps more than any other, because it is about home.

You will need to pre-plan. Do not wait until it is time to teach.

Decide on a field trip and call ahead to confirm.

Find an empty map of your state that you can print on cardstock. Links to websites of maps are available on the *GO GLOBAL* Resource page.

Find some non-fiction EASY books on your state. Books with minimal text and maximum illustrations are best.

Find some fiction picture books that are about your state, or are based in your state or region and show some of its attributes. See the introduction for a review on the definition of a living book. Ask your librarian for help. She will probably be able to direct you to some books that use story or narrative to capture the child's interest.

Consider what is somewhat unique about your state and search (or ask your librarian) for books about that topic.

- Is there an animal that is associated with your state/ area? (moose, California condor, type of bear, armadillo, roadrunner, alligator, etc.)

- How about a natural region, habitat or landform? (everglades or any marshes, seashore, Great Lakes or any significant freshwater, mountains, forests, glaciers, volcanos)

- Is there an interesting people group to learn about—the Native Americans in your state, the Amish, a significant immigrant group?

- Are there any industries that you would like to highlight?

As you can see the problem will be limiting what you study, not finding something to study. To help you decide, consider what is MOST important to you personally, and what can be sparked by wonderful living books. This week is to give your child a TASTE of what she can learn about in her state. Don't overwhelm with too much information.

Get at least one book to prepare your child for the field trip. The more she is primed, the more she will enjoy the trip.

In addition to the books, try to think of some things that the kids can DO. Your books are your allies here; they can and will spark ideas. Do not make it too hard. Sometimes it can be playing what they just learned about—either with blocks, Legos, and figurines, or with full body dramatizations.

MATERIALS

Books

1. Non-fiction book(s) on your state. Look for ones without too much text, but interesting illustrations.
2. "Living books" based in your state or region.

Secondary Books

1. More living books.

SUPPLIES

1. Map of your state. Links available on the *GO GLOBAL* Resource page.
2. Colored pencils.

DAY 1   OVERVIEW AND PHYSICAL GEOGRAPHY

EVERYONE

1. Look at a map of your state. What are the main cities, mountain ranges, rivers? Find them on the map. Are there forests, deserts, or farm lands? Where have you been? What have you seen?
2. Fill in a blank map of your state. What habitats do you have? Add the images for mountains, forests, plains, deserts. Add important rivers and cities that your child knows, and, at the least, his home town and the state capital. Do NOT overwhelm your child with information. Emphasize the locations they already know such as cousins' or grandparents' home towns, camping locations, etc.
3. Read a "living book" about your state, city, or region. It can be about the geography or land forms in your state, but does NOT have to be. Discuss. Add any appropriate activities.

DAY 2   LIVING BOOKS AND ANIMALS

EVERYONE

1. Read one or two of the "living books." They can be, but do NOT have to be about animals. Discuss. Add any appropriate activities.
2. Do you have a state bird, state animal, state reptile, state flower, or state tree? Find a picture to cut out or draw one for your state map.

DAY 3 — LIVING BOOKS AND CULTURAL GEOGRAPHY

THE HUMAN COMMUNITY, WHICH INCLUDES
HISTORY, ECONOMICS, GOVERNMENT, IMMIGRATION, AND URBANIZATION

EVERYONE

1. Read one or two of the "living books." They can be, but do NOT have to be about people in your state. Discuss. Add any appropriate activities.

2. Discuss economics in your state. RELAX. This is easy—you will just discuss what people do for a living. Do you know any farmers or owners of small businesses? Anyone in high tech industry? (They work on computers; even a four-year-old understands that.) Is there a military base, farm fields, or a factory nearby? How about a mine, smelter, or lumber mill? The goal here is NOT mastery. Even young children understand that people work, and that there might be some special things done in your state that are unique. For instance, here in Arizona we point out the cotton fields, the citrus groves, the copper mines, the cattle (and sheep) herds to our child as these are the historic main jobs in Arizona. Of course, they are no longer the force they were (Hello, high tech industry!), but they are still important.

3. Make your state flag. Find out what the colors and symbols on your flag represent.

DAY 4 — FIELD TRIP

EVERYONE

1. Visit an interesting outside location in your state. This could be a National or State Park, a botanical garden, or just a beautiful river or mountain. Kids love to get out and see what makes their home state exceptional. Find out about the animals and plants in a fun way.

2. OR, visit a historical museum for your state. Look for one that does tours for *younger* children. Invite a family to join you if you need a few more kids to make the minimum number for a trip.

3. Consider taking a whole month to explore your state. This would be a wonderful summer activity. What are the main industries? Can you take a tour of a farm, mine, smelter, factory? Perhaps you can visit your state capital and meet your state representatives. Visit your state parks and any national parks or monuments in your state. And always find these places on a map!

WEEK 5
NORTH AMERICA
CANADA

BIG PICTURE

It is time to turn our attention to the nearest neighbors of the USA. These neighbors share geography (Rocky Mountains, the two oceans, the Great Lakes), and the colonization in the east by Great Britain (and France), and colonization in the southwest by Spain.

Canada is our neighbor to the north. While they were first colonized by the French, the majority of their immigrants were British. Thus, the USA shares a lot of history as well as a long border with Canada. The indigenous people in Canada, Greenland, Alaska, and Siberia are commonly referred to as Eskimo. Since many aboriginal people view the term Eskimo as derogatory, it is common to teach your child to use the term First Nations, First Peoples, or by the tribal names such as Inuit (IN-yoo-it) (which refers to the largest grouping of Native Americans in Canada) or Yupik (YOO-pik) (Alaska).

Canada is known for its rich forests and mountains, and the wildlife that inhabit them. You will make a Canadian flag with its maple leaf, have a Canadian breakfast, and learn about moose, as well as Canadian Mounties. Then you will learn about the Arctic region, including the Inuit people, polar bears, igloos, and the northern lights. And of course, there will be a hockey activity!

If your child asks, Greenland is part of North America and is the largest island in the world. Australia is not an island; it is a continent. In 2009, Greenland assumed responsibility for self-governance, but Denmark maintains control of foreign affairs.

MATERIALS

Books

1. *Beginner's World Atlas 3rd Edition*, National Geographic. 2011.
2. *Very First Last Time*, Jan Andrews. Ages 5–9. Wonderful story of Inuit girl hunting for mussels under the ice.
3. *Over in the Arctic*, Marianne Berkes. Ages 4–8. Discover animals in the Arctic—both the tundra, icecap, and Arctic Ocean. Counting, singing, animals, maps, activities, and extra information in the end notes!
4. *The Blizzard's Robe*, Robert Sabuda. Ages 4–9. Arctic tale of the origin of the northern lights with wonderful batik art.
5. *The Polar Bear*, Jenni Desmond. Ages 4–9. Lusciously illustrated nonfiction book about polar bear bodies, habits, and habitats.

Secondary Books: Find *some* of these excellent books to read aloud and make available to your children for their quiet times. * means especially recommended.

1. ****House of Snow, Skin, and Bones**, Bonnie Shemie. Ages 4–12. Simple pictures with simple text alternate with pages of more information for older children and adults. Before reading, ask your child what the First Peoples might have used to build their homes since there is not much wood in the far north. [Answer: Snow, ice, animal skins, animal bones, rocks.]
2. ***Immi's Gift,** Karin Littlewood. Ages 4–7. Sweet story of young Inuit ice fishing and finding a brightly colored wooden bird. Connects two cultures delightfully. If you use this book make sure to read slowly. Let the children tell you what animals they know that are in the sea, and the ones who come to visit her at her igloo.
3. ***A Sled Dog for Moshi**, Jeanne Bushey. Ages 4–8. Modern day story of Inuit girl and her family's sled dogs. Lovely illustrations, a map of the arctic area, and cultural aspects and vocabulary.
4. ***Polar Bears**, Gail Gibbons. Ages 4–8. Comprehensive and yet young child friendly book with map.
5. ***My Little Polar Bear**, Claudia Rueda. Ages 2–6. Sweet pictures with all the important information on the polar bears.
6. **Ulaq and the Northern Lights**, Harriet Taylor, Ages 5–9. Fox hears legends of the northern lights from various animals. Real explanation on last page.
7. **Arctic Lights, Arctic Nights**, Debbie S. Miller. Ages 5–9. Book explains the unusual daylight patterns and the northern lights.
8. **The Longest Night**, Marion Dane Bauer. Ages 4–8. Which animal will call the sun back during the winter solstice?
9. **Northern Lights,** Nick Hunter. Ages 5–10. A nonfiction book that will delight your child who likes nonfiction, science, and always asks, "why?"
10. **The Fiddler of the Northern Lights,** Natalie Kinsey-Warnock. Ages 5–8. Grandfather in north Canadian woods tells story of fiddler whose music brings the northern lights.
11. **Dogteam**, Gary Paulsen. Ages 4–9. Lovely water colored poem of a nighttime winter run.
12. **Out of the Woods**, Rebecca Bond. Ages 4–10. True story of 1914 fire in Canadian woods where everyone, even the animals, waded into the lake to survive.
13. **Eh? to Zed: A Canadian Abecedarium**, Kevin Major. Ages 5–12. Amusing book about all things Canadian. I did not know many of them, but fortunately there is some explanation at the back of the book.
14. **This Place is Cold**, Vicki Cobb. Ages 4–9. Land, animals, plants, climate, and some history of Alaska. Much of the information applies to other Arctic locales.
15. **On Mother's Lap**, Ann Herbert Scott. Ages 2–5. Sweet picture book about Inuit mother rocking her children. Not much about Canada or the Inuit People (other than the reindeer blanket), but a sweet reminder how alike we all are. Ask your child if he has a doll (or stuffed animal), a play car (the boy has a boat and you can look back to see there is a big boat outside of his house, not a car), a pet, a blanket, and a rocking chair.
16. **Survival at 40 Below**, Debbie S. Miller. Ages 5–9. A look at the animals during the frigid winter months in the northern portion of Alaska.
17. **Looking for a Moose**, Phyllis Root. Ages 3–6. Find the moose. Fun with information on the appearance of the moose.
18. **Moose (North American Animals)**, Annie Hemstock. Ages 3–5. Photographs and simple text.

19. ***Busy, Busy Moose***, Nancy Van Laan. Ages 4–7. Easy reader about animals in forest during the four seasons.
20. ***Ice Bear: In the Steps of the Polar Bear***, Nicola Davies. Ages 4–8. Poetic language with soft lifelike paintings.
21. ***Polar Bears***, Julie Murray. Ages 5–8. Factual, interesting, photographic book.

SUPPLIES

1. Breakfast: Canadian bacon, blueberries, pancakes, and maple syrup
2. Map of North America from last week, available on *GO GLOBAL* Resource page
3. Northern lights art: high quality watercolors, watercolor paper, brushes, sponge, black construction paper, Polar bear silhouette. Tutorial and silhouette are available on the *GO GLOBAL* Resource page.
4. Red construction paper and Canadian leaf template, available on the *GO GLOBAL* Resource page
5. Safari TOOB Fun & Frigid Figures Arctic. Link for purchase available on the *GO GLOBAL* Resource page.
6. Simple costume for Canadian Mountie play: red jacket, hat, and stick horse or broom (if you have them on hand)
7. Polar bear foot prints: printable available on the *GO GLOBAL* Resource page
8. Marshmallow igloo supplies: Styrofoam bowl, miniature marshmallows, and simple icing
9. Blubber experiment supplies: lard/Crisco, plastic bag, and ice water
10. *GO GLOBAL* Game

DAY 1   OVERVIEW AND NORTHERN LIGHTS

EVERYONE

1. Start the day with a "Canadian" breakfast with back bacon (Canadian bacon), your favorite pancakes with maple syrup, and blueberries.
2. Read ***Beginner's World Atlas***, pages 24–25.

    a) Find Canada on a map. Talk about how Canada was settled by the British and French. Explain how most of the population (90%) is along the southern border. Ask your child if she can guess why. Let her guess, and perhaps give her some hints. [Answer: It is very cold in the northern area.]

    b) Add a star for the capital Ottawa to your map. Review Rocky Mountains, Great Plains, Great Lakes. Point out and name Alaska, making sure she realizes that it is part of the United States of America.

3. Play ice hockey with socks and rags to clean the kitchen floor. Just spray the floor and let them have fun. Use hockey sticks, or some kind of stick. Add a puck, which could be a clean peanut butter lid. The cleaning of the floor won't be perfect—but it can do some good and they will enjoy it!
4. Read ***Over in the Arctic***. Enjoy the book. In a subsequent reading look for the hidden animals on each page that are told about at the end.

> Most children do not want you to read the end pages of information. But the parent should read these and be ready to impart some of the information informally.

Use this book to explain the terms tundra and icecap. Tundra is an area of very cold temperatures and such a short season above freezing temperatures that trees cannot grow. Only a few very small shrubs, grasses, mosses, and lichens might grow. Few animals live in this area, most ones of note are included in this book. Ice cap is an area where the temperatures never get above freezing, and so nothing grows.

Review your globe to see the tundra and icecap areas.

ADD FOR SIX-YEAR-OLDS AND UP

5. Read one of the picture books about the northern lights.

    a) Watch the video of ***Above the Northern Lights*** by Mannheim Steamroller. Watch again and talk about which pictures are photographs and which are drawings/paintings. Link available on the *GO GLOBAL* Resource page.

    b) OPTIONAL: Paint the northern lights

    1. Carefully wet a piece of white cardstock (or watercolor paper) with a sponge to help the paint "dance" on the page.

    2. Use liquid watercolors (brighter than traditional watercolors) to make the blue, green, pink, purple swirly strips. Cover the entire page.

    3. After they are done, the parent can carefully use a clean damp sponge to help blend. Do NOT go across the colors or it will all mix together.

    4. After drying, Add black construction paper mountains, or a strip of black land on the bottom of the page with a black polar bear icon walking along. This will highlight the northern lights and add perspective. The polar bear silhouette and an art tutorial are available on the *GO GLOBAL* Resource page.

    > Help for the mom: Very little paint is needed—if they make it too goopy, it will all blend together. Encourage your children to make big patterns of each color—stripes, circles, or wavy stripes.

ADD FOR SEVEN-YEAR-OLDS AND UP

6. Talk like a Canadian. Here are a few words to get you started.

Word	Pronunciation	Meaning
about	a-BOOT	about
eh?		<used at end of sentence> Don't you agree?
washroom		bathroom
gut-foundered		hungry
pencil crayon		colored pencil
queue	Q	a line of people
kerfuffle		awkward situation, or a commotion
knapsack	NAP-sack	backpack
mountie		policeman

DAY 2 — FOREST, FLAG, AND MOOSE

EVERYONE

1. Canada is well known for its beautiful forests. Make a Canadian flag out of construction paper and talk about the maple leaf. Remember how we had maple syrup yesterday? This syrup comes from the maple tree!

   The maple leaf is lobed, with palmate veins and serrated edges. Ask your child to look at your ear lobe. Then look at the maple leaf. Can he see the lobes? Show her an unlobed leaf. The maple leaf has palmate veins. Show your palm with the fingers spread out. Some leaves have veins that spread out from the branch like your fingers from your palm. Other leaves have veins that branch out from a central vein (pinnate) and other leaves have the veins start at the base and then meet at the top of the leaf (parallel). Finally show a bread or steak knife. Tell your child this is a serrated edge. The maple leaf edge is also serrated. Other leaves have smooth edges. This is great vocabulary building for mom and child! Use these words and explain their meaning as the child is tracing and cutting out a maple leaf. Pattern of maple leaf available on the *GO GLOBAL* Resource page.

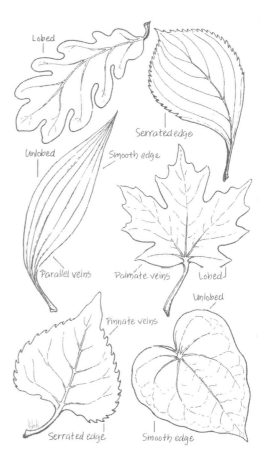

2. Have your child describe a moose. If needed, prompt them:

    a) What color are they?

    b) How tall do you think they are?

    c) Describe their face, their antlers.

    d) Then read a book about a moose. This should be a book that has the moose in their natural habitat, such as **Looking for a Moose**, or **Moose (North American Animals)**. (This is in contrast to *If You Give a Moose a Muffin*, which while a delightful book, does not provide the educational value we want.) The book can be illustrated with sketches, paintings, or photographs, but needs to have an emphasis on the real animal.

   While reading one or more books about moose, make sure to impart these facts:

    a) Moose are brown and quite large (800 to 1,600 lbs.). Ask your kids: How much do you weigh? How much does Dad weigh? How many dads would it take to weigh as much as a moose?

    b) Moose are in the deer family.

    c) They are herbivores (eat plants).

    d) They have a peanut shaped head.

    e) They have long legs and large flat feet that help them wade in the water.

    f) The male bull moose has a hump on its shoulders and unique antlers which are palmate, shaped like your hands with fingers extended. Your child might find it interesting that leaves and moose antlers can be palmate!

ADD FOR SIX-YEAR-OLDS AND UP

3. Look at a picture of a member of the Royal Canadian Mounted Police, or as they are more commonly known, a Canadian Mountie. There is a small picture of the Mounties in the **Beginner's World Atlas**, page 24. Note his distinctive dress uniform and hat. Why do you think the coat is red? [Possible answers: It is pretty. They can see each other in the fast forests of Canada. It contrasts to the blue-clad US army, but is similar to the British military who wore redcoats.]

   Their hat is a campaign hat which is a wide Stetson with a flat brim and a "Montana crease." This hat departed from a traditional British hat to one developed in the North American west. Ask your children why this hat would be better. [Answer: It keeps the sun off the face and neck. The crease would help the rain to pour off rather than pool in the middle.]

   How are the Mounties different from other police forces? [Answer: They historically rode horses, and they are both local and federal civilian officers.]

   Dramatize. Wear a red jacket or t-shirt, a high crowned, broad brimmed hat (pinched in all four corners), and ride stick horses through the forest to maintain order.

DAY 3 — INUIT AND IGLOOS

EVERYONE

1. Read ***Very First Last Time***. Most of these discussion prompts will only work with children five years and up. But even your preschoolers will enjoy the story.

    On the first read, savor this story and possibly discuss these questions.

    a) On the first page, ask your child how Eva could walk on the bottom of the sea. Why would she want to do so? Then turn the page and continue the story.

    b) On the third page spread mussels are mentioned. Ask if your child knows what they are. You do not need to tell her. She will find out as the story progresses.

    > These short pauses can heighten the excitement and expectation of the story.

    On the subsequent readings, you may use some of these discussion prompts.

    c) On the first page spread ask your child if they know where this story takes place. [Answer: Where it is cold, and in Canada since that is what we are studying this week.] Then ask if it is in present time, or a long time ago? The clues might be the telephone poles / electrical lines. Don't give it away, if they do not notice. You will ask the same question on the next page.

    d) After you have read the entire book, find the real location on your globe: Ungava Bay. It is not part of Hudson Bay, but is the bay on the northern coast of Quebec.

    e) How can a first time be a last time?

    f) Ask your child if there is something she is looking forward to doing all by herself.

    g) Why was Eva afraid? Did she have a good reason to be afraid? What did she do when she was afraid? [Answer: She covered her eyes.] What do you think she did when she closed her eyes and put her hands to her face? [Hint: There is a picture on the wall in her kitchen on the first page spread. And though only a few buildings are shown in the small village, there is a church.] What do you do when you are afraid?

    h) You might talk about being afraid of the dark. Eva had reason to be afraid of the dark. But do you have reason to be afraid of the dark at night when you are in your room?

    i) Watch a BBC video of Native Peoples collecting mussels under the sea ice. Link available on the *GO GLOBAL* Resource page.

    j) Find the strange shadow shapes: the wolf, bear, seal. Other pages also have strange shadow faces and shapes to find.

    k) Ask your child if she thinks it would be easy or hard to collect mussels. Why or why not? [Answer: It is hard because they attach to a surface so tightly they are almost impossible to detach unless one uses a tool. Draw your child's attention to the tools in the book.]

    l) Eat mussels, if you so desire.

2. Act this story out with your Safari TOOB toy figurines. This would be an excellent activity for your child to do in her free play, and again when dad comes home.

3. Make a marshmallow igloo. (Even a two-year-old might be able to do this.) First, look at books that have pictures of igloos and talk about how they are made. Art tutorial available on the *GO GLOBAL* Resource page.

   Materials
   - Miniature marshmallows
   - Paper/Styrofoam bowl
   - Plate or piece of cardboard covered with aluminum foil
   - Glue/Icing: powdered sugar mixed with water into paste.

   Process

   Provide a base covered with aluminum foil

   a) Cut "door" in a bowl

   b) Make icing for "glue"

   c) Glue miniature marshmallows on the bowl. You can dip the marshmallows and then stick them on.

   > News Flash: This is a pincher activity that develops prewriting skills.

   d) Sprinkle powdered sugar on top, if you can handle the mess.

   e) Add some arctic figures, if you have them. Allow your child to play with this while you are preparing dinner tonight.

DAY 4 — POLAR BEAR

EVERYONE

1. Have your child describe a polar bear. After she tells you what she knows, read ***The Polar Bear*** by Jenni Desmond.

   a) Read this book slowly. It is a living book, even though it is nonfiction. Because it is not a story with a sequential plot, you can interrupt your reading even on the first read through to discuss or even do something.

   b) On the second full spread, you can ask your child the name of the small animal by the girl. Ask your child if she thinks it is a baby polar bear. Why not? [Answer: It has a bushy tail, slender legs; it is an arctic fox.] What are those green swirls in the sky? [Answer: Northern lights.]

- c) On the third full spread page, the author lists where the polar bear lives. Get your globe and find these places.
- d) On the fourth full spread, they mention that the polar bears growl, roar, chuff, hiss, whimper, and purr. Let your child make all those noises.
- e) On the page talking about the weight of the polar bear let your child count the children on the pages.
- f) On the page where he tracks the animals, let your children trace the dotted lines to the prey!
- g) On the page with the bears sleeping, stop when you read about how they stretch out on their back with their feet in the air. Have your child assume this position and then ask her if she could sleep like that. Then ask how she thinks the Polar Bear sleeps when it is cold. Most children will curl up in a ball and you can affirm their intuition. I then told my littles that the bear covers his snout with his paw. I told them to do so and then asked them why the bear would do that. [Answer: It holds their warm breath next to their nose and mouth and keeps them warmer.]

2. You want to make sure to include learning/discussing these facts:
    - a) Polar Bears live at the North Pole area only—NOT at the South Pole, where the penguins live.
    - b) They are large (780–1550 lbs.). That is about the same as how many adults?
    - c) They are carnivores (eat meat).
    - d) They have white fur, but black skin.
    - e) They have elongated faces with large black noses and small ears.
    - f) They have enormous feet.
    - g) They are good swimmers and able to jump from one floating ice block to another.

3. Pretend to be a polar bear.
    - a) Jump from ice block to ice block. Mom can make a game out of it with chalk "ice blocks" drawn on the sidewalk, or with paper "ice blocks" taped to the floor inside.
    - b) Go hunting and sneak up on a seal, crawling on your belly. Make sure to cover your big black nose with your white paw so the seal will not see you coming. This behavior is legendary, but too much fun to ignore.
    - c) Hold your breath. Polar bears can swim underwater for three minutes. How long can you hold your breath?

4. Polar bear feet are huge! Make a drawing of a polar bear foot, which can be as big as 12" by 18". Then have your child make her foot print inside of the polar bear foot print to see the difference. Ask your child if she knows why the polar bear's feet might be so huge. [Answer: The polar bear's large feet can act like snow shoes to enable them to walk on top of the snow instead of sinking into it.] Polar bear foot print is available on the *GO GLOBAL* Resource page.

ADD FOR SIX-YEAR-OLDS AND UP

5. Polar bears have two different layers of fur—an under layer of dense fur that keeps them warm and an over layer of course hair that keeps the inner fur dry. Very importantly they have a layer of body fat that keeps them warm. Do this experiment with your child to learn about the value of this blubber.

   Materials
   - Lard (i.e. Crisco)
   - Zip lock plastic bag
   - Bowl of ice water

   Instructions

   a) Cover one hand with lard, making sure the fingers are well covered. Then cover with a zip lock bag.

   b) Place the uncovered fingers into ice water. How long can the child stand it? Time him!

   c) Now place the lard covered plastic bagged fingers in the water. How does the hand covered with "blubber" feel different? How long can your child stay in the cold water now? Time her!

6. Why is the polar bear white and the moose brown? Place a toy figure of each animal first on a white sheet, then on some brown material. Have your child stand 6 to 10 feet away and tell you which animal they can see each time. This is called camouflage—which is the way the animal is designed for protection from their enemies, or to be hidden from their prey.

WEEK 6
NORTH AMERICA
MEXICO

BIG PICTURE

This week turn your attention to the southern neighbor of the USA. Mexico shares geography with the United States. The US mountains and desert extend into Mexico. The same large bodies of water are to their east and west.

Mexico was colonized by the Spanish who also colonized much of California, Arizona, New Mexico, Texas, Nevada, Utah, and parts of Oklahoma and Colorado. Mexico has two strips of mountains and is mostly desert, with some rainforests in the south. The body of water to their east is called the Caribbean Sea. You will learn about geologically-recent volcanic activity in Mexico, and will learn some Spanish words. Throwing a Mexican fiesta with decorations, food, dancing, and a piñata will conclude the week!

MATERIALS

Books

1. ***Beginner's World Atlas 3rd Edition***, National Geographic. 2011.
2. ***Hill of Fire***, Thomas Lewis. Ages 4–8. Easy-to-read true story of a farmer plowing a field in Mexico and having a volcano erupt.
3. ***Fiesta!***, Ginger Foglesong Guy. Ages 3–8. Wonderful counting and vocabulary book gathering items for a party (fiesta). Both Spanish and English words, so usable even if you do not speak Spanish. Colorful folkloric artwork complements this story which will build excitement for creating your piñata!
4. ***I Don't Like Snakes***, Nicola Davies. Ages 4–9. A unique snake loving family convinces the littlest sister of the value of snakes that delightfully slither, shed, see, smell, hunt, eat, and produce babies. Rich vocabulary, charming pictures, and tons of interesting facts make this book a winner.

Secondary Books: Find *some* of these excellent books to read aloud and make available to your children for their quiet times. * means especially recommended books

1. *****Adelita***, Tomie DePaola. Ages 4–9. Delightful Cinderella story infused with Mexican culture and art. Even includes some Spanish words, with a pronunciation guide at the back of the book.
2. *****Papa's Pastries***, Charles Toscano. Ages 4–7. Miguel's father bakes pastries and when he cannot sell them, gives them away to those even more needy than his family. Sweet story of kindness and sharing highlighting the generous and hospitable nature of the Hispanic culture.
3. *****The Tortilla Factory***, Gary Paulsen. Ages 4–8. Exquisite cycle-of-life story from seed to plant to tortilla. And the cycle from the harvesting farm workers, to the tortilla machine operators, to the deliver truckers who deliver the tortillas back into the hands that will plant the seeds.
4. *****Erandi's Braids***, Antonio Madrigal, Tomie dePaola. Ages 3–7. While financially poor, this Mexican family is rich in love and sacrifice for each other.

5. ***Mañana Iguana**, Ann Whitford Paul. Ages 4–7. Retelling of the little red hen with desert animals and a happy ending that will delight your children. Integrates Spanish words with a glossary and pronunciation guide.
6. A nonfiction book about rattlesnakes such as **Buzzing Rattlesnakes**, Ruth Berman. Ages 4–7. Look for one with photographs or realistic illustrations and simple, short text.
7. **What Can You do with a Rebozo?** Carmen Tafolla. Ages 3–6. Sweet book about the traditional Mexican shawl which includes Hispanic culture, a piñata, Mexican dance, and costume.
8. **The Cazuela That the Farm Maiden Stirred**, Samantha Vamos. Ages 4–10. A farm girl prepares a cazuela (pot) of rice pudding with help from the animals. Spanish words are presented.
9. **Pumpkin Fiesta,** Caryn Yacowitz. Ages 3–6. Fable set in Mexico about a hard worker who teaches a fool about pumpkins.
10. **Frida Kahlo: The Artist Who Painted Herself**, Margaret Frith/ Tomie DePaola. Ages 6–9. Bio of the most famous female Mexican artist. Parents might want to read first as it mentions Day of the Dead, though in thoughtful way.
11. **Nine Days to Christmas, A Story of Mexico**, Marie Hall Ets. Ages 5–6. Old-fashioned story of a little girl in Mexico who gets her first posada and piñata.

SUPPLIES

1. Map of North America from last week
2. Copy of Mexico seal for flag, available on the *GO GLOBAL* Resource page
3. Materials for volcano: jar/cup; baking soda, vinegar, liquid detergent, and red tempera paint
4. Materials for snake: green construction paper or paper plate; OR Neck tie snake: old neck tie, plastic grocery sacks, long chenille wire, red felt, googly eyes, needle and thread, jingle bells, thin pole to push in stuffing. Tutorial available on the *GO GLOBAL* Resource page.
5. Diluted glue for "snake skin"
6. Materials for piñata: paper sack, small toys/candy, tissue paper, glue stick, scissors, newspaper for stuffing, stapler, and string/yarn. Tutorial available on the *GO GLOBAL* Resource page.
7. Spanish language tutorial available on the *GO GLOBAL* Resource page
8. Mexican hat dance tutorial and music, which are available on the *GO GLOBAL* Resource page
9. Food ingredients for Mexican fiesta
10. Costumes for Mexican fiesta (optional)
11. *GO GLOBAL* Game

DAY 1 — OVERVIEW AND VOLCANO

EVERYONE

1. Look at your map of North America to find Mexico. Point out that it is mostly desert with two strips of mountains. Also point out that Central America is mostly forest. Color the vegetation symbols on Mexico and Central America. Explain that we will be learning about the rainforest in a few weeks!

    Draw a star for the capital city, Mexico City.

2. Read **Hill of Fire** and then make a volcano.

Materials

- Cup or small jar
- ½–2 oz. washable tempera red paint, can add some yellow if you would like
- 6 drops liquid detergent
- 4 Tbsp. baking soda
- 1 C. vinegar

Process

    a) Make a mound outside with sand, gravel or dirt and place the cup inside the top of the mound. Do not have sand, gravel, or dirt in the cup. You could also make a "mountain" with play dough formed around the cup. If you do this inside you need to have the volcano in a large lipped pan.

    b) Fill cup ½ full of warm water and add paint, detergent, and baking soda.

    c) Slowly pour vinegar into cup. You should be able to do a couple of eruptions.

3. Read one or more of the books about or based in Mexico.

DAY 2 — FLAG AND LANGUAGE

EVERYONE

1. Mexico's flag consists of three vertical bands in green, white, and red. The Mexican coat of arms, which shows an eagle on a prickly pear cactus with a snake in its beak and talons, is in the center of the white band. Make a Mexican Flag for your fiesta tomorrow. Pattern of snake emblem is available on the *GO GLOBAL* Resource page to print off and color.

2. Read ***I Don't Like Snakes***. As you read aloud take breaks to move as inspired by the book. This activates the children's learning, keeps everyone motivated, increases anticipation, and is fun, too!

    a) For instance, after learning about the three ways that snakes slither on pages 8–9, instruct everyone to get down on the ground and slither those three ways!

    b) Have your child flick their tongues as they learn about how the snake smells.

    c) Constrict around a stuffed animal when you read about constrictors.

    d) Apply diluted glue to your child's arm when you start to read the book. When you get to the pages about shedding skin let your child peel off the "old skin".

3. Rattlesnake art tutorials available on the *GO GLOBAL* Resource page.

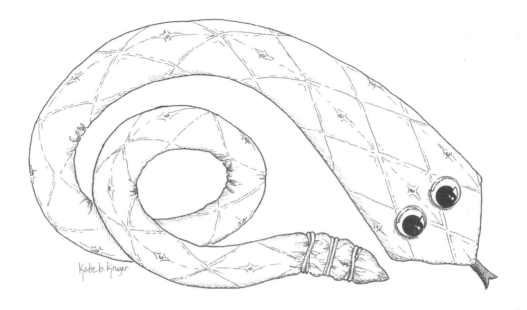

Easiest: Construction paper or paper plate rattlesnake. Cut with triangular head, draw diamonds along the back and a rattle at the end of the tail.

OR

Harder: Rattlesnake Stuffed Animal

Materials

- Inexpensive necktie(s) from a thrift store. You want a wide tie so the head will be big. Diamond pattern or spots would be great, but you can use your imagination.
- Filling: old plastic grocery sacks OR batting
- Long skinny pole/stick to push the stuffing into the snake/tie.
- Needle and thread
- Tongue: red felt
- Eyes: googly eyes OR buttons. CAUTION: choking hazard for babies/toddlers
- Fabric glue
- OPTIONAL: backbone/vertebrae: long thick chenille wire
- OPTIONAL: Rattle: Jingle Bells
  CAUTION: Choking hazard for babies/toddlers.
  CAUTION #2: Our preschool boys smacked each other with the tails—which is potentially painful and dangerous with the bells.

Process

1) Open tie at the wide end. Carefully snip the thread in the center where the lining is connected to the tie. DO NOT use a seam ripper to rip open the seam. (I know this from experience.)

2) OPTIONAL: Add the vertebrae. First, have your child feel his sibling's backbone, or yours. Tell him that snakes are vertebrates and have a back bone. This step will enable your child to bend the snake and have the snake wrap around things.

3) Stuff the tie. Use batting if you want a soft stuffed animal feel, realizing that you, the parent, will do most of the work. Plastic grocery sacks provide a crinkly feel, are less messy, and allow the child to do more of the stuffing. Use a skinny, smooth stick (such as a curtain rod) to push down the batting/sacks.

4) Sew the lining to the wide end of the tie.

5) Add the eyes (fabric glue) and tongue (sew or fabric glue).

6) OPTIONAL: sew on the jingle bells if they want their snake to be a rattler.

4. Watch a fun video from the father-son duo at What's Inside of what is inside a rattlesnake's rattle. Link available on the *GO GLOBAL* Resource page.

5. If rattlesnakes live in your area, take this time to discuss safety precautions.

    a) Never place your hands, arms, feet, or legs where you cannot see them when outdoors.

    b) Wear closed toed shoes when walking through areas with snakes.

    c) Walk around logs instead of blindly stepping over them.

    d) Remain calm if you see a snake. It wants to get away from you as much as you want to get away from it.

    e) Do NOT poke at a snake. It can strike the distance of half its body length. So, a four-foot snake can strike two feet.

    f) Learn to recognize the poisonous snakes in your area. For instance, rattlesnakes have a large triangular shaped head as well as their rattle. They can strike even if they are not rattling.

    g) Learn the seasons and locations where you are most likely to encounter them. In the spring and the autumn snakes are active, but still sluggish, and may strike because they cannot get away from you fast enough.

    h) If you encounter a snake while riding your bike lift your legs and coast, so the snake will strike at the wheels and not your legs.

    i) If bitten, immobilize the limb, keep it lower than the heart, and call 911.

    j) Relax, Mom. Over half of all rattlesnake bites occur when a person is trying to tease, probe, or catch the snake. And less than 1% of all the people bitten by a rattlesnake die.

ADD FOR SIX-YEAR-OLDS AND UP

6. Learn some Spanish. Just try the easy ones if you have not had any exposure to the language. You may continue learning Spanish while studying South America and while studying Spain in Europe. Language tutorial available on the *GO GLOBAL* Resource page.

Spanish word	Pronunciation	Meaning
hola!	OH-lah	hello
adios	ah-dee-OHS	good-bye
fiesta	fee-EHS-tah	party
sombrero	sohm-BREHR-oh	hat
piñata	pee-NYAH-tah	container of toys/candy for game
taco	TAH-koh	corn tortilla with meat filling
olé!	o-LAY	hurray

Harder

por favor	pohr fah-VOR	please
gracias	GRAH-see-yahs	thank you
si	see	yes
no	no	no
Mexico	MEH-hee-coh	Mexico

Advanced

Cómo está?	KOH-moh ehs-TAH	How are you?
Estoy bien.	ehs-TOY bee-EHN	I am fine.
Cómo se llama?	KOH-moh seh YAH-mah	What is your name?
Me llamo Juan.	meh YAH-mo Wahn	My name is John.
español	es-pan-YOHL	Spanish

DAY 3 — FIESTA PREPARATIONS

EVERYONE

1. Make a "no mess" piñata. Traditionally, piñatas are made of papier-mâché which is messy, multi-stepped, and difficult for young children to do. This project is simple, fairly quick, and not messy. Let your little ones do as much as they are able. They will love helping put in the toys, and the crumpled paper. Cutting the fringe and gluing on the strips are great ways to build their hand strength and dexterity in preparation for writing. If you prefer to buy a piñata, get a classic one such as a bright colored donkey, parrot, sombrero, sun, or star. Tutorial available on the *GO GLOBAL* Resource page.

    Materials
    - Paper bag (large grocery bag)
    - Candy and/or small, unbreakable toys

- Newspaper
- Bright colored tissue paper
- Craft glue, scissors, and stapler
- String or yarn

Process

a) Open bag and put candy/small toys in the bottom—no more than half way full so it is not too heavy. Fill rest of bag with crumpled newspaper.

b) Pinch the top of bag together and roll down two or three times. Staple shut.

c) Cover bottom of bag with tissue paper. Cut paper so that it is about 2 inches larger than the bottom of the bag all the way around. Glue the bottom and the sides. You can fold the corners like you are wrapping a gift.

d) Cut strips of tissue paper that are long enough to go around the bag, and are about 4 to 6 inches wide. You will need about five strips of paper. Use bright colors!

e) Use scissors to cut fringe along one long edge of tissue paper. The cuts should be about half way through the tissue paper and they should be about one inch apart.

f) Glue first strip just above the piece of tissue paper along the bottom by putting glue on the non-fringed part of the paper. The fringes should hang over the other tissue and even lightly hang over the bottom edge of the bag. Continue with each piece of tissue paper until the entire bag is covered and looks like a 1920's flapper dress! To make your piñata appear fuller, use more strips glued closer together.

g) Punch two holes along the top folded edge of the bag. Using a 2–3-yard piece of string or yarn thread through the holes. Knot the string firmly so that it will not come apart when you hang it.

h) Cut several strips of tissue paper about one inch by six inches and glue to the bottom of bag.

i) Hang the piñata. Blindfold one child at a time and let him swing using a stick or plastic bat. OPTIONAL: hang the piñata with a piece of rope/string to be able to pull up the piñata so everyone gets a turn. If your children have a hard time breaking the bag, weaken the bag with a few discreet cuts.

2. Read some of your Mexico books again.

3. Learn the Mexican hat dance. Tutorial and music available on the *GO GLOBAL* Resource page.

    Hands on hips, alternate putting one foot out with the heel on the ground. (3x) Clap. (2x) Swing your partner or throw a sombrero on the floor and hold alternate hands to dance around the hat. Change directions for fun. Shout out, "Olé!"

4. Practice your Spanish.

DAY 4   FIESTA DAY!

EVERYONE

1. Costumes are OPTIONAL. Do not stress about this. Just a bright scarf or play silk tied around their waist will make them feel festive and happy!

    For the boys: Dark pants (perhaps with silver braid or brads down the sides), white shirt, red sash belt, sombrero. VERY OPTIONAL: Add maracas for him to hold and perhaps draw on a small mustache.

    For the girls: a full dress/ skirt (could be layered ruffles) with at least some bright red. White, bright green, and bright yellow are good colors to add. You can use a white skirt and add a bright colored (red alone or with other bright colors) sash around her waist. Add a red flower in her hair above one ear. Her hair can be loose or in a bun on the side where the flower is bobby pinned.

2. Plan the meal. Let your children do as much themselves as possible.

    > As your children build their own tacos, they will practice and strengthen the pincher grasp, which is a prewriting exercise. They want to do it themselves, and this is an important exercise as well.

    <u>Tacos or Tostadas</u>: Tostada or taco (hard or soft) shells; refried beans will help the other toppings to stick; cooked, crumbled ground beef (or turkey/chicken) with package of taco seasoning. Top with shredded lettuce, diced tomatoes, and grated cheese. OPTIONAL: sliced black olives, sour cream, and salsa. Let your kids build their own tostados or tacos. Serve with tortilla chips and guacamole.

    <u>Sangria</u>: ½ C. grape juice; ¼ C. orange juice; ¼ cup Sprite/7up. One or more cut up fruit: orange slices, maraschino cherry, peeled pear slices, sliced strawberries, and raspberries.

    <u>Chocolate</u> for dessert. Did you know that cacao has been cultivated for at least three thousand years in Mexico?

3. Decorate: as simple as putting out your flag, piñata, snake art, and food. You can add some streamers in the bold Mexican colors.

4. Have the fiesta: Break the piñata, practice your Spanish, dance, and eat some fun Mexican food. Play the *GO GLOBAL* Game adding the North American cards into the mix!

WEEK 7
CATCH UP OR TAKE A BREAK!

WEEK 8
SOUTH AMERICA
GENERAL & ANDES MOUNTAINS

BIG PICTURE

South America has the world's largest chain of mountains, the Andes Mountains, along its whole west coast. It also has the largest (but not longest) river in the world, the Amazon River. Much of South America is covered with rainforests—hot damp forests or jungles. And it has the driest desert in the world—the Atacama Desert. There is also an area of grasslands called the Pampas in the southeast section of the continent where there are vast cattle herds and the cowboys of South America called gauchos.

The Andes Mountains are the second highest mountains in the world—only the Himalayas are taller. In the north, close to the equator the mountains are warm and humid. In the south, they are cool and damp. In the central region, the climate is dry. The indigenous people farmed on narrow terraces built into the hillsides and raised llamas, alpacas, and sheep.

Lake Titicaca (TEE tee kah kah), located in the Andes Mountains in Peru, is the world's highest lake. It is deep enough for large ships to use.

Llamas are a South American relative of the camel, though they do not have a hump. They were domesticated in South America around 4000 BC near Lake Titicaca by the Indians who predated the Incas. Llamas are used as pack animals in the Andes as they can carry heavy loads, walk sure footed on the steep mountain, and endure long distances. They are herbivores, eating grass, and are about as tall as a man. They also provide wool for rugs, fabrics, and rope.

Llamas are social creatures and like to be around other llamas or even other animals. Though they are good beasts of burdens, they will simply sit down if you load them up too much. They hum when they are happy and spit if they are angry or scared.

MATERIALS

Books

1. ***Beginner's World Atlas 3rd Edition***, National Geographic. 2011.
2. ***Up and Down the Andes: A Peruvian Festival Tale***, Laurie Krebs. Ages 6–8. A simple story with vibrant pictures that demonstrate South American culture and history as a group of children climb the mountains to a summer solstice celebration of the sun god. Map and end notes for further info. Parents need to be ready to talk about how people are religious by nature and want to worship God. More information in the lesson plans.
3. A non-fiction book on llamas such as ***Llamas*** (A True Book) Emilie Lepthien. Ages 6–10. You might need to talk about the pictures rather than read the complete text.

4. ***Love & Roast Chicken: A Trickster Tale from the Andes Mountains***, Barbara Knutson. Ages 4–7. Story of Guinea Pig and Fox in the Andes. Spanish words.
5. ***Lost City: The Discovery of Machu Picchu***, Ted Lewin. Ages 5–9. Beautifully illustrated story of Hiram Bingham's discovery of this lost city.

Secondary Books: Find *some* of these excellent books to read aloud and make available to your children for their quiet times. * means especially recommended.

1. ***Is your Mama a Llama?*** Deborah Guarino. Ages 2–6. A baby llama asks his friends if their mama is a llama. Shows various baby animals in their natural surroundings.
2. ***The Littlest Llama***, Jane Buxton. Ages 3–7. Delightful story of a little llama looking for friends. The little llama meets other animals in the Andes, and even some of the native people.
3. ***Maria Had a Little Llama***, Angela Dominguez. Ages 3–8. Story of Andean girl and her pet llama.
4. ***Patterns in Peru: An Adventure in Patterning***, Cindy Neuschwander. Ages 6–11. Pretend adventure of finding a mythical Inca city in the Andes. Fun math activities.
5. ***Harley***, Star Livingstone. Ages 5–8. Early reader for the child to read aloud. Story of a llama in the modern USA that is used to herd sheep.
6. ***Papagayo: The Mischief Maker***, Gerald McDermott. Ages 4–7. Mischievous parrot leads the quiet, nocturnal jungle animals to stop the ancient night monster dog. A trickster tale that might be scary for sensitive children.
7. ***This Place is High: The Andes Mountains of South America***, Vicki Cobb. Ages 7–11. Good information on altitude, climate, food, animals, Inca history, and culture of the Bolivian and Peruvian Andes.
8. Nonfiction book such as ***Guinea Pigs***, Katie Marsico. Ages 6–10.

SUPPLIES

1. Map of South America (available on the *GO GLOBAL* Resource page) printed on card stock
2. Weaving kit OR metal cooling rack and ribbons
3. Blue paper, sandpaper, and scissors
4. *GO GLOBAL* Game

DAY 1 — OVERVIEW

EVERYONE

1. Read ***Beginner's World Atlas***, pages 26–31.
2. Using a printed copy of the South America map provided on the *GO GLOBAL* Resource page,
   a) Point out that the Pacific Ocean is to the west, the Atlantic Ocean to the east, and the Southern Ocean to the south. The parent or the older children can label these water bodies. Mention the Caribbean Sea to the north. Let them color the water blue.
   b) Color the mountain symbols that stretch along the western edge of the continent all the way from the northern edge to the southern tip. Label the Andes Mountains.
   c) Color the Amazon River blue. Label the river.

d) Color the grass plant symbol to the pampas area. Pampas are in Argentina and Uruguay in the southeastern portion of South America.

e) Color the rainforest/jungle trees in the Amazon rainforest area, and to the eastern portions of Brazil as indicated on the map on page 29 of the ***Beginner's World Atlas***.

f) Add small strips of sandpaper to the desert regions marked with a "d".

3. Learn about the different amount of rainfall in the rainforest and the desert.

a) Parent should measure and cut 15 one-inch by ten-inch strips of blue paper. Mark each strip into one-inch squares.

b) Let your child cut four of the strips into one-inch squares.

c) Make a bar graph by taping the squares on your wall.

- One column on your wall indicates the average annual rainfall in your home town

- A second column indicates the average annual rainfall in the Amazon Forest (70–110 inches)

- A third column indicates the average rainfall in the US desert (Phoenix gets about 7 inches)

- A fourth column indicates the average rainfall in the Atacama Desert in Chile, the driest desert in the world. Parts of the desert have not seen a drop of rain since record keeping began. The average for this desert area is 0.6 inches of rain per year. So, you will need to cut one of the squares in half!

Have your child explain this to you first and then to dad when he comes home from work! Leave this up on your wall for the whole time that we are studying South America. We will refer to it again.

DAY 2 — ANDES MOUNTAINS

EVERYONE

1. Tell your child that the Andes are the longest mountain range on Earth. These very tall mountains (taller than any mountains other than the Himalayas in Asia) rise steeply from the coast of the Pacific Ocean. The ancient people who lived in the South American Andes in the 15th and 16th centuries are called the Incas. They built a great city called Machu Picchu around AD 1450 which was not discovered until 1911.

Read ***Lost City: The Discovery of Machu Picchu*** to give your children a sense of the history of this area. Make sure they understand that this wonderful water color picture book is about real people and real places. This true story will mesmerize everyone, from your preschoolers to the adults in your home! Mark Machu Picchu on your map.

2. Read ***Up and Down the Andes*** to get a sense of this area and these people. The children go to a summer solstice celebration of the sun god. Parents need to be aware and ready to talk about how people are religious by nature and want to worship God. Many primitive cultures worshipped the sun. This is why some Christians, called missionaries, go overseas to tell people the Good News about the Son of God.

> These are the kinds of discussions we want to have with our children, and this book provides a good opportunity to develop a Christian world view.

DAY 3 — LLAMAS

EVERYONE

1. Read one or more of the llama books and discuss the information provided in this week's introduction.

    a) Llamas sit down when you overload them.

    b) Llamas hum when they are happy.

    c) Llamas spit when they are angry. (Just pantomime.)

    d) Llamas take a "bath" by rolling in the dust!

    e) Llamas neck wrestle. They try to push each other to the ground just using their necks!

    Pretend to be llamas.

2. To celebrate the llama, weave a bright colored scarf out of "llama" wool. Either purchase a kit or do this easy weaving activity. Tutorial available on the *GO GLOBAL* Resource page.

> This is not only fun, but again, develops and strengthens the important pincher grip for your child, which is a necessary skill for writing.

Materials

- Yarn, ribbon, or pipe cleaners in vibrant colors (blue, green, red, yellow, black, dark orange, white, maroon) and various widths
- Metal cooling rack

Process

Have your child wind the yarn or ribbon in and out of the metal grid.

DAY 4 — GUINEA PIGS

EVERYONE

1. Read **Love and Roast Chicken**. This is a trickster tale where a small animal uses his brains to trick a stronger animal. Trickster tales are oral traditions and occur worldwide! We will also read some trickster tales from Africa when we study that continent. There is a pronunciation guide at the back of the book since there are a few Spanish and Quechuan words.

   Before you read, while looking at the cover:

   a) Ask your child who she thinks are the two main characters. [Answer: The guinea pig (she might say mouse) and the fox.] Ask which one she thinks will be the trickster.

   b) Ask if she thinks this will be a happened-in-real-life (nonfiction) story or a fantasy (fiction) one?

   > This question can be used regularly as you read with your young child. It is important that they can differentiate between real and pretend. Any time animals talk it is pretend.

   While you read the book:

   a) During the clay figure scene, ask why she thinks Cuy's paws stuck to the clay doll. Does this remind her of another story? [Answer: *Brer Rabbit and the Tar Baby*.]

   b) On the page with Tio Antonio in the den, ask your child what she thinks the Tio will find when he exits the den. [Answers will vary; give the child an opportunity to guess.]

   c) What does Tio think he will miss the most if the world ends? [Answer: Dancing in the moonlight with the village girls and chicken dinners. You do not need to tell your child that this is foreshadowing. But she will remember that is what Cuy uses to tempt Tio later.]

   After reading:

   d) Ask your child who gets fooled in this story? When she gives one answer ask her how that individual was fooled. Then gently ask if anyone else was fooled. The point here is to get her to think and analyze. The point is NOT for you to instruct her. [Answer: Tio, the farmer, and Cuy.]

   e) Have your child describe the countryside (the Andes Mountains) in this story. [Possible answer: tall mountains with snow, rocky terrain, steep mountains where you can see down into the valleys.] This will help solidify the concepts of the physical geography of the Andes Mountains.

   f) Have your child describe the houses and people of this poor, rural area in the Andes Mountains. [Possible answer: a simple farm without a town, candles rather than electricity, bare feet or sandals, simple clothes.] This will help solidify the cultural geography of the region.

2. Read a non-fiction book about guinea pigs such as **Guinea Pigs**, by Katie Marsico.

- a) The guinea pig is neither a pig nor from Guinea. These rodents originated in the Andes Mountains and were domesticated as early as 4000 BC for food. They have been popular pets for centuries: even Queen Elizabeth I had one in the early 17th century.
- b) Visit the pet store this week to see some real guinea pigs.

3. Read the books from earlier this week, or any others you found.
4. Play the *GO GLOBAL* Game to review continents, oceans, and North America.

WEEK 9
SOUTH AMERICA
RAINFOREST

BIG PICTURE

South America has some of the largest and most important rainforests in the world. This week the focus is on the Amazon rainforest, which is warm throughout the year with high humidity. Your family will learn about the parts of the rainforest: the floor, the understory, the canopy, and the emergent layer.

The floor is the musty ground of the rainforest that lacks fresh air and sunlight due to the dense layers above. Few plants live here. Instead the floor is littered with fallen leaves, rotting fruit, and fungi. Insects such as ants, earthworms, termites, and bacteria thrive here with ground dwelling birds, snakes, and mammals. There are many pools, ponds, and rivers flowing through this area with their own wildlife. Tree buttresses, which are like roots that are growing above the ground, stabilize many of the trees in this moist soil.

The understory is the height of the small trees such as palms and strangler figs (about 60 to 120 feet above the floor), which have thinner trunks and narrow crowns. This area gets just a little sunlight and provides a home for the jaguars, anteaters, frogs, and snakes. Many of these trees have dangling aerial roots that the monkeys use to swing through the forest.

The canopy of the forest is the largest portion of the tree tops and is considered the umbrella or roof of the forest. This thick layer rises from about 100 to about 165 feet above the floor. Ninety percent of the forest animals live in here including birds, monkeys, sloths, snakes, frogs, insects, and lizards. Many of these animals NEVER touch the floor. The top of the canopy has strong sunlight and it is here that the bees and butterflies flit through the bright flowers.

The emergent layer includes the few trees that emerge above the canopy, basking in the ample sunlight, wind, and rain. Here birds, bats, butterflies, and some monkeys dwell. The harpy eagle, however, rules all as it surveys the rest of the rainforest and sweeps down to find its prey in the top of the canopy.

Although only 7% of the earth is tropical rainforest, more that 50% of the world's plants and animals live there! For the next two weeks, you will learn about some of this unique wildlife.

While a jungle is technically slightly different from a rainforest, the distinction does not need to be explained to elementary aged children. For the parents: The jungle does not have the layers, and the floor is more thickly vegetated. There is jungle in South America, but it is mostly known for the rainforest. The same symbol will be used for the jungle and rainforest.

MATERIALS

Books

We will use these books again next week.

1. ***The Umbrella,*** Jan Brett. Ages 4–10. Carlos walks in the rainforest while animals collect in the umbrella he left as he climbed the canopy.
2. ***The Rainforest Grew All Around***, Susan Mitchell. Ages 4–8. The circle of life from the floor to the canopy. Includes many animals and the kapok tree, liana vines, and bromeliads.
3. ***"Slowly, Slowly, Slowly," Said the Sloth***, Eric Carle. Ages 2–7. Delightful book about the sloth, lots of rainforest animals, and a delightful verbal answer in the end.
4. A nonfiction book about sloths with photographs, such as **Baby Sloth**, Aubrey Lang. Delightful book full of easy-to-understand information and photographs, or **Being a Sloth**, Julia McDonnell, or **Find It in a Rain Forest**, Dee Phillips.
5. ***Jungle Song***, Miriam Moss. Ages 4–8. Story of baby tapir exploring the rainforest in South America. Wonderful variety of over two dozen animals, rich vocabulary, and sweet illustrations. Endnote with additional information about the Amazon jungle.

Secondary Books: Find *some* of these excellent books to read aloud and make available to your children for their quiet times. * means especially recommended.

1. ****Over in the Jungle: A Rainforest Rhyme**, Marianne Berkes. Ages 4–8. Counting, fabulous illustrations of 10 rainforest animals, rich vocabulary, and end pages filled with additional information.
2. ****In the Rainforest**, Kate Duke. Ages 4–8. Child friendly with great information that will cover much of what we learn in this lesson. Rainforest structure and plants as well as animals.
3. ***Nature's Green Umbrella,** Gail Gibbons. Ages 6–10. Great information and pictures. Parents will need to read and simplify for younger children, but that can be done easily with this book. Rainforest structure and plants, as well as animals.
4. ***Find It in a Rain Forest**, Dee Phillips. Ages 3–7. Simple text on the rainforest and animals including sloth, iguana, tapir, toucan, jaguar, parrot, monkey, and viper.
5. ***Here is the Tropical Rain Forest**, Madeleine Dunphy. Ages 5–7. Lyrical story and lush naturalistic paintings.
6. ***Meet the Howlers!** April Pulley Sayre. Ages 3–7. Fun, rhyming, nonfiction book with lots of information on howler monkeys. Simple text for younger children with more information for older kids.
7. **We're Roaming in the Rainforest**, Laurie Krebs. Ages 4–8. Similar to **The Umbrella** and **The Rainforest Grew All Around**. Maps and extra info in the back of book. Information on rainforest structure, indigenous peoples, and animals.
8. **So Say the Little Monkeys**, Nancy Van Laan. Ages 3–7. Brazilian folktale of little monkeys who play all day provides an important moral. Lyrical structure, amusing rhymes, and charming onomatopoeia ("Plinka, plinka goes the rain") make this a wonderful read aloud. Onomatopoeia is a word that imitates, resembles or suggests the sound it describes.
9. Nonfiction books on the Amazon animals that interest your child. Look for books with realistic picture and simple text such as **Capybara**, Anita Ganeri; or **Capybaras**, Grace Hansen.
10. **Rain, Rain, Rain Forest,** Brenda Guiberson. Ages 4–8. The sounds and animals of the rainforest.
11. **Can You See Me?** Ted Lewin. Ages 4–7. Easy reader. Find the animals hidden in the rainforest.

Video

1. **The Second Voyage of the Mimi** stars a 12-year-old Ben Affleck going on a fantastic adventure learning about the Mayans and the Central American rainforest. This educational television program includes a 15-minute story segment and a 15-minute science presentation. It is only on YouTube and the programs are grainy. This program is aimed at upper elementary/ middle school, but we have found all ages like it. The storyline is exciting, and they are very informative. The second half of episode 11 (In the Canopy) and last half of episode 10 (Up in a Tree) are especially relevant for this study. Link available on *GO GLOBAL* Resource page.

SUPPLIES

1. Dramatization props: blue cloth, green crepe paper, flowers or floral cloth
2. Multiple copies of the South American animal chart, available on *GO GLOBAL* Resource page
3. Chocolate covered Brazil nuts: 4 oz. semi-sweet chocolate, 8 oz. shelled Brazil nuts

DAY 1 — AMAZON RAINFOREST

EVERYONE

1. Review the amount of rain that falls in the rainforest. Look at your blue squares and recount them.
2. Read ***The Umbrella*** and ***The Rainforest Grew All Around***. Talk to your children about the layers of the rainforest.
3. Dramatize the Amazon rainforest. This activity will teach your child the parts of the rainforest as well as a lot about the animals and even a bit about the indigenous people who have inhabited the area for centuries.

    a) First define your habitat. Find a place either inside or outside where your child can move up and down four levels. The four levels you teach your child will be the floor, the understory, the canopy, and the emergent layer.

    - You can do this outside with a climbable tree or a jungle gym.

    - Inside bunk beds would be ideal—the floor of the room is the floor, the lower bunk is the understory, the ladder and laying on the top bunk is the canopy, and sitting up with your arms up is the emergent layer.

    - A sofa could also work. The floor of the room is the floor, loose cushions on the floor are the understory, the sofa seat is the canopy, and the arms or back of the sofa are the emergent layer.

    Realize that where ever you set this up and teach them, they will go back and play without you, so make sure that it is a safe environment for your children.

    b) You do not need to add much decoration—perhaps a blue play silk, or blue cloth, on the floor to be the pond or river. For safety reasons, we should not use any real rope to approximate vines in the understory, but perhaps some green crepe paper would be fun and safe! The top of the canopy is where the bright flowers live and bloom—so place some artificial flowers or some flowered material up there.

    c) Have your child climb to each area and tell you its name. Then play a game with him by calling out a place to go. Let him go back and forth to various levels. As he is in the level, have him describe it. Is it dark or light? Is there a breeze? How humid is it?

    d) Ask your child if he knows what plants are in the rainforest. Does he know what layer they are in. What animals are there? Do not worry if he doesn't know… that is what we are going to be learning. Today it is enough to know the four layers.

4. Read more of your Amazon rainforest books and talk about the animals. Tomorrow we will start a list.

DAY 2 — SLOTH AND AMAZON ANIMALS

EVERYONE

1. Read **"Slowly, Slowly, Slowly," Said the Sloth** and read a nonfiction book about sloths.

    a) Have your child act like a sloth (hang upside down on the sofa, move very slowly) while you read the **Slowly, Slowly** book.

    b) If possible, look at a nonfiction book about sloths to see photographs and learn more about this interesting animal.

    c) Information that you should impart to your child about the sloth:

    - He moves slowly.
    - He hangs upside down from a tree, and therefore his hair grows in an unusual direction.
    - The sloth is a habitat (home) for many other organisms including moths, beetles, cockroaches, fungi, and algae.
    - He eats mostly buds and leaves.
    - He has low energy and sleeps 15–19 hours per day.
    - He can swim and only comes down from his tree about once a week.
    - He is quiet, only making a gentle sigh—"ah-eee."

    d) Talk about the words the sloth uses to describe himself: Lackadaisical, dawdle, dillydally, unflappable, languid, stoic, impassive, sluggish, lethargic, placid, calm, mellow, laid-back, relaxed, tranquil, slothful. Ask your child which words he knows. Ask him which words he likes! Do not make it a test. Perhaps you can use some of these words in your everyday talk.

    e) On another reading of the book see if your child can name some of the other animals in the book: they are all listed on the back-end pages. Let him pick two other animals to dramatize.

2. Have your child START to make a chart of life in the rainforest. DO NOT do this for him. You may do the writing, but let him do the dictating. The first column should read "Animal", second column is "Location" and third column is for the child to draw a picture. Add a few animals every day! Printable available on *GO GLOBAL* Resource page.

Animal	Location	Drawing
Sloth	Understory	

    a) Location is where the animal lives: Emerging Layer, Canopy, Understory, Floor.

    b) Start with the sloth. You have already discussed the animal's behavior. And you have already dramatized the sloth. Mom can write down the name and location if the child prefers not to write; the purpose of this exercise is to talk and learn about the animal, not a handwriting exercise. But don't just fill in the information. Make sure he knows what layer the animal lives in. Then the child can draw a picture of the sloth.

c) Now ask your child what additional animal he wants to add to the list. Elicit information from your child... You can talk about anything about the animal that you or your child finds interesting. This could include what the animal likes to eat, its color, how it moves, etc. Make sure to discuss how you would dramatize this animal. An extensive chart is provided below with suggestions for the parent. But do not *just* use this chart, or just teach this information. You want to let your child have an opportunity to be creative and to tell you what he thinks! And you DO NOT have to cover all these animals. Younger children might only add one animal a day.

Your child might want to act out some of the animals himself. He might prefer to use stuffed animals to act out other animals. Allow for creativity and personal preference!

3. Continue to slowly add animals to your chart. Use the rainforest books to help you think of animals and collect information.

4. Dramatize the Amazon rainforest.

Name an animal and have your child go to the level where that animal lives and act like that animal. Only use the animals that you have read about and talked about. You will play this every day this week, and perhaps next week as well! Continue to add animals as you learn about them.

You do not need to learn all of these—but we wanted to supply you with a list.

Animal	*Location*	*Behavior*
Army Ants	Floor	March along in a line.
Leaf-cutter Ants	Floor	Bite off leaf sections and carry back to nests.
Anaconda	Understory/ Floor	Largest snake in the world by weight. Constricts and suffocates prey by wrapping around it. Likes to live in the swamp/water. Eats fish, rodents, tapirs, capybaras, deer, birds, and even jaguars. Gives birth to 20–40 live young.
Anteater	Floor	Flicks its tongue 160 times/min to avoid ant stings. Eats about 35,000 ants and termites each day. Uses large claws to dig and for self-defense.
Bat	Understory/ Canopy	Do not have feathers and are not birds; but do have wings and fly. Eat insects or fruit. Hang upside down
Boa Constrictor	Understory/ Canopy	Hides among the leaves of a tree wrapped around a branch. Slithers and then wraps around something and squeezes. Carnivore. Gives birth to live young.
Rhinoceros Beetle	Floor	Can carry 850 times its weight. Uses horn to dig his way out of thick floor matter. Also known as the Hercules Beetle.
Morpho Butterfly	Emergent/Canopy	Flits and flutters. (Use some play silks to dramatize.)

Animal	Location	Behavior
Caiman	Floor	Crocodile-like animal that lives in small streams or hidden in hollow logs or undergrowth. Carnivore.
Capybara	Floor	Largest rodent in the world; herbivore who eats grasses and river plants. Has webbed feet and can swim. Nocturnal. Jumps into the water when frightened.
Coati	Canopy/ but travels to Emergent & Floor	Raccoon-like animal with prehensile tail. Sleeps high in the canopy. Omnivores who likes to eat insects (like tarantulas), fruit, small birds and eggs. Chirps, snorts, grunts. Hides nose to show submission. Bares teeth to show anger.
Electric Eel	Floor in the water	Uses its electric shock to stun its prey.
Poison Tree or Red Eyed Frog	Understory/Canopy	Sticky pads on their toes help them cling to branches and leaves. They leap about to catch flying insects to eat. Bathes in bromeliads. Squat and jump!
Jaguar, also known as a panther	Floor/Understory	Hunts for fish by stirring water to disturb the fish. Sometimes, it uses its tail as bait to get the fish to come to the surface. Carnivore, nocturnal, buries its food for later consumption.
Kinkajou	Canopy	Scampers in the trees, nocturnal. Eats fruit and sips nectar from flowers with tongue. Also known as Honey Bear.
Howler Monkey	Canopy	Loudest land animal; Howls can be heard up to 3 miles away, scratches under arms. Herbivore—leaves and fruit.
Spider Monkey	Canopy	Swings arm over arm (brachiates), scratches under arm and chatters!
Marmoset	Canopy	Highly active monkey. Eats fruit, insects, and leaves. Loves to chew the tree trunks to eat the gum inside. Likes to climb to the top of the canopy to feed on the insects up there.
Ocelot	Understory/Floor	Likes to climb on tree branch. Pounces and bounces!
Piranha	Floor in the water	Carnivore: meat-eating fish that can tear apart an animal in minutes. Eats mollusks, fish, birds, lizards, rodents.
Tapir	Floor	Herbivore. Raises his nose and shows his teeth to detect scents. Likes to spend time in and under the water. Most active at dusk and dawn.
Sloth	Canopy	Hangs upside down, along a branch. Moves very slowly.
Tarantula	Floor	Can be as big as a man's hand. Scurries on the ground.
Harpy Eagle	Emergent/ Canopy	Sits on the high tree and swoops down to the canopy to grab some dinner! Carnivore who eats sloths, monkeys, iguanas and other birds.

Animal	Location	Behavior
Scarlet Macaw	Canopy	Nests inside tree trunks; Stamps foot and takes short sidewise steps (along a branch), flies through the canopy. Screeches/ squawks!
Hummingbird	Canopy/ Emergent	Darts about sipping nectar from flowers. Beats wings very quickly as it hovers to eat.
Quetzal	Canopy	Brightly colored—red belly, iridescent green wings and neck area. Long tail feathers. Eats fruits, berries, insects, and small frogs. Weak flyer.
Toucan	Emergent/ Canopy	Roosts in tree holes. Playful and mimics other sounds. Loves to bathe in pools of water that collect in the tree hollows. Uses beak to reach the fruit in the trees. Omnivore uses tongue to get ants. Lives in flocks.

DAY 3   MONKEYS, LIANAS, AND STRANGLER FIG

EVERYONE

1. Read some of the rainforest books.
2. Continue to add animals to your chart. Use the rainforest books to help you think of animals and collect information.
3. Dramatize the Amazon rainforest.

    Name an animal and have your child go to the level where that animal lives and act like that animal. Only use the animals that you have read about, talked about, and/or added to your list.

4. Talk about the "New World" monkeys. The monkeys in Central and South America have prehensile tails—which means they can use their tails like another arm/leg. They can grasp or hold objects with their tails. They can even hang and swing from their tails. The monkeys in Africa and Asia do NOT have prehensile tails. Be on the lookout for other animals that have prehensile tails such as tree porcupines, rats, possums, chameleons, geckos, alligator lizards, snakes, salamanders, or seahorses.

ADD FOR SIX-YEAR-OLDS AND UP

5. Vines are plants that trail along the ground or climb a tree, a fence, a wall, etc. A liana is a long-stemmed vine that is rooted in the soil and grows up using trees to climb to the canopy to get access to the sunlight. Animals like to use the liana to climb up the tree, as the base of the liana, near the ground, is usually woody and stiffer, though still small in diameter.

    Hemi-epiphytes are a group of plants that are like vines, but grow from the top down. These plants, such as orchids and strangler figs, start life in the canopy and grow down to the ground. Often their seeds grow in the crevices atop other trees—where there is a lot of light. Strangler figs grow slowly, with their roots growing downward and wrapping around the host tree. Once the roots reach the ground, the plant grows even faster. And sometimes the original support tree dies, so the strangler fig becomes a free standing "tree" with a hollow central core!

Are there any vines or epiphytes in your town? If so, go find them!

Look in your books for lianas, orchids, and strangler figs. See if your child remembers that lianas grow from the ground up.

DAY 4 — TAPIR AND BRAZIL NUT

EVERYONE

1. Read *Jungle Song* and add more animals to your list. Tapirs are large animals related to the horse! Adults are about seven feet long. Tapirs have a proboscis. While looking at a picture of the tapir, point to the nose and ask your child if it reminds him of another animal. [Answer: Elephant.] Tell him that this kind of a nose is called a proboscis. The tapirs live on the floor of the rainforest, like to be in mud, and are vegetarians. The babies are striped to be able to hide better from the jaguars and crocodiles who like to eat them. We will revisit the tapir to contrast it to the capybara in a few days.

    On a subsequent read, have your child

    a) Point out the animals as you read the book.

    b) Talk about the jungle—the light filtering through the leaves.

    c) Describe the thick vegetation.

    d) Point out the water. [Answer: Rain, lake, water dripping from plants when it is not raining, the mist.]

    e) Describe how the animals are camouflaged.

    f) Compare and contrast the termites and the ants, the bees and the hornet, the frog and the toad, the tree frog and the bull frog.

    g) Note that the morpho butterfly is as big as a hand. You might mention that we will make one next week!

2. The Brazil nut tree is one of the largest trees in the rainforest, reaching about 160 feet tall, with a trunk up to 6 ½ feet in diameter. Chocolate comes from the cacao (or cocoa) tree, which is a small (20 feet tall) evergreen tree native to Central and South America.

    Make and eat chocolate covered Brazil nuts.

    ### Ingredients

    - 1 pkg. (4 oz.) semi-sweet chocolate
    - 8 oz. shelled Brazil nuts, skins removed

    ### Process

    Melt chocolate as directed on package (Mom). Remove from heat and let your children dip each nut halfway into chocolate; place on sheet of wax paper. Refrigerate 15 minutes to set.

3. Dramatize the Amazon rainforest.

    Name a few animals and have your child go to the level where that animal lives and act like that animal. You might want to add green crepe paper streamers for the lianas and epiphytes. Only use the animals that you have read about, talked about, and/or added to your list.

ADD FOR SIX-YEAR-OLDS AND UP

4. Learn about capybaras; compare and contrast them to the tapirs. How are they similar and how are they different? Don't just tell your child. Look at pictures and guide him to observe and answer. You might ask him to describe the noses, tails, or body shape. You might ask him if they eat similar things or different things. Let your child reason this out!

    [Possible answers: Differences: Capybaras are rodents, tapirs are more closely related to horses! Tapirs are much bigger—seven feet long, while capybaras are four feet long. Tapirs have a proboscis, a long snout, while capybaras have a blunt nose. Tapirs have a short tail, capybaras have no tail at all; baby tapirs are striped while baby capybaras are colored like the adults. Similarities: both have long, narrow bodies described as pig-like; they live side-by-side in South America; both like mud; both are herbivores; both are food for jaguars and crocodiles.]

WEEK 10
SOUTH AMERICA
RAINFOREST, PART II

BIG PICTURE

Your exploration of the Amazon rainforest will continue this week. There was a lot of information shared last week, and you will continue to look even deeper into the plants and animals of the rainforest, emphasizing frogs, bromeliads, tropical birds, and butterflies.

This is a craft heavy week. Next week will be a lighter load so you can finish projects.

MATERIALS

Books

1. The books from last week.
2. **Red-Eyed Tree Frog**, Joy Cowley. Ages 4–7. Exquisite photographs of animals from the Central American rainforests. Simple text with extra end notes. Additional animals include macaw, toucan, iguana, katydid, caterpillar, and boa. The picture of the frog in the red bromeliad is worth the hunt for the book.

Secondary Books

1. The books from last week.
2. **My Amazon River Day**, Kris Nesbitt. Ages 6–11. Photo essay of a typical day of Peruvian children who live on the banks of the Amazon. Map and wildlife described.
3. **Amazon Boy,** Ted Lewin. Ages 6–10. Young native boy visits the big city and appreciates his home in the Amazon forest.
4. **The Frog with the Big Mouth,** Teresa Bateman. Ages 3–5. Retelling of the traditional tale of the wide-mouthed frog who meets a toucan, coati, capybara, and jaguar.
5. Nonfiction book on tropical birds such as the toucan, the macaw, or the harpy eagle.
6. Additional nonfiction books on the Amazon animals that interest your child.

SUPPLIES

1. Pineapple and other tropical fruit
2. Safari Rainforest TOOB, link available on *GO GLOBAL* Resource page
3. Toucan bird supplies: board, pool noodle, tongs, fruit, and candy "bugs" in a jar
4. Macaw bird supplies: pliers and nut
5. Harpy eagle supplies: sidewalk chalk, measuring stick, hot dog, and carving fork
6. Bird art supplies: brightly colored cardstock/construction paper (1 sheet each black, red, orange, green, white blue, yellow, gray) If making two sets add extra sheet of red. Compass or other way to measure circles. Tutorial available on *GO GLOBAL* Resource page.

7. Butterfly art supplies: white cardstock, blue and turquoise tissue paper, glue, black marker or paint, brown crayons, scissors, hole punch. Optional: silver glue-glitter. Tutorial available on *GO GLOBAL* Resource page.

DAY 1   AMAZON PINEAPPLE AND TREE FROG

EVERYONE

1. Use a fresh pineapple to talk about how it grows. A stalk grows out of the plant and the pineapple grows "impaled" on this stalk. Pineapple was first grown in one portion of South America and spread throughout Central and South America centuries ago. Columbus encountered it in 1493 and took it back to Europe. It was introduced into the Philippines, Hawaii, Zimbabwe, and Guam, where it is an important food and export.

   Pineapples are bromeliads, which are plants that form a rosette on top, where water is caught and stored. There are hundreds of different kinds of bromeliad plants that provide water for the animals that live high in the rainforest. Place your pineapple in a sink or bowl and try to capture water in your pineapple by spraying the pineapple with a spray bottle. This is the perfect location for a tree frog. It is the nursery for some of the frog eggs and tadpoles. The strawberry poison dart frog lays her eggs on a leaf on the ground, and the daddy frog cares for the eggs until they become tadpoles. At that point, the mother frog carries the tadpoles on her back and puts them in a bromeliad pool.

   Dramatize the lifecycle of the tree frog. Read **The Red-Eyed Tree Frog**, if available.

   Tonight, use the pineapple top (or the whole pineapple) with a little plastic tree frog as your dinner's centerpiece and have your child explain the life cycle to his dad.

2. Have a tropical fruit salad with fruits that come from the Amazon rainforest such as pineapple, banana, mango, passionfruit, coconut, guava, or papaya.

3. Read one of your Amazon rainforest books; add more animals to your list.

4. Dramatize the Amazon rainforest.

   Name a few animals and have your child go to the level where each animal lives and act like that animal. Only use the animals that you have read about, talked about, or added to your list.

DAY 2   AMAZON BIRDS (AN ART DAY)

You do NOT have to do all the art projects, but do cover the material and dramatize the birds. Photographs of the five birds and the butterfly are on the *GO GLOBAL* Resource page if you do not have them in your library books.

EVERYONE

1. Learn about the toucan. Have your child find pictures of the toucan in your rainforest books. Try to have at least one book with photographs of the toucan.

    a) Ask your child to describe the toucan.

    b) If she does not mention the beak, point it out. Ask her how long the bird's beak is compared to the bird's height. [Answer: Over half his height.] Ask your child if she could hold up her head if her nose was as wide as her face and two feet long! Then ask her to guess how the toucan hold up his head. Let your child think about this and give some answers.

    > This is an important step to developing their mental capabilities. Learning is more than regurgitating facts. Learning includes being able to reason to an answer.

    c) After she comes up with some answers have her hold a somewhat long and heavy board up to her nose. Then have her hold up a pool noodle to her nose. Though the noodle is even longer, she can hold it up easily. While the toucan's beak is incredibly huge, it is very lightweight.

    d) So, what is the purpose of this beak? God designed him this way… but why? Let your child think of answers before you guide her. [Answers include: To reach food, to play catch with their mate.]

    Toucans prefer to eat fruit. With their bills they can reach the end of the branches where the fruit is located. Toucans have 6-inch-long tongues, which in addition to the beak helps them reach deep inside of trees to find and capture insects that they also like to eat. Measure your child's tongue and compare that length to 6 inches.

    e) Using some long tongs as their beak, have your child reach for fruit "out on a branch" and then "dig" for (candy) bugs deep inside a tree (deep jar).

    f) Your child might also find it interesting that toucans do not fly much. Their wings are small. They are perching birds with some toes forward and others pointed back so that they can grasp a tree branch.

2. Make a collage toucan out of brightly colored paper circles. Tutorial available on *GO GLOBAL* Resource page.

   Materials
   - Cardstock or construction paper: black, bright orange, bright green
   - Glue sticks, scissors, and compass or some way to measure circles

   Process
   - a) Cut circles out of cardstock or construction paper. Parents should measure and draw circles if it is too difficult for the child.
     1. One 5" black circle, cut in half for body
     2. One 3.5" orange circle, cut in half for beak
     3. One 3.5" black circle, cut in half for wing
     4. One 1" bright/light green circle for eye
     5. One 0.25" black circle for pupil
   - b) Assemble bird.
     1. Glue large, black half-circle to orange half-circle for beak.
     2. Add black half-circle for wing.
     3. Add green and black circles for eye.

3. Learn about the scarlet macaw. Have your child find pictures of the scarlet macaw in your rainforest books. Try to have at least one book with photographs.
   - a) Ask your child to describe the macaw.
   - b) Point out the brightly colored plumage (feathers) if she does not notice it. Ask her to name all the colors. Also, note the length of the tail and the shape of the beak. Their long wings and tails help them fly through the rainforest.
   - c) So, what is the purpose of this beak? God designed him this way… but why? Again, let your child think of answers before you guide her. [Answers include: To bite into fruit and to crack open the nuts and seeds that they like.]
   - d) His beak is short, strong, and curved to crack nuts. Use some pliers to crack open a nut for you to eat.

   > A child effortlessly expands her vocabulary as an adult uses rich words such as *plumage, perching, beak, impaled* while looking at books and real objects.

4. Make a collage scarlet macaw out of brightly colored paper circles. Tutorial available on *GO GLOBAL* Resource page.

Materials

- Cardstock or construction paper: red, white, black, yellow; two contrasting colors: yellow, orange, blue, or light green
- Glue sticks, scissors, compass or some way to measure circles

Process

a) Cut circles out of cardstock or construction paper.
   1. Five 3.5" red circles, cut two in half
   2. Two 3.5" circles in yellow, pink, blue, or light green. Cut all in half.
   3. One 2.5" white circle for eye
   4. One 0.5" black circle for pupil
   5. One 3.5" circle of orange, cut in quarters for beak

b) Assemble bird.
   1. Glue two large red circles to be head and body. Add red half circles for wings.
   2. Add 3–5 half-circles for the tail.
   3. Add white and black circles for the eye.
   4. Add yellow quarter for the beak.

5. Dramatize the Amazon rainforest.

Name a few animals and have your child go to the level where each animal lives and act like that animal. Only use the animals that you have read about, talked about, or added to your list.

ADD FOR SIX-YEAR-OLDS AND UP

6. Learn about the harpy eagle—the largest eagle in the world. Have your child find pictures of the harpy eagle in your rainforest books. Try to have at least one book with photographs.

   a) Ask your child to describe this eagle.

   b) Point out the powerful build of this bird: the strong wings, the hooked beak, the huge talons, and the hooded eyes. Compare this bird to the more well-known bald eagle. Ask your child how they are alike and how are they different. [Answer: Their build, beak, talons, and hooded eyes are similar. Differences are coloring and the crest.]

   c) This bird is about 3½ feet long, with a wingspan of up to 7 feet. Have your child lie down so you can measure and mark his body length and arm span using sidewalk chalk. Then mark the body length and wing span of this bird on top of your child's. The wing span is actually small for an eagle. This smaller wingspan enables the harpy eagle to maneuver in the thick rainforest.

   This eagle's talons are 3–4 inches long—the same size as a grizzly bear's claws.

   d) Ask your child what and how she thinks this bird would eat. [Answer: He eats tree dwelling mammals such as sloths and monkeys, occasionally birds like macaws, and reptiles like iguanas and snakes by swooping down and catching them in his talons.] Tell your child that this is a bird of prey.

    e) Let your child pretend to be a harpy eagle and swoop in with a large meat carving fork to see if she can spear a hot dog resting on a cutting board.

7. Make a collage harpy eagle out of paper circles. If you have more than one child, you might have your younger child make the first two birds while your older child makes the last two birds. Tutorial available on *GO GLOBAL* Resource page.

    Materials
    - Cardstock or construction paper: grey, white, black
    - Glue sticks, scissors, and compass or some way to measure circles

    Process

    a) Cut circles out of cardstock or construction paper.
        1. Two 3.5" grey circles, one cut in half
        2. One 2.5" white circle, cut in half (tail)
        3. One 2.5" grey circle, cut in half (tail)
        4. Five or six small triangles of grey (crown)
        5. One 0.5" black circle, cut in half (eye)
        6. One 3.5" circle of black, cut in quarters and then modified to be "hooked" (beak)

    b) Assemble bird.
        1. Glue two large grey circles to be head and body. Add triangular snips of grey to make the crown on the bird. Add one grey half-circle for wing.
        2. Add 3–5 half white and grey circles to be tail.
        3. Add black half circle for "hooded" eye.
        4. Add modified black quarter for beak.

ADD FOR SEVEN-YEAR-OLDS AND UP

8. Learn about the resplendent quetzal. Have your child find pictures of the quetzal in your rainforest books. Try to have at least one book with photographs.

    a) Ask your child to describe the quetzal.

    b) Point out the brightly colored plumage (feathers) and the very long tail if she does not mention it. Ask her to name the colors. The coloring is iridescent from green-gold to blue-violet. Use the word iridescent and make sure your child knows the meaning. The quetzal is unique for the male's two long tail feathers. The quetzal bird is 14–16 inches long, with the tail feathers adding an additional 26 inches to its length.

9. Make a quetzal out of brightly colored paper. Tutorial available on *GO GLOBAL* Resource page.

Materials
- Cardstock or construction paper in bright or iridescent: green, red, yellow, white
- Glue sticks, scissors, and compass or some way to measure circles

Process

a) Cut circles out of cardstock or construction paper.
1. One 3.5" red circle, cut in half (body)
2. One 1.5" green circle (head)
3. One 1" green circle (chest)
4. One 2" green circle, cut in half (wing)
5. One 0.5' x 2" x 2" white triangle (tail)
6. One small yellow triangle (beak)
7. Two long, narrow green strips the length of your paper, pointed at one end (tail feathers)

b) Assemble bird
1. Cut tiny triangles off the top of the head, the chest, and wing to make them look like feathers. Glue to body.
2. Glue tiny beak and a tiny black eye.
3. Glue white triangle to bottom of the body to start the tail.
4. Glue long strips of green to be the tail feathers.

DAY 3 — AMAZON INDIANS AND THE BLUE MORPHO BUTTERFLY

EVERYONE

1. Read **My Amazon River Day**, if available. Talk about the Amazon Indians and add them to your dramatization of the rainforest. The activities below are for Indians who are still living in the jungle. Explain that many of the Amazon Indians are now living in less primitive situations than as portrayed in **My Amazon River Day.**
2. Things to know about the Amazon Indians:
   a) They live on the floor of the rainforest.
   b) Some hunt with a blowpipe and poisoned darts.
   c) They wade in the water and spear or net fish.
   d) The collect fruit and dig tubers (like potatoes or turnips) in the jungle.
   e) They pound on hollow logs to communicate with each other.

3. Learn about the morpho butterfly. Have your child find pictures of the blue morpho butterfly in your rainforest books. Try to have at least one book with photographs.

    a) Ask your child to describe this butterfly.

    b) Point out the brightly colored blue wings that are edged with black. The blue morpho is one of the largest butterflies in the world—with wing spans of five to eight inches. The vivid, iridescent-blue coloring is only on the back of the wings. The underside is dull brown with "eyespots" providing camouflage when the wings are closed.

4. Make a blue morpho butterfly. Tutorial available on *GO GLOBAL* Resource page.

    Materials

    - Eight-inch circle of white cardstock/ poster board
    - Scissors, glue
    - Various shades of blue and turquoise tissue paper
    - Brown water color paint
    - Circles of black, brown, white, or yellow tissue paper for the eyespots
    - Black marker or black paint
    - White hole punched circles to decorate the black portion
    - OPTIONAL: silver glitter glue

    Process

    a) Make a big v and little v on the circle as shown. Cut out notches.

    b) Color the "underside" brown first.

    c) Use black paint or marker to draw the body.

    d) Paste on the eyespots.

    e) Turn butterfly to the front. Tear tissue paper into small pieces and glue covering the front of the wings.

    f) Use black paint or marker to draw the body and outline the wings. Add white dots and glitter glue, if you want.

    g) Fold the butterfly so it can close its bright blue wings to "hide" from its predators. Will its eyespots scare the predators away?

5. Add animals to your list and dramatize the Amazon rainforest.

DAY 4 — REVIEW RAINFOREST

EVERYONE

1. Finish any of the art projects.
2. Dramatize the Amazon rainforest.

Review the levels of the rainforest, then name animals and have your child go to the level where each animal lives and act like that animal.

3. Have your children pick their favorite books from the Amazon rainforest to read again.
4. Celebrate the rainforest by eating some more tropical fruit.

WEEK 11
SOUTH AMERICA
PAMPAS AND THE PEOPLE OF SOUTH AMERICA

BIG PICTURE

In the last week in South America you will learn about the Pampas, the South American grasslands where the gauchos (South American cowboys) herd cattle. In addition, you will read books about children living in South America so your child can develop empathy for others. This light week will give you time to finish projects and books and review South America. Consider visiting a local zoo this week to see South American animals that you have learned about.

MATERIALS

Books

1. ***My Mama's Little Ranch on the Pampas***, Maria Cristina Brusca. Ages 5–10. A year on a small Argentinian ranch. Includes a visual dictionary of Spanish words and geographical terms used in the book.
2. ***A Pen Pal for Max***, Gloria Rand. Ages 5–10. A Chilean boy sends a personal note with the grapes from his family farm that are headed to the US.

Secondary Books Find some of these excellent books to read aloud and make available to your children for their quiet times. The * means especially recommended.

1. ***Abuelo***, Arthur Dorros, Ages 3–7. Sweet story of a boy and his grandfather based in Argentina.
2. ***Carolina's Gift: A Story of Peru***, Katacha Diaz. Ages 4–9. Peruvian girl goes to market to find a gift for her grandmother. Wonderful pictures and information about Peruvian culture in story form and from a child's perspective.
3. ***Waiting for the Biblioburro***, Monica Brown. Ages 5–8. Based on true story of a teacher/librarian who takes books to children in rural Colombia; or ***Biblioburro: A True Story from Columbia***, Jeanette Winter. Ages 5–8.
4. ***Mia's Story,*** Michael Foreman. Ages 4–9. Sweet and moving story of a little girl in Chile in the foothills of the Andes who grows and sells flowers.
5. ***Saturday Sancocho***, Leyla Torres. Ages 3–7. Maria Lili's family collects the ingredients for chicken sancocho at the village street market. Recipe at the end!
6. ***Miranda's Day to Dance,*** Jackie Jasina Schaefer. Ages 3–6. Cute counting story as a little dancer feeds the South American animals South American foods.

SUPPLIES

1. Conga dance tutorial available on *GO GLOBAL* Resource page
2. Rain stick supplies: cardboard tube, nails, duct tape, dried beans, and rice. Tutorial available on *GO GLOBAL* Resource page.
3. *GO GLOBAL* Game

DAY 1   PAMPAS

EVERYONE

1. Review your map of South America. Can your child remember the name of the mountains? The large river? Where is the driest desert in the world?

   Tell your child that the Pampas are the fertile South American grasslands much like the North American Great Plains. The area close to the Amazon River plain gets more rain, while the area in the south is drier. There is a lot of farming here, and ranching in the drier areas. South American cowboys are called gauchos. Play gauchos and herd your cows or sheep.

2. Read ***My Mama's Little Ranch*** if you can find it, or another picture book on South America.

    a) Read it first for the story.

    b) On subsequent readings, you can use some (but not all) of the following discussion prompts

      - The first line begins, "One steamy afternoon in January…" See if your child knows, or can guess, why it is steamy in January. On the third page is another clue: "Mama, Guillermo, and I were going to stay there all summer." On page 11, "The summer passed too quickly, and before we knew it, it was March, time … to go back to school." Use the information on the seasons on the front and end pages of the book and your globe to review the seasons in the northern hemisphere and southern hemisphere. Do not worry if they don't really get it. They will eventually.

      - Ask about the setting—where and when the story happened.

        We know it is in Argentina so find the country on your globe. The setting is also in the countryside rather than a city. Ask your child how we know that. [Answer: Windmills, an electric generator, no schools, riding horses and a sulky rather than cars all the time, dirt/mud roads, kerosene lantern.]

        When did the story take place? Is this in our time or a long time ago? [Answer: Recently is hinted because of the modern looking car.]

      - Be ready to discuss anything that stands out to your child: the difference between beef and dairy cows, the differences and similarities between gauchos and North American cowboys, windmills, branding cattle, the clothing, the birthing of the large calf.

3. The Conga dance came from the Cuban carnival dance. It is more of a march and is an easy and fun activity for young children.

   Learn the EASY Conga Dance. Tutorial and music are available on *GO GLOBAL* Resource page.

   > Right, left, right, touch left with toe.
   > Left, right, left, touch right with toe.
   > Add swing arm up to the opposite way of the touch.
   > Make a Conga line.

4. Practice some Spanish.

DAY 2 — CHILE

EVERYONE

1. Read ***A Pen Pal for Max*** or one of the other books about the life of a child in South America from the book list.

    a) Find the locations on a map that are mentioned in the book: Chile and the Andes Mountains.

    b) What work do the parents do? What is a vineyard?

    c) Locate the mountains in the background of the pictures. Review that Chile has a narrow strip of farmable land between the ocean and the Andes Mountains.

    d) Why is it summer in North America while it is winter in South America?

    e) Do you know what an earthquake is?

    f) Do you have a pen pal? Would you like one? You will have a chance to make that happen this week.

    g) Ask your child to compare his life with Max's. How is your life different? How is it similar?

2. Practice some Spanish.

DAY 3 — RAIN-STICKS

EVERYONE

1. Read a story about the life of a child in South America from the book list. As you read this book talk to your child about how their lives are similar and different than these children. Practice some Spanish.

2. Make a rain-stick, which was traditionally made by poking the spines into the wood skeleton of a cactus by the Mapuche Indians in South America. These rain-sticks were used to encourage rain to come to a dry land. You might ask your child if he thinks playing the rain-stick will make it rain. The answer, of course, is no. But it does sound like rain, doesn't it? Rain-sticks are also found in Southeast Asia, Australia, and Africa. Tutorial available on *GO GLOBAL* Resource page.

Materials

- A heavy cardboard 2" diameter mailing tube
- About 70 flathead nails that are just shorter than the diameter of the tube. 1¾"
- A hammer
- About 1 cup of dried, uncooked pinto beans, about ½ cup of uncooked rice. Using a mixture of different sized beans/rice will make more interesting sound.
- Duct tape
- Materials to decorate the outside of the tube: paint, crayons, yarn, or colored duct tape

Process

a) The parent should use a marker to draw dots about ½ inch apart along the spiral seam of the tube. Then supervise the child to carefully nail nails into tube on these dots. Do not collapse the tube by pressing too hard. It will still work if the nails are sporadic, but there will be a more melodious sound if the nails are on a spiral. Poke the nails all the way down, but they should not poke through the other side of the tube. A child under six may need help starting the nails. They can even just push the nails in with their fingers.

b) Seal one end and add the beans and rice, which should only take up about 1/10 of tube.

c) Close ends, seal everything with duct tape.

d) Decorate, if you would like.

DAY 4 — SOUTH AMERICA WRAP-UP

EVERYONE

1. Consider sponsoring a child through Compassion International which is a reputable child advocacy ministry that pairs compassionate people with those who are suffering from poverty. The ministry releases children from spiritual, economic, social, and physical poverty, and enables them to become responsible and fulfilled adults. You as a family can sponsor a specific child from one of 26 countries in Central and South America, Africa, or Asia. As well as financially sponsoring a child you can exchange letters and photos. Link available on *GO GLOBAL* Resource page.

   If you choose to support a child whose native language is Spanish, practice some words in preparation for communicating with your Compassion International child.

2. Ask your child to tell the favorite things he learned about South America. You might need to give your child some prompts such as: What did you learn about the Andes Mountains? The Amazon rainforest? The Pampas?

   > This is a verbal (and painless) quiz. Having your child tell you what they learned about is called narration and is an important skill. It requires practice to be able to synthesize what you have learned in order to communicate it to others.

3. Reread a favorite South American book.
4. Play the *GO GLOBAL* Game. Add South American as well as North American cards.

WEEK 12
CATCH UP
OR TAKE A BREAK!

WEEK 13
ANTARCTICA
PART I

BIG PICTURE

Antarctica is the coldest, driest, and windiest continent on Earth. It is located around the South Pole and is almost totally enclosed by the Antarctic Circle. Scarcely touched by humans, the frozen land is made up of breathtaking scenery, broken by only a handful of scientific bases and a "permanent" population of a small number of scientists.

Antarctica was not discovered until 1820 and was largely neglected until the 20th century. Ernest Shackleton led the Nimrod Expedition in 1907, which reached the South Magnetic Pole. Richard Byrd led several voyages to Antarctica in the 1930's and 1940's.

Antarctica is a desert. The area's moisture is all tied up in frigid seawater and the huge sheets, shelves, and packs of ice which cover nearly all of the continent. There is little snowfall in the interior of the continent, and even less rain.

Antarctica is accessible in the southern summer season (November to March) when enough sea ice melts to allow the ships to dock. During these summer months, there will be 24 hours of daylight, and the coastal temperatures might rise to 50° F. During the winter season (May to August) there can be 24 hours of darkness, and the coastal temperatures fall to -40°F. The temperatures in the interior are even colder with summer highs around 5°F and winter lows plummeting to -112°F.

Antarctica is notable for being the only continent with little significant land plant life—only some lichens and mosses. And there are no native land mammals, reptiles, or amphibians. There are no polar bears; they are only at the *North* Pole. However, Antarctica's shoreline serves as a nesting ground for many species of migratory birds and penguins. The Southern Ocean which surrounds Antarctica is the home to many fish and marine mammals, including whales and seals.

This first week you will emphasize the continent itself and the animals that live there, especially the penguins.

MATERIALS

Books

1. ***Beginner's World Atlas 3rd Edition***, National Geographic. 2011.
2. ***Here is Antarctica***, Madeline Dunphy. Ages 4–9. Great introduction to the web of wildlife in Antarctica. Great vocabulary, illustrations, and read aloud potential for all ages.
3. ***Antarctic Antics: A Book of Penguin Poems***, Judy Sierra. Ages 4–9. Delightful funny poems illustrating the life of the emperor penguins. A read out loud must!

4. *The Emperor's Egg*, Martin Jenkins. Ages 4–8. Fabulous story of the emperor penguin taking care of his egg/chick.
5. *Mr. Popper's Penguins*, Richard & Florence Atwater. Ages 5–10. Slapstick story of the Popper family and their penguins. First published in 1938 and so tells of another time—which just adds to its charm. If you can't do the book, skip the movie; the movie is dreadful.

Secondary Books: Find *some* of these excellent books to read aloud and make available to your children for their quiet times. * means especially recommended.

1. ***March of the Penguins***, Luc Jacquet. Ages 4–9. Excellent story of the life cycles of the penguins with highest quality National Geographic pictures. Companion book to the movie. Do NOT get the movie. See Week Fourteen for an analysis of Antarctica movies.
2. ***The Blue Whale,*** Jenni Desmond. Ages 5–8. We will revisit this book from week two!
3. ***If You Were a Penguin***, Wendell and Florence Minor. Ages 3–7. Darling book with additional fun facts on last page.
4. ***Baby Penguin***, Aubrey Lang. Ages 4–8. Story of a baby king penguin with photographs. Wonderful. Not located in Antarctica, but on islands in the South Seas.
5. ***Penguins!*** Gail Gibbons. Ages 5–9. Good overview of various penguins from around the southern hemisphere.
6. **About Penguins: A Guide for Children,** Cathryn Sill. Ages 4–8. Overview of all penguins, not just the ones living in Antarctica. Lovely pictures, simple text, with additional information in the last pages.
7. **Penguins! Strange and Wonderful**, Laurence Pringle. Ages 7–10. Good general information on penguins.
8. *A Mother's Journey*, Sandra Markle. Ages 4–8. Story of the emperor penguin emphasizing the work of the mother.
9. *The Emperor Lays an Egg*, Brenda Cuiberson. Ages 6–8. Good information and entertaining; Not quite as endearing as the Emperor's Egg.
10. **Emperor Penguins**, Roberta Edwards. Easy reader.
11. **Emperor Penguins: Antarctic Diving Birds,** Laura Hamilton Waxman. Ages 7–10. Good book for older children who like non-fiction. Readers will compare and contrast key traits of emperor penguins to other birds encouraging the reader (or listener) to make connections and draw conclusions about these animals.
12. *A Penguin's World*, Caroline Arnold. Ages 3–7. Though I do not care for the simplistic paper-cut illustrations, it is a nice story of the Adelie penguin with map and glossary.
13. *A Penguin Story*, Antoinette Portis. Ages 2–5. Edna the penguin is looking for color to break up the palette of blue and gray in her world. Cute book that teaches colors as well as a bit about penguins.
14. **Little Penguin: The Emperor of Antarctica**. Jonathan London. Ages 4–8. Another cute book on emperor penguins.

SUPPLIES

1. Map of Antarctica printed on cardstock, available on the *GO GLOBAL* Resource page
2. Penguin Bingo, link for purchase available on *GO GLOBAL* Resource page
3. Small foam footballs, or something else to represent penguin eggs perched on your feet
4. Flashlight and globe

DAY 1 — GENERAL AND SOUTH POLE

EVERYONE

1. Find Antarctica on your globe. Ask your child to find the North Pole. Review what the North and South Poles are, and review that the earth rotates on its axis. Have your child rotate on her axis.

2. Ask your child if she can think of why there are no cities, and only a few science stations (with less than 1,000 permanent residents) in Antarctica. [Answer: The temperatures in Antarctica rarely get above freezing, even in the summer. The only plants that grow there are mosses and lichens.]

3. Read **Beginner's World Atlas**, pages 56–59.

4. Using your printed map of Antarctica mark the South Pole and the Ross Ice Shelf. Trace the Transarctic Mountains symbol. Color the whole continent with icecap symbol.

ADD FOR SIX-YEAR-OLDS AND UP

5. Continue Activity 1 by discussing both revolving and rotating. See if your child can rotate on her "axis" and revolve around the "sun" (which is you holding a flashlight) at the same time.

6. Using a flashlight and your globe demonstrate again to your child how the south pole is dark for most of the day and night in half of the year, and mostly light day and night for the other half of the year. IF YOU DEMONSTRATE using the globe, they might even understand why they have winter during our summer, and summer during our winter.

   If you watch the video mentioned on Day 4, there is a portion where they set up a camera to catch the sun never setting, but simply circling on the horizon. This segment starts at 31 minutes. An older child might understand this bit if you do the activity first. Parental Warning: The next segment on the video discusses the death of some of the early explorers. You might want to just show the one segment.

DAY 2 — ANTARCTIC ANIMALS AND PENGUINS

EVERYONE

1. Read **Here is Antarctica**. This is a great read aloud book (in the style of *The House that Jack Built*) that introduces the land and the animals of Antarctica.

   a) Read it a second time and notice that the pictures not only reveal what the current text is talking about, but also foreshadow the next page. For instance, on pages 2–3 that are about the icebergs, you can see the leopard seals which will be featured on the next page spread, and on that page spread you can see the orca peering out from under the ice in the bottom right of the illustration. Then on the next pages highlighting the orca, you can see the macaroni penguin fleeing to the left. And so on through the book. Have your child identify each foreshadowing element. They do NOT need to know the term "foreshadowing." They learn the concept now, and when the term is introduced much later they will understand it.

    b) You could read the book a third time (perhaps later in the day) and ask your child if she could tell you the names of the animals… and what they eat. Make sure your child understands that there are predators who eat prey! They will be able to use this information for play later.

2. Read ***Penguins!*** (Gibbons) or another book that talks about the different kinds of penguins. While there are 17 different kinds of penguins, no one needs to know all of them. They simply should understand there are different kinds and should be able to distinguish a few. Everyone should know the emperor penguin. Other popular ones could be: macaroni penguin, chinstrap penguin, Adelie penguin.

3. Play Penguin Bingo to learn the breeds of penguins, the other animals, and features of Antarctica.

ADD FOR SIX-YEAR-OLDS AND UP

4. Start to read ***Mr. Popper's Penguins*** out loud to your children. Read two chapters per day. The best read aloud times are usually right before nap/quiet afternoon rest time or bedtime. This is a 20-chapter book, though the chapters are short (less than 10 minutes to read aloud), and so this pace will take you 10 days to read the entire book. You will need to read on all seven days in the week, if possible. Hopefully your child will begin to ask for "just one more chapter" and you could be done even sooner! If your oldest child is not into the story by chapter four, you might need to put it aside until she is a bit older.

DAY 3   PENGUINS AND EMPEROR PENGUINS

EVERYONE

1. Learn some of the characteristics of penguins. Ask your children if they realize the penguin is a bird even though it does not fly. You could ask your child what all penguins have in common; then ask them why God designed penguins this way. The younger the child, the more simplistic this discussion will be. As they describe penguins make sure to cover the following.

    a) Why do penguins have webbed feet with claws? [Answer: To help them swim, and to help them grip the ice.]

    b) Why do they have small wings that do not help them fly? [Answer: To help them swim.]

    c) How do they use their beaks? [Answer: To eat, to protect themselves, to preen (which is to clean and straighten their feathers), to be able to move their eggs, to break out of their shells.]

d) How do their feathers help them? [Answer: They keep them warm and dry.]

e) What is the purpose of the penguin's body shape? [Answer: It is hydrodynamic in the water.]

2. How long can you hold your breath? Time everyone. Who can hold their breath the longest? Then share that penguins can hold their breath for up to an hour.

3. Learn about the emperor penguin's life cycle by reading ***The Emperor's Egg***.

    Here is some additional information for you, the teacher. In May or June (which is the beginning of winter in Antarctica), the males and females march onto the interior portion of of Antarctica, up to 100 miles from the water's edge. There the penguins choose their mates. The female lays the egg, places the egg on the male's feet, and heads to the ocean where she will eat, eat, eat. Meanwhile the male protects the egg from the ice and wind by balancing it on his feet and covering it with his brood patch, a flap on his belly. He takes care of the egg and then the hatchling for TWO WHOLE months while the female is away eating. When it really gets cold all the males huddle together to keep warm. Even after the chick hatches the male keeps the chick warm. At long last, the female returns and trumpets her hello. The male trumpets back and the chick whistles. The penguins recognize their own family's voices. Then the female takes care of the chick, and the male heads to the ocean to have a big meal. Finally, the parents take turns feeding the chick.

    a) Dramatize the daddy penguin and time how long you can incubate the eggs on your feet, using small foam footballs as penguin eggs.

    b) When Dad comes home have the kids tell their dad what they learned about penguins. This is great review, solidifies the learning, and also builds the relationship with their dad.

ADD FOR SIX-YEAR-OLDS AND UP

4. Continue to read ***Mr. Popper's Penguins*** out loud to your children.

5. As a continuation of Activity 1, talk about the penguin's coloring. Ask your child if she can think of a reason why the penguin has dark-colored backs and light-colored bellies. [Answer: Camouflage coloring protects them while they are in the ocean. The black backs makes them difficult to see from above against the dark sea. The white bellies make them hard to see from below against the light sky.]

DAY 4   PENGUINS

EVERYONE

1. Read more penguin books; There are so many great ones! Read the ones your child likes over and over again! Repetition of information is great at this age. And seeing and hearing from different sources is helpful. While you should emphasize engaging books with a story, make sure you have at least one book with photographs of penguins, such as ***Baby Penguins*** or ***March of the Penguins***.

2. Reread ***The Blue Whale*** from week one. The blue whales live all over the world, including in Antarctica, though this book does not mention Antarctica. You will also remember that they eat krill…. Just like the leopard seal and penguins.

3. ***Antarctic Antics*** is a favorite read-aloud for all ages because of its hysterically funny poems. Even a four-year-old will get into guessing the predator with these easy rhymes, and everyone will chortle about regurgitation. Make a game of trying to use these great vocabulary works in your everyday conversations!

ADD FOR SIX-YEAR-OLDS AND UP

4. Continue to read ***Mr. Popper's Penguins*** out loud to your children. Read over the weekend as well.

WEEK 14
ANTARCTICA
PART II

BIG PICTURE

You will continue to learn about Antarctica focusing on the expeditions. This week you will also learn a bit about snow, ice, glaciers, and icebergs.

MATERIALS

Books

1. **Something to Tell the Grandcows,** Eileen Spinelli. Ages 4–8. Delightful story of Byrd's trip to the South Pole from the cow's perspective. Fun, simple overview.
2. **Mr. Popper's Penguins**, Richard and Florence Atwater. The book, NOT the movie.
3. The books from Week Thirteen can be used this week as well.

Secondary Books

1. *__Sophie Scott Goes South__, Alison Lester. Ages 5–9. Nine-year old Sophie sails to Antarctica with her dad, the captain of an icebreaker. Richly illustrated journal entries interspersed with photographs make this informational and entertaining.
2. **Who was Ernest Shackleton?** James Buckley. Ages 7–12. Interesting read for an older child on the exploration of Antarctica.

Videos

1. **Antarctica, An Adventure of a Different Nature**. 1991. 40-minute documentary on Antarctica. The action of the animals, and the sweep of the landscape makes this a worthwhile watch. The music is a bit cheesy, but your kids won't mind. There are a few parts you might want to skip because they talk of the death of some explorers. Details are below in the activity.
2. We DO NOT recommend the other penguin movies: *Happy Feet* or *Mr. Popper's Penguins*. They are both crass, crude, and lacking in educational value.
3. We DO NOT recommend *The March of the Penguins*. While the book is listed, and the images National Geographic captures are breathtaking, this movie is not good for young children for two main reasons. First, the movie anthromorphizes the animals: The commentary by Morgan Freeman encourages the audience to think of the penguins as if they were humans. Secondly, the film starkly shows the brutality of nature—many of the penguins and their babies freeze to death, are graphically killed and eaten by other animals, etc. And this is not just once or twice, but all through the film. This can be disturbing to children, and to some adults as well. It is also incorrect. We need to be careful not to imbue animals with human rights. And as much as it is disturbing to see the cute penguins eaten by other animals, that is part of the cycle of life. At the same time, it is not helpful to see such extensive brutality.

SUPPLIES

1. Penguin Bingo, link for purchase available on the *GO GLOBAL* Resource page
2. Safari TOOB Penguin figures, link for purchase available on *GO GLOBAL* Resource page
3. Plastic tray/ cookie sheet/ cake pan
4. Ice and snow: make by pulsating ice in your blender
5. *GO GLOBAL* Game

DAY 1 — ICE AND SNOW

EVERYONE

1. Ask your child to tell you the difference between ice and snow. Guide him with some further questions:

    a) What happens if we put an ice cube in a cup and leave it on the kitchen counter? [Answer: It melts into water.]

    b) What happens if we put snow in a cup and leave it on the kitchen counter? [Answer: It melts into water.]

    c) Ask him again, what is the difference? Listen for the answer: Snow is lighter/weighs less/ is airier. The scientific explanation is that ice is frozen liquid water, while snow is flakes of frozen water vapor that is fluffy.

2. Make "snow" with your heavy-duty blender, if it can crush ice. Place a few ice cubes in the blender and pulse it until it is a snowy texture. Freeze water in traditional ice trays, or use silicon muffin tins to make excellent ice blocks.

    Snow accumulates in Antarctica and rarely melts. Eventually it becomes a glacier, a huge mass of ice moving across land. An iceberg is a large floating piece of ice that has broken away from a glacier.

    a) Pack down some snow on a piece of wax paper and freeze it. Explain to your child that the snow in Antarctica (and other very cold places) accumulates and is pressed down and freezes. It is then ice. Take your now frozen ice sheet out of the freezer and have it slide down a slope (a cookie sheet). Explain that it is now a glacier.

    b) Next, have an ice cube floating in the pan of water that is representing the ocean. Tell your child that when a chunk of ice breaks off from the glacier and and is floating in the water, it is called an iceberg.

    While you can teach your child this information directly, you can and should include these words when you are playing with your child with the snow, ice, and penguin figures.

> This is dynamic (active, natural learning) rather than didactic (sit, listen, and repeat). While there is a place for didactic instruction, dynamic learning opportunities are more powerful. Your child can "play" again and explain all of this to dad in the evening!

3. Encourage your child to play with the penguin figurines, ice, snow, and water. Use a very large cookie sheet or cake pan, ice cubes, a nice amount of snow, and the penguin figurines. (A small pan of water is optional, and messier.) Let your child play. Watch and see what they include. Do NOT step in, but see the natural review activity that happens after they have been steeped in the stories. Let them play while you make lunch or dinner! Watch to see how many of the following elements they include. If they miss some of them you might ask a question to such as, "What is the mama penguin doing?" Or you might grab a figurine and jump into the play with them!

   a) March the penguins inland to have lay their eggs and have papa penguin watch the eggs while mama penguin goes to the sea to eat. Verbalize what she is eating.

   b) Mama comes back and feeds the baby, while the papa goes to the ocean to eat.

   c) The mama and papa penguins trumpet while the baby whistles. Can your child whistle? I am sure he can trumpet!

   d) The penguins dive off the cliffs into the sea.

   e) The penguins look out for their predators in the ocean below. Your child might pull out the orca whale from the arctic region Safari TOOB set!

   f) The predators miss the penguins because they are camouflaged.

   g) The penguins swim in the water, and both walk and hop on the ground and slide on their bellies. But they never fly.

ADD FOR SIX-YEAR-OLDS AND UP

4. Continue to read *Mr. Popper's Penguins* out loud to your children.

DAY 2 — EXPEDITIONS

EVERYONE

1. Read *Something to Tell the Grandcows*, a funny story loosely based on Admiral Richard Byrd's expedition to Antarctica. This delightful story will review Antarctica as this cow sees the snow, icebergs, icicles, seals, whales, petrels, and penguins. Your children will review that during part of the year the sun shines all day and all night, and that at other times of the year the sun does not shine at all. Even the aurora australis (southern lights) is shown on one page. You do NOT need to explain all this, in fact you should not turn a great fun book into a lecture or lesson. It is enough to expose your children to this information. And be ready if they ask questions!

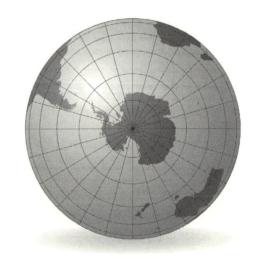

a) After reading the book find the locations on your globe/ maps: Virginia and Little America which was their base camp on the Ross Ice Shelf.

b) You might ask your child what is real and what is imaginary in this story. He may think the whole thing is made up, which it is not.

2. Read, or reread, more penguin books.

3. Pull out the ice, snow, and penguins to let your child play again.

ADD FOR SIX-YEAR-OLDS AND UP

4. Continue to read *Mr. Popper's Penguins* out loud to your children.

DAY 3 — EXPEDITIONS

EVERYONE

1. Go on an "expedition" of your own. It can be at a local park, a nature preserve, or just in your neighborhood.

    a) Ask your child how he should dress. Does he need a hat (for warmth or for protection from the sun)? Gloves? A sweater or coat? What kind of shoes would be best?

    b) Ask your child what he should take. Let him pack his backpack. Water? A snack? Tissue or handkerchief? A pair of binoculars? A compass? A tablet and pencils to sketch or take notes?

    c) Ask him what he is he hoping to see. (birds, bugs, flowers, etc.)

    d) Now, go on your expedition!

ADD FOR SIX-YEAR-OLDS AND UP

2. Continue to read *Mr. Popper's Penguins* out loud to your children.

DAY 4 — EXPEDITIONS

EVERYONE

1. Watch a movie/Video/DVD about Antarctica.

    Antarctica, An Adventure of a Different Nature. 1991. Recommended. Cheesy music, but interesting photography and great breadth of coverage of the topic. Information on the climate, geography, and exploration of Antarctica, including historic footage and photographs of early expeditions to the pole. Also includes some great footage of a variety of Antarctic animal life. There is some discussion of climate change, but only one excessive excerpt from about 23 minutes to 28 minutes.

Much of this video will probably not entice your small children and so you may just want to play a few parts for him—especially the animals and some of the scope of the land. The end of the movie dramatizes the death of some of the early explorers; though it ends with a statement of faith in God, this might be too intense for your children. Please preview. Link available on *GO GLOBAL* Resource page.

2. Play the *GO GLOBAL* Game with the North America, South America, and Antarctica cards.
3. Play with the penguins and ice.
4. Play Penguin Bingo.
5. Read your favorite books over again.

ADD FOR SIX-YEAR-OLDS AND UP

6. Continue to read **Mr. Popper's Penguins** out loud to your children.

WEEK 15
CHRISTMAS AROUND THE WORLD

BIG PICTURE

Most schools lighten the load between Thanksgiving break and the new semester in January. This section is designed to be less stress for the teachers/ parents while providing great reading and discussions topics. Be flexible with this month and this list of books and activities. While we do not provide any craft/art projects, you can easily add those, if desired.

Here you will find an extensive list of books that tell of the Christmas story in a way to enable you to emphasize geography. This includes the geography of the nativity story and how this story is celebrated across the world. All the books have been previewed and are good, both morally and aesthetically. The starred ones are the best! We have tried to include enough information in the description for you to be able to choose books that will work best for your family. Many are about the nativity, some are just the biblical text, while others have more fanciful inclusions, such as how the animals in the crèche were feeling. Some of the books tell true stories about how people celebrate Christmas in various part of the world. Some mythical, pretend, and realistic fiction are included. There are only a few books listed that do not clearly touch upon the Christian story of Christmas, and this is indicated in the description.

Use your globe to find where the story is located, where the characters in the story originate from, and any countries mentioned.

Consider learning about the traditions you already have and talk about their geographic origin. This can include everything from decorations, to songs, to gift-giving traditions, to cookies and other foods.

Do NOT try to read all these books in one year; we have listed 50 books! Read a dozen or less. You can always revisit some of these in coming years. Many of these books are available in libraries, but may be difficult to find if you wait until December, so start looking and requesting in November.

THE ULTIMATE LIST OF CHRISTMAS BOOKS

The Nativity

We want to infuse our Christmas readings with stories of the historic Nativity. This year emphasize the where of the story—Nazareth, Bethlehem, Jerusalem, and even Egypt and the East. Grounding your Christmas reading in the real story of Bethlehem will give your children a firm foundation. While the imaginary, legendary, and fictional stories can be wonderful, children need to clearly know and understand the true, unadorned story. Many wonderfully illustrated books are listed for your perusal.

Find the locations of Israel, Nazareth, Bethlehem, Jerusalem, Egypt on your globe and other maps. You will cover the Middle East (and Israel) during the Asia unit. But this Christmas talk about the area of Israel. For instance, how cold is it there? [Answer: Though there are snow-capped mountains in the north, the southern area of Israel is desert-like. Both Bethlehem and Jerusalem have a Mediterranean climate which means they have hot dry summers and mild wetter winters. It rarely snows there.]

1. **The Christmas Story,** Gennady Spirin. All ages. Gorgeously illustrated with words straight from the King James Bible with rich symbolism and imagery.
2. **The Story of Christmas,** Pamela Dalton. All ages. Exquisite scissor-cut illustrations in Pennsylvania-German folk-art tradition accent the King James nativity account.
3. **Father and Son: A Nativity Story**, Geraldine McCaughrean. Ages 4–9. Nativity story from Joseph's viewpoint—from Bethlehem to Egypt to Nazareth. A powerful perspective honoring Joseph.
4. *The Nativity*, Ruth Sanderson. Ages 5–10. Biblical text with vivid, detailed illustrations.
5. *The Christmas Story*, Metropolitan Museum of Art. All ages. The Christmas story retold through paintings from their collection, and excerpts from the King James Bible.
6. *A Child is Born: The Christmas Story*, Elizabeth Winthrop. All ages. Faithful adaption of the Biblical nativity account with beautiful, haunting illustrations.
7. *The Christmas Story,* James Bernardin. Ages 3–7. Short texts from the King James Bible and lifelike art work (no halos and blurry silhouetted wingless angels).

The Nativity—with fanciful additions

1. **All for the Newborn Baby**, Phyllis Root. Ages 5–10. An exquisitely illustrated lullaby for Jesus. Animals that factor into Christmas legends and miracles from Italy, France, Belgium, England, Puerto Rico, Germany, and Spain are pictured. The author's note on the last page explains some of legends and where they are from.
2. *The First Christmas: An Angel Came to Nazareth,* Anthony Knott; Illustrated by Maggie Kneen. Ages 3–7. This creative take on the nativity story centers around giving four animals their choice of rider.
3. *Who Built the Stable? A Nativity Poem*, Ashley Bryan. Ages 4–8. A lovely poem imagining an African shepherd boy building a stable for his animals and welcoming the holy family. The whole book is with bright African colors, costumes, and faces.

The Gift Givers

There are many stories of people bringing gifts to the Christ Child, and other stories of giving gifts in His name. We can be inspired by the generosity of the Wise Men mentioned in the Bible, the little drummer boy, and St. Nicholas.

The Wise Men (also known as the Magi and the Three Kings) are mentioned in the Gospel of Matthew. While the Biblical text does not tell how many Magi there were, traditionally we refer to three men because of the listed three gifts of gold, frankincense, and myrrh. The Bible states that they came from the east. Traditionally named Melchior, Caspar, and Balthasar, their individual lands of origin vary in tradition: perhaps Persia, India, Arabia/ Yemen, Sheba, Ethiopia, Egypt, or Mongolia.

St. Nicholas lived in the third century in Turkey and was raised by wealthy parents to be a devout Christian. He was orphaned while still young and used his inheritance to help the poor. Nicholas entered the ministry and eventually became a bishop in Myra, Turkey. Nicholas was a generous and loving Christian minister. One legend tells of a poor man with three daughters who did not have money for their dowries. Secretly Nicholas tossed bags of gold through an open window which landed in the girl's stockings hung to dry. This money provided dowries enabling the girls to marry. This is why we hang stockings, receive small gifts, and traditionally receive an orange to symbolize the bag of gold. If you do not use the Santa legend, you will still want to talk about St. Nicholas. You should consider explaining to your children that some families do pretend he is real. You have an opportunity to teach your children to be gracious.

1. ***Santa, Are You For Real?* Harold Myra. Ages 3–7. Children discover there really was a Saint Nick. The older 1977 version is better—more text and we like the illustrations better.
2. *We Three Kings,* Gennady Spirin. All ages. Luxurious paintings perfectly fit the words of the carol.
3. *Carol of the Brown King: Nativity Poems,* Langston Hughes. All ages. Simple poems celebrating the first Christmas with luminous bright paintings in characteristic African colors. Many of the characters are depicted as Africans. This poem is available in many anthologies as well.
4. *The Story of the Three Wise Kings,* Tomie DePaola. Ages 4–10. The basic story with such lovely illustrations—look for the partridge and the pear.
5. *The Third Gift*, Linda Sue Park. Ages 6–10. A fictional story of a boy who collects myrrh resin with his father. A simple moving tale of ordinary people involved in an extraordinary event.
6. *Amahl and the Night Visitors*, Gian Carol Menotti and Michele Lemieux. All ages. The honored composer tells the story of his most famous opera, inspired by his own miraculous recovery from lameness as a child. This story can also be found in collections such as *Joy to the World*, Ann Keya Beneduce, illustrated by Gennady Spirin. If you like opera music, find and listen!
7. *The Little Drummer Boy*, Ezra Jack Keats. Ages 3–8. The traditional sweet story.

Around the World Christmas—General and Carols

Here is a general book about celebrating Christmas around the world and another about various Christmas carols. The first known Christmas hymns date from 4th century Rome. Under the influence of Francis of Assisi in the 13th century a strong tradition of popular Christmas songs in regional native languages developed in France, Germany, and Italy. Christmas carols in English first appeared in the 15th century.

1. *Christmas Around the World,* Emily Kelley. Ages 7–9. Christmas customs and activities in eight countries.
2. *Tasha Tudor's Favorite Christmas Carols*, Tasha Tudor. All ages. Tudor's exquisite illustrations enhance the words and simple arrangements of seventeen traditional carols. A short historic note is included for each carol.

Around the World Christmas—Italy and France

Italy and France have several lovely Christmas traditions, legends, and tales.

<u>The Crèche</u>—Saint Francis of Assisi is credited with creating the first live nativity scene in the 13th century to emphasize the worship of Christ rather than secular materialism and gift giving. The first crèches were staged with live people and animals. Eventually statues were used to represent the animals and people in the Nativity scene.

<u>Befana</u> (known as Babushka in Eastern Europe/Russia) is visited by the Wise Men and invited to come along to see the newborn King. After saying no to the Wise Men, the old woman has a change of heart. She then bakes cookies and candies to deliver to the Christ Child. Because she tarried to first sweep and then bake, she flies quickly to catch up with the kings. But alas, she never does, and is still searching. As she continues her search for the Christ Child, she delivers sweets to the children she encounters.

1. ****_Jingle the Christmas Clown_,** Tomie dePaola. Ages 3–10. Left behind by the circus, Jingle the little clown and his baby animals make Christmas Eve special for the poor villagers in an impoverished Italian town.
2. *****_The Clown of God_**, Tomie dePaola. All ages. French legend of juggler offering the Christ Child the only gift he has.
3. **_Saint Francis and the Nativity_**, Myrna Strasser. Ages 4–7. The fictional story of Mario, a young shepherd boy is woven with the historical first nativity.
4. **_The Legend of Old Befana,_** Tomie dePaola. Ages 5–10. Italian fable of grumpy Befana flying across the sky looking for the Christ Child. She cannot find him and so delivers gifts to children she does find.
5. **_Strega Nona's Gift_**, Tomie dePaola. Ages 4–9. A story of Strega Nona celebrating Italian Christmas traditions from the Feast of St. Nicola in early December to Epiphany in January with an emphasis on the food and liturgical calendar. The end pages include extra information on the various Christmas feasts in Italy.

> Remember—just read a few of these books! You can always revisit others in coming years!

Around the World Christmas—United Kingdom

Great Britain is the home of many Christmas traditions such as decorating with holly and ivy, eating Christmas (plum) pudding, the arrival of Father Christmas (their St. Nick), and the first English carols.

1. **_The Friendly Beasts_**, Tomie dePaola. Ages 4–8. A 12th century English Christmas carol with exquisite Italian style pre-Raphaelite illustrations.
2. **_The Twelve Days of Christmas,_** Helen Haidle. Ages 4–9. This book explains the Christian truths concealed in the familiar carol.

3. ***Letters from Father Christmas***, J.R.R. Tolkien. Ages 5–10. Beautifully illustrated letters to Tolkien's children. It encourages the Father Christmas myth, with delightful Tolkien additions of the North Polar Bear and attacking goblins. It is all fantasy with no Christ story.

4. ***Smudge and the Book of Mistakes: a Christmas Story***, Gloria Whelan. Ages 6–10. Set in Ireland in the Middle Ages, Brother Cuthbert is mistakenly chosen to be the scribe for an illuminated manuscript of the Nativity story.

Around the World Christmas—Russia

1. *****The Miracle of St. Nicholas***, Gloria Whelan. Ages 5 and up. Fictional story of a 20th century Russian boy who sees a Christmas miracle when his church has the first service in decades. Sobering, inspiring, and a wonderful glimpse of the Russian Orthodox church. You will use this book again when studying Russia.
2. *****Babushka: A Christmas Tale,*** Dawn Casey. Ages 5–8. A Russian tale of an old woman who is seeking the Christ Child and distributing gifts to boys and girls as she journeys on.
3. ***Shoemaker Martin***, Leo Tolstoy and Bernadette Watts. Ages 5 and up. After showing kindness to three strangers, the Russian shoemaker learns that Jesus visited him.

Around the World Christmas—Germany and Eastern Europe

The Germans originated many of our favorite traditions. Advent calendars (with little doors hiding pieces of chocolate) hail from Germany. Aromatic evergreen Advent wreaths provide a timely progression as an additional candle is lit each week. The family gathers around each evening to sing, talk, have a dessert, and pray. Gingerbread houses, cookies, and Christmas markets also hail from Germany.

The most well-known German tradition is the <u>Christmas tree</u>. According to legend, in AD 722 Boniface encountered some pagans who were about to sacrifice a child at the base of a huge oak tree. He cut down the tree to prevent the sacrifice and a fir tree grew up at the base of the oak. He stated that this evergreen, with its branches pointing to heaven, was a holy tree—the tree of the Christ child, and a symbol of His promise of eternal life. Another legend is that one Christmas Eve, about AD 1500 Martin Luther was walking through the snow-covered woods and was struck by the beauty of the snow-glistened trees. Their branches, dusted with snow, shimmered in the moon light. When he got home, he set up a small fir tree and shared the story with his children. He decorated the Christmas tree with small candles, which he lighted to honor Jesus, the light of the world.

<u>Silent Night</u> was written and then first performed in Germany with a simple guitar accompaniment.

The ancient story of King Wenceslas and the modern story of the Berlin Candy Bomber will delight your children.

1. *****An Early American Christmas,*** Tomie dePaola. Ages 4–10. The German immigrants bring their Christmas traditions to early 1800s New England.
2. *****Mercedes and the Chocolate Pilot,*** Margot Theis Raven. Ages 5–10. The true story of the Candy Bomber from the perspective of a little German girl who received candy.
3. ***Christmas from Heaven; The True Story of the Berlin Candy Bomber***, Tom Brokaw. Ages 5–10. True story of Berlin Airlift and the pilot who started to drop candy for the starving Berliners.

4. ***Silent Night: A Christmas Carol is Born,*** Maureen Brett Hooper. Ages 5–7. Story of the origin of the famous Christmas Carol written in Austria in 1818.

5. ***Good King Wenceslas***, J.M. Neale, illus. by Jamichael Henterly. Ages 4–8. The good king generously shares with a peasant family. This 19th century carol is based on the story of 10th century Wenceslas who lived in Bohemia, the modern Czech Republic.

6. ***Stephen's Feast***, Jean Richardson. Ages 4–8. The youngest page at the court of Wenceslas accompanies his king on a mission and learns compassion and generosity.

7. ***Good King Wenceslas,*** John M. Neale, illus. Tim Ladwig. Ages 4–8. The story of the kind-hearted King who sets out to help a poor man and experiences a miracle.

8. ***Gingerbread Christmas***, Jan Brett. Ages 3–6. A gingerbread baby takes a band to a Christmas festival in Germany. Secular, but fun, and captures the mood of Christmas in Germany!

> Remember—Use your globe and map to include a geographical perspective to this year's Christmas.

Around the World Christmas—Scandinavian Countries

From the cold Scandinavian countries, we have two historic legends that have birthed Christmas stories and celebrations. In the 4th century when Christians were persecuted in Rome, Lucia was a brave young woman who took food to the Christians hiding in dark tunnels. She wore candles on her head to light the way. In Scandinavia on Saint Lucia Day the oldest daughter in the family dresses in white with an evergreen wreath and seven lighted candles on her head and then serves coffee and sweet rolls to her family.

1. ***The Race of the Birkebeiners,*** Lise Lunge-Larsen. Ages 6 and up. Norwegian skiers save a child prince (who is in danger from his evil uncle who wants to claim the throne) and brought peace to their country. It all starts on Christmas day in AD 1206.

2. ***Kirsten's Surprise (American Girl),*** Janet Shaw. Ages 7–11. Kirsten has recently immigrated from Sweden to Minnesota and is excited to introduce her cousins to St. Lucia Day.

3. ***The Christmas Wish***, Lori Evert. Ages 3–7. A magical story of Nordic Anja receiving help from animals like a polar bear, an ox, and a reindeer on her way to help Santa. If you like the Santa myth, this book has breathtaking photographs of Arctic northern Europe.

Around the World Christmas—South of the Border

Poinsettias, posadas (dramatizations of the Holy Family looking for a place to stay), piñatas, luminarias (small paper lanterns lining the walkway to guide the spirit of the Christ child to one's home), and yummy tamales are all part of the celebrations south of the border.

1. *****The Legend of the Poinsettia***, Tomie dePaola. Ages 4–9. A poor Mexican girl wants to give a gift to the Christ child. Her modest gift of weeds become beautiful red stars to adorn the manger.

2. *****Uno, Dos, Tres, Posada! Let's Celebrate Christmas***, Virginia Kroll*. Ages 3–7. A charming introduction to a Hispanic tradition celebrated on the nine nights before Christmas. Some Spanish words, but easily understandable to an English-only audience.

3. ***Too Many Tamales,*** Gary Soto. Ages 4–8. A cute story of Hispanic family making tamales for Christmas.

Around the World Christmas—USA

While we consider the USA our home, we have many wonderful Christmas stories that might be cross-cultural for your family. These stories include some traditions that were brought to the US from other countries. Most sources think candy canes came from Germany when a local candy maker was requested to make sugar sticks to keep the children quiet during worship services. According to legend he made them in the shape of a shepherd's cross, with the color white to signify the purity of Jesus, and the red to signify His blood shed for us.

1. ****An Early American Christmas,*** Tomie dePaola. Ages 4–10. The German immigrants bring their Christmas traditions to early 1800s New England.
2. ***The Year of the Perfect Christmas Tree: An Appalachian Story,*** Gloria Houston. Ages 5–9. A story of courage and the power of family and community in 1918 Appalachia.
3. ***The Trees of the Dancing Goats,*** Patricia Polacco. Ages 5–10. During a scarlet fever epidemic, a Russian Jewish family help make their Christian neighbors' Christmas special and have their own Hanukkah even more blessed.
4. ***Christmas Soup***, Alice Faye Duncan. Ages 4–8. The Beene family dreams of a Christmas feast while Baby Fannie prays, 'Bless our home with something more.' Soon, two hungry strangers arrive and are invited to share the family's meager soup.
5. ***Legend of the Candy Cane,*** Lori Walburg. Ages 4–7. An endearing story that emphasizes the Christian meaning of Christmas, with historical information in the end pages.

WEEK 16
AFRICA
OVERVIEW, SAHARA, AND NILE

BIG PICTURE

Africa was referred to as the Dark Continent in the mid-19th century because it was mysterious and unknown to those who did not live there. The mysterious veiled jungle, the immense Sahara Desert, and the vast savanna grasslands contain many exotic and interesting animals such as lions, elephants, and giraffes. This second largest continent is home to a large diversity of ethnicities, cultures, and languages. And while it is quickly becoming modernized, there is still a large portion of the population living without many of the modern conveniences. While you will emphasize the diversity of land, people, and animals, you will also use this as an opportunity to learn about life without some of our modern conveniences such as running water, indoor plumbing, central heating, stoves, refrigerators, cars, and phones.

The Sahara Desert is the largest desert in the world. It is about the same size as the United States of America. Some of the sand dunes in the Sahara are hundreds of miles long. In addition to sand dunes there are plateaus of rock and even some snowcapped mountains. The desert is very hot during the day with temperatures as high as 130°F, but the temperatures drop significantly at night, and it sometimes gets so cold that frost forms. It rains rarely in the desert. An oasis has a supply of water, usually a natural spring that enables this small area to grow plants which provide for animals and people. Most of the people in the desert live in these oases which dot the Sahara.

Nomadic people have lived in the Sahara for thousands of years. They herd their camels, goats, sheep, and donkeys, looking for good pasture land. They wear loose fitting robes, hooded cloaks, and slippers to withstand the harsh climate. They live in simple skin tents with little furniture so they can move easily. Caravans can be up to a mile long with camels carrying goods to trade to distant locations.

The Nile River is the longest river in the world. And it is the home of one of the most famous early civilizations, ancient Egypt. We will briefly explore the ancient Egyptians touching on the pyramids, mummies, hieroglyphics, as well as the interesting wildlife such as the Nile crocodile and the Egyptian cobra. We do not encourage delving deeply into the Egyptian religion in the elementary years. That is best suited for older students. Books discussing religion are noted, and you should preview these books before using them. The suggested books have all been vetted, and though some may contain some Egyptian and Arabian mythological and religious elements, these elements are not dominant or overwhelming and the rest of the content is powerful.

MATERIALS

Books

General

1. ***Beginner's World Atlas 3rd Edition***, National Geographic. 2011.
2. ***Africa is Not a Country***, Margy Burns Knight. Ages 5–12. The first two pages are a great overview of the continent of Africa. The rest of the book is one- to two-page vignettes of children's lives in various countries in Africa demonstrating the variety of cultures. This is not a book to sit and read through in one setting. But your children will enjoy looking at the pictures and hearing the stories if told over a few days.
3. ***African Animal Alphabet,*** Beverly & Dereck Joubert. Ages 4–8. National Geographic provides high quality photographs of African animals with just the right amount of text and clever alliteration.

Sahara Desert

4. ***A Collection of Rudyard Kipling's Just So Stories***, Candlewick Press. This gorgeously illustrated collection of Kipling's origin stories are fanciful tales which tell of how various phenomena came about. Buying this collection is encouraged as we will read four selections for Africa and one for Australia. You can read about the whale and the Amazon armadillo from the continents we have already studied. This week we will read **How the Camel Got His Hump,** a playful tale of the arrogance and downfall of the lazy camel.
5. ***This is the Oasis***, Miriam Moss. Ages 4–8. Great explanation of the Sahara, oasis, nomadic peoples, and the animal life there.

Nile

6. *We're Sailing Down the Nile: A Journey through Egypt*, Laurie Krebs. Ages 5–8. Interesting book with a lot of information. Parental Caution: contains information on the Egyptian religion and gods.
7. ***Croco'nile,*** Roy Gerrard. Ages 5–8. Siblings in ancient Egypt have a pet crocodile and become artisans to the Pharaoh. Fun introduction to ancient Egypt for little kids. The illustrations give a great sense of the art, culture, and life in ancient Egypt.
8. ***13 Buildings Children Should Know***, Annette Roeder. Ages 8–12. While geared towards older children, this book is a gem, and could be used with younger children as they explore many buildings we study in this curriculum, including: The Great Pyramid, Notre Dame Cathedral, the Leaning Tower of Pisa, the Tower of London, St Peter's Basilica, the Taj Majal, Neuschwanstein Castle, and the Eiffel Tower.
9. Bible story of Joseph, such as ***Joseph***, Brian Wildsmith. Ages 4–10. Incredibly detailed illustrations of this biblically accurate story will delight all ages. Consider purchasing for your family library!
10. Bible story of Moses, such as ***Exodus***, Brian Wildsmith. Ages 4–10. Companion piece for Joseph. Intricate illustrations will teach much about Egypt, and the promised land! Consider purchasing for your family library!

Secondary Books: Find *some* of these excellent books to read aloud and make available to your children for their quiet times. * means especially recommended. This list is very long—even just two or three of these books can add to your week.

1. *****Ashanti to Zulu: African Traditions**, Margaret Musgrove. Ages 4–7. Caldecott winner. Beautiful pictures in an ABC format covers 26 people groups in Africa. Though not a story, each tribe description includes an illustration with a man, a woman, and a child in native dress, as well as an animal, an artifact, and living quarters.
2. **Off to the Sweet Shores of Africa: and other Talking Drum Rhymes.** Uzo Unobagha. Ages 3–6. Rhymes about Africa in the spirit of Mother Goose.
3. **Africa**, Allan Fowler. Easy Reader. Simple overview of Africa.
4. **Calabash Cat**, James Rumford. Ages 4–7. West African cat crosses a desert, grassland, jungle, and ocean seeking the world's end. Illustrations in the style of the calabash engravers from the country of Chad make this a very worthwhile read.
5. **A Triangle for Adaora: an African Book of Shapes,** Ifeoma Onyefulu. Ages 3–7. Winsome photographs of two girls finding shapes in Africa.
6. **African Critters**, Robert Haas, National Geographic. Ages 6–9. Perhaps a bit too much information to read to young children, but they will love to flip through the excellent photographs of leopards, elephants, wild dogs, lions, hyenas, cheetahs, hippos, rhinos, and other small critters.

Sahara Desert

7. *****Muktar and the Camels,** Janet Graber. Ages 5–8. A gentle story of a Somali orphan in Kenya returning to the nomadic life of his people by taking care of camels. Written in a way to help a modern western child understand and empathize with someone from a different culture. Lovely dream-like illustrations.
8. **Ali, Child of the Desert,** Jonathan London. Ages 5–10. Ali finds courage and friendship in this realistic survival adventure in the Sahara Desert.
9. **The Butter Man**, Elizabeth Alalou. Ages 6–9. True story of a child in the Atlas Mountains of Morocco during a drought.
10. **What's the Matter, Habibi?** Betsy Lewin. Ages 3–8. Delightful story of a camel and his master set in the north African bazaar. The camel just wants a FEZ!
11. **The Storyteller**, Evan Turk. Ages 5–9. Lovely illustrations enhance this engaging folktale of a storyteller who brings water back to the desert. As in many folktales there is magic, including the Sahara Desert as a Djinn. Parents might want to preview first.
12. **Deserts: Surviving in the Sahara**, Michael Sandler. Ages 6 and up. Great overview of deserts, the Sahara, Timbuktu, and desert animals.
13. Nonfiction book on camels and the desert such as: **Camels are Awesome,** Allan Morey. Ages 4–8. **Camels,** Kate Riggs. Ages 4–6; **Camels**, Susie Dawson. Ages 5–10. **Peoples of the Desert**, Robert Low. Ages 6–8.

Nile and Egypt

14. **Crocodile Listens**, April Pulley Sayre. Ages 4–8. Mama crocodile takes care of her hatching babies. Set in the Nile with added information on end pages.
15. **Bill and Pete Go Down the Nile**, Tomie DePaola. Ages 4–6. Bill the crocodile learns about his home in Egypt and captures the bad guy during a field trip. Egyptian motifs fill this delightful book.

16. ***Seeker of Knowledge: The Man Who Deciphered Egyptian Hieroglyphs***, James Rumford. Ages 5–9. True tale of the man who first deciphered hieroglyphs.
17. ***The Nile River,*** Allan Fowler. Ages 4–8. Easy Reader. Great intro with good age-appropriate information.
18. ***Egypt, True Books***, Elaine Landau. Ages 7–10. A simple book with a great overview of Egypt. Parents could quickly read beforehand and then explain to younger children while they look at the pictures.
19. Nonfiction book about crocodiles such as ***Crocodiles: Built for the Hunt***, Tammy Gagne. Ages 5–9.
20. Nonfiction book about cobras such as ***Killer Snakes: Egyptian Cobra***, Jessica O'Donnell. Ages 4–8 or ***Amazing Snakes: Spitting Cobras***, Emily Rose Oachs. Ages 4–8.
21. ***The Scarab's Secret***, Nick Would. Ages 6–9. The tiny scarab beetle uncovers a plot to kill an Egyptian prince in this lavishly illustrated book. Parental caution: References Egyptian gods.

Movies

1. ***Prince of Egypt***. Disney. While this animated movie might be frightening for some sensitive children, and has some small historical inaccuracies, it is a great movie that showcases the beauty and majesty of ancient Egypt.

SUPPLIES

1. Map of Africa (available on the *GO GLOBAL* Resource page) printed on cardstock, sand paper
2. Materials for pin prick activity: push pins, Styrofoam plate or cork plate, small map of Africa, available on the *GO GLOBAL* Resource page
3. Template for camel art on the *GO GLOBAL* Resource page.
4. Multiple printed pages of the African animal chart, available on the *GO GLOBAL* Resource page
5. Outdoor sand box, or indoor bin with sand, drinking straw or turkey baster
6. Spinach beef couscous ingredients: deli roast beef, couscous, spinach, soy sauce
7. Timeline materials: Washi tape, printed dates and pictures, available on the *GO GLOBAL* Resource page
8. Bag of white paper cups OR blocks
9. Playdough

DAY 1   AFRICA OVERVIEW AND AFRICAN ANIMALS

EVERYONE

1. Read ***Beginner's World Atlas***, pages 44–49.

    a) Find Africa on the globe. Ask your child name the other continents you have studied. Can she also name the oceans around Africa? Using the map of Africa provided on the *GO GLOBAL* Resource page, label and color the Atlantic and Indian Oceans. Also, find, color, and label the Mediterranean Sea and the Red Sea.

    b) Color the mountains on your map: the Atlas Mountains in the north, the mountains along the Great Rift Valley, and the Drakensberg Mountains in the far southeast. Do NOT expect your child to learn the names. It is enough to know that there are mountains.

   c) Color and label the Nile River. Color and label Lake Victoria.

   d) Add small sand strips on the Sahara Desert. Add sand strips to the Kalahari Desert.

   e) Color the jungle symbol to the sub-Saharan portion of Africa.

   f) Color the grassland symbol for savanna.

2. Read ***Africa is Not a Country.*** You will need more than one sitting to get through this book. Older children might enjoy finding the countries on your globe. Talk to your child about how these children are different and similar to them.

3. Pin prick a map of Africa. As is beautifully expressed in ***Africa is Not a Country,*** Africa is pretty much impossible to pin down in a neat little one-dimensional box. But that won't keep you from pinning it down in the most literal of ways! Using cork tiles (or cleaned Styrofoam plates/pans) make a perforated outline of Africa. This classic Montessori activity is a great way to work on coordination, concentration, fine-motor skills, the pincher grasp needed to hold a pencil, and strengthening the muscles used with handwriting. If the children punch close together, the map will "cut out" like a perforated picture.

While they are poking holes you can point out some of the shapes and land forms—the Horn of Africa and the Cape of Good Hope. And you can read a story from the African books.

Materials

- Map of Africa available on the *GO GLOBAL* Resource page
- Push pins
- Styrofoam or cork sheet

Process

   a) Print one map of Africa for each child from the *GO GLOBAL* Resource page.

   b) Layer the map on top of the Styrofoam or cork sheet. Secure with tape or paper clips so it will not slide as they make the pinpricks.

   c) Have your child carefully poke holes along the border of the continent. Discuss and/or read about Africa while the child pokes the holes.

   d) Give your children the opportunity to explore and play with their Africa map cutouts if so desired.

   e) Display art work.

ADD FOR SIX-YEAR-OLDS AND UP

4. Have your child start to make a chart of animals from Africa. DO NOT fill it all out for her. You may do the writing but let her do the dictating. The first column should be "Animal", the second column is "Location" and the third column is for your child to draw a picture. You will want to discuss the behavior of the animals. Add a few animals every day! A printable for this list of African animals list is available on the *GO GLOBAL* Resource page.

a) Location is where in the animal lives: desert, savanna, or jungle. You might include desert oasis.

b) Behavior to discuss can include anything interesting about the animal that your child mentions; this could include what the animal likes to eat (is it an herbivore, carnivore or omnivore?), its color, if it is solitary or lives in community, etc. Make sure to discuss how you would dramatize this animal. I have included some suggestions below, but do NOT just fill in the chart. You want to let your child have an opportunity to be creative and to tell you what she thinks.

c) Slowly add to this list by asking your child what animal she would like to add. Then you can learn more about this animal. Or you can slowly add to this list in the next few weeks as you learn about the animals.

AFRICAN ANIMAL CHART

Animal	*Location*
Aardvark	savanna, jungle
African elephant	savanna, jungle
Agama lizard	desert
Antelope/ impala/ gazelle	savanna, jungle, desert
Cobra/ Sahara sand viper	desert
Baboon	savanna, jungle
Camel	desert
Chameleon	jungle, savanna, desert
Cheetah	savanna, desert
Chimpanzee	savanna
Colobus Monkey	jungle
Crocodile	Nile River
Dassies	desert
Dung Beetle	desert
Fennec Fox	desert
Giraffe	savanna
Gorilla	jungle
Hippopotamus	jungle, savanna
Honeyguide	savanna
Honey badger	savanna
Hyena	savanna

Animal	*Location*
Jackal	savanna, jungle, desert
Leopard	savanna, jungle
Lion	savanna
Mongoose; meerkat	desert, savanna
Mandrill	jungle
Ostrich	desert
Rhinoceros	savanna, jungle
Scarab Beetle	desert
Warthog	savanna
Wildebeest	savanna
Zebra	savanna, jungle

DAY 2 SAHARA DESERT, CAMELS, AND CARAVANS

EVERYONE

1. Read *This is the Oasis, Ali Child of the Desert,* or another book about the Sahara and oases.

    a) Discuss the vastness of the Sahara. The Sahara is as big as the United States of America!

    b) Discuss sandstorms and the dangers in the desert.

    c) Discuss the animals of the desert and the oases.

    d) Discuss how one dresses in the desert. [Possible answers: loose light weight clothing that covers and protects from the sun.]

    e) *Ali* mentions some unique Berber/Muslim beliefs of leaving one long lock of hair on their otherwise bald heads so that they can be grabbed and pulled into heaven. It is easy to skip over it, or you might want to take the time to discuss superstition, and that God does not need a handle of hair to save us!

2. Make sand dunes in a plastic bin or out in your sand box. Use a straw to blow in one direction across the top of the sand. Compare your dunes with pictures of the Sahara. If you do not have access to sand, you could use cornmeal in a lipped cookie sheet. Do this activity outside, if possible. Rather than blowing through straws you could use a turkey baster to create the wind.

3. Read *How the Camel Got His Hump.* Soak in the rich vocabulary and wonderful story.

4. Easy Camel Art. Art Tutorial available on *GO GLOBAL* Resource page.

    ### Materials

    - Cardstock/construction paper: One sheet of any color you would like

- Template available on *GO GLOBAL* Resource page

Process

    a) Fold paper in half and cut out camel body with the top of his body on the fold. Cut out ears and insert. Template provided on the *GO GLOBAL* Resource page.

    b) Draw eye, nostril, and mouth.

5. Read some of the other listed books about camels. Known as the *Ships of the Desert*, camels can carry large amount of goods and people. Your child should learn:

    a) Camels are mammals. The Bedouins (nomadic peoples of the Saharan and Arabian Deserts) drink their milk.

    b) Camels are domesticated—which means that they are willing to live with and work for people.

    c) They spit when they are mad!

    d) They travel steadily at a moderate pace—about 25 miles a day at the rate of three miles per hour. An average man can walk at about the same pace—if he has no pack, is not in the desert, and for just one day.

    e) Camels can have one or two humps. The humps store fat and help them survive on a long trip without eating or drinking—up to 30 days!

    f) They have adaptations to help them live in the desert.

- They can close their nostrils to keep the sand from going up their noses.
- Their eyelashes shade their eyes and they have three eyelids to protect against the sand.
- The two toes on their feet spread out so they do not sink into the sand.
- Their thick but loose wool keeps them warm in the cold desert nights and cool during the day.
- They have thick lips so they can eat thorny bushes in the desert. They are herbivores and only eat plants.

6. Go on a caravan. A caravan is a group of people and animals traveling together on a long journey through the desert. People usually took camels since these animals are so well suited for life in the desert.

    a) Ask your child what she would take on the caravan trip. Remind her that she will be in the desert, and she or her camel must carry everything she needs.

    b) Designate someone to be the camel to carry the food, blankets, water, and goods.

    c) Ask your child how she would dress. Will she wear a hat? What kind? Why?

    d) Go on a caravan through the neighborhood! Will there be a sandstorm? If it is long enough you might send someone ahead to make an "oasis" with shade, dates, and water.

    e) Afterwards discuss the difference between the expedition in Antarctica and the caravan in the desert. [Answer: While both are difficult, one deals with extreme cold and the other with extreme heat. Water is important in both. The Antarctic expedition was to discover and learn about things such as wildlife. A caravan is to transport people and goods from one place to another.]

7. OPTIONAL—Eat Couscous, a North African dish of small balls of pasta. There are many more complex recipes on line. I like this quick and SIMPLE one:

Ten Minute Spinach Beef Couscous (serves 4)

Ingredients

- 1 lb. deli sliced roast beef
- 32 oz. frozen chopped spinach (or fresh spinach sautéed)
- 2 C. Couscous
- Soy Sauce

Instructions

a) Chop beef into strips, sauté in oil. Sprinkle with garlic. Add drained defrosted spinach or fresh sautéed spinach.

b) Cook couscous by stirring into 2 cups boiling water, return to boil, cover, remove from heat, let stand 5 minutes. Fluff with fork.

c) Fluff couscous with fork and place on a plate, top with beef/spinach and sprinkle with soy sauce.

DAY 3 ANCIENT EGYPT, NILE RIVER, AND PYRAMIDS

EVERYONE

1. Discuss when the ancient Egyptians lived by making a timeline, so your children can see the flow of history. Timelines are crucial to understand the scope of time and to understand how the different aspects of culture are interrelated (political history, art history, music history, history of science, biblical and church history, etc.) Just as we want our children to understand their place in our world, we also want them to understand their place in time. Oversized books with filled in timelines have too much information for a child to understand. Creating a timeline is the best way to build an understanding of time. While you will want to have a more complex time line in the later elementary years, it is enough to make a simple, small timeline at this stage.

Attach one seven-foot piece of Washi tape slanted upward along your wall, with a corresponding descending seven-foot strip making an upside-down v shape. Add a 2.5-foot piece of Washi tape ascending straight from the bottom left slanted piece. This small piece will be for the "Prehistory" events before 2000 BC. Mark each four-inch segment with a black marker to represent every 100 years. Labels and figures for the timeline, as well as photographs of completed timelines, are available at the *GO GLOBAL* Resource page. Print off labels for each 500-year segment. Make a cross of two thin sticks lashed together with twine.

- a) Talk about how time is divided by when Christ lived. Add the cross between BC and AD. Tell the children that the time to the left is BC, i.e., Before Christ. Explain that BC stands for Before Christ and that AD stands for Anno Domini, or the year of the Lord. Add the large BC and AD letters to the appropriate side.

- b) Label the 500-year increments.
  - Descending from the top on the BC side: 500 BC, 1000 BC, 1500 BC, 2000 BC,
  - Descending from the top: Cross AD side: AD 500, AD 1000, AD 1500, AD 2000, Present
  - Ascending from the bottom of the BC line: no 100-year marks, Prehistory

- c) Ask your child about famous/ familiar people they know, such as Grandma & Grandpa, Bible figures such as David & Goliath. Did they live before Jesus or after Jesus? Add just a few people to your time line, including a picture of your own family. Templates for timeline figures some historical figures and events are available at the *GO GLOBAL* Resource page. The goal here is to *begin* to build a framework—not fill in every event that they know.

- d) Add a few significant historical figures, IF they already know them. Perhaps the Pilgrims arriving at Plymouth in 1620 and the Declaration of Independence in 1776. This gives some context of when the USA was formed.

- e) Add Egyptian people/places/ events to the time line *as you learn about them.*
  - The Sphinx and Great Pyramid of Giza were built around 2500 BC.
  - Joseph the Patriarch lived around 1900 BC.
  - Moses lived around 1500 BC.

2. Read ***We're Sailing Down the Nile*** and/or ***Croco'nile***.

    - a) Ask your children if they think these Egyptians lived before or after Jesus? Before or after Jonah? Before or after David? Before or after Moses?

       Egypt became a unified kingdom in 3150 B.C. The kingdom fluctuated but lasted through 332 BC. Point out the beginning and ending on your time line.

    - b) On a second reading point out and discuss the plants and animals such as papyrus, lotus, and the scarab beetle.

3. Point out pyramids and the sphinx in ***We're Sailing Down the Nile*** or ***Croco'nile***. Read ***13 Buildings Children Should Know***, pages 4–7. You can read just the large print and look at the pictures if your child is young. If she is interested, read the smaller print, too.

Add the Great Pyramid to your timeline. It was built around 2550 B.C.

4. Build a pyramid out of Lego or Duplo blocks. (easiest activity)

OR

Let your child make a pyramid out of paper cups. (Still easy, but more open ended) Give her the cups and let your child explore how to make it. She might make a line of cups on the ground and stack cups making one triangle. She might start with a square of cups on the ground and build a more three-dimensional pyramid. There is NOT one right way to build this.

DAY 4   ANCIENT EGYPT AND NILE CROCODILE

EVERYONE

1. Read books and learn about the Nile crocodile.

    a) It is 16 feet long. Measure this to see how big it really is. OPTIONAL: Let your child draw a life-sized crocodile on your sidewalk or driveway with chalk.

    b) It swims 18 miles per hour. That is about three times faster than an Olympic swimmer.

    c) It can hold its breath for two hours. How long can you hold your breath? Most children can't last more than 30 seconds. Some people might be able to last two minutes. See if your child remembers how long the polar bear (three minutes, which we learned in week 5, day 4) or the penguins (an hour, which we learned in week 11, day 3) can hold their breath.

    d) It can jump several feet into the air and snap birds for a dinner. Measure your child's vertical leap.

    e) It only eats about once a week. Ask your child if he would like to try eating as often as a crocodile eats.

2. Read the story of Joseph. Make sure your children understand the when and where of this narrative. Look at your globe and timeline! This story tells how the Hebrews ended up in Egypt. Add Joseph to your timeline.

3. Read the story of Moses' life—his birth and the deliverance from Egypt. It is important to integrate the events of the Bible with regular history. You can talk about how the Israelites were conscripted to build for the rulers in Egypt. (Exodus 5)

Children should realize this is a not a fictional story, but a true historical event. Joseph brought the Hebrews into Egypt and Moses brought them out. Reading the story rather than just watching a cartoon movie will help this understanding.

Add Moses to your timeline. Then, using your timeline show the time between these two patriarchs.

4. If you choose to watch **Prince of Egypt**, be sure to read/tell the true narrative before watching. As with all movies, discuss afterwards what parts are true, false, and conjecture (could be true, but not assuredly so).

ADD FOR SIX-YEAR-OLDS AND UP

5. Using your Egyptian books, point out the art and writing which is called hieroglyphics.

    a) Stand like Egyptians. Body facing forward, legs and face turned 90° to one side. Stiff arms with fingers showing. This is fun and hones good coordination skills.

    b) Make a "tablet" by rolling out some playdough. Give your child some stamps or instruments to "make" hieroglyphs. Find inspiration in your books for this activity. The purpose of this activity is to understand that hieroglyphs represent words and objects; do not expect them to copy the actual hieroglyphs.

6. Read about cobras.

    a) Review what you learned about snakes while studying Mexico and South America.

    - Snakes are vertebrates.

    - They slither on the ground because they have no legs or arms.

    - Some are venomous.

    - Some are constrictors.

    b) Look at pictures and talk about the cobra's hood. The snake can make the area right below the head flatter and wider. It makes the snake look scarier.

    c) The Egyptian cobra is five to eight feet long. Measure this size!

    d) This snake likes to live in hot places with water—in oases and near the Nile River.

    e) A cobra has fangs and injects venom. The bitten animal or human will die in about 15 minutes unless given an antivenom drug.

    f) A cobra hunts at night and eats small animals like mice, rats, frogs, birds, lizards, and other snakes.

    g) A cobra makes loud hissing noises when cornered and sways back and forth when its enemy moves.

WEEK 17
AFRICA
SAVANNA AND EAST RIFT

BIG PICTURE

The African savanna is mostly grasslands with some low bushes, water holes, and a few trees. Many of the people who live in the eastern portion of Africa live a simple life where the men hunt, fish, herd the animals, and build the homes. The women cook, take care of the children, weave, and tend the family garden. Most live in mud homes with roofs of straw, bamboo, and leaves. This contrasts with West Africa where people tend to wear more modern clothes and live in apartments.

This week we will learn about the savanna (also known as African plains), Mount Kilimanjaro, and the animals in the plains, with an emphasis on the elephant.

We will learn about the Maasai people, a semi-nomadic tribe who live in Kenya and Tanzania near the Great Rift area. They herd cattle, sheep, or goats which historically provided all their food needs with the animals' milk, meat, and sometimes blood. In the modern age livestock no longer provides for all their needs and they have added rice, potatoes, and cabbage to their diet. The Maasai live in small villages enclosed with a kraal, a low thorn bush fence surrounding their wattle and daub dwellings. Their round homes are built with interwoven sticks and grass covered with a mud paste, and topped with straw roofs. Clothing varies with the tribes, but includes a piece of usually red or blue, rectangular cloth wrapped around the body. Men and women wear elaborate woven and beaded bracelets and necklaces. Men, women, and children participate in the Maasai jumping dance. But for the men it is also an athletic competition that determines who will be the leader of the hunt. To protect their livestock, they sometimes need to hunt a lion with just spears.

MATERIALS

Books

1. **We All Went on Safari: A Counting Journey through Tanzania,** Laurie Krebs. Ages 4–9. A group of Maasai people travel across Tanzania and encounter the animals. Lovely illustrations capture the African plain. Pages in back have additional information on animals, Maasai people, Swahili names, and a map of Tanzania.
2. **Mama Panya's Pancakes: A Village Tale from Kenya**, Mary Chamberlin. Ages 4–9. Story of sharing and life in Kenya. Pages in back about the people, village life, school, plants and animals, common greetings, a pancake recipe, and a map of Kenya.
3. **Bringing the Rain to Kapiti Plain**, Verna Aardema. Ages 4–8. A wonderful read-aloud tale from Kenya about ending the drought on the Kapiti Plain.
4. **This is the Mountain**, Miriam Moss. Ages 4–8. A story of the people, plants, and animals on and around Mt. Kilimanjaro.

5. ***My Rows and Piles of Coins***, Tololwa M. Mollel. Ages 4–9. A modern Maasai boy in Tanzania works and saves his money to buy a bicycle.
6. ***A Collection of Rudyard Kipling's Just So Stories***, Candlewick Press. This week we will read ***The Elephant's Child.***

Secondary Books: Find *some* of these excellent books to read aloud and make available to your children for their quiet times. * means especially recommended.

1. ****Over in the Grasslands: On an African Savanna,*** Marianne Berkes. Ages 4–8. Ten animals in the grasslands with ten additional hidden animals for your child to find. Extra information is on the end pages.
2. ****The Tree of Life: The World of the African Baobab***, Barbara Bash. Ages 6–10. Starting with the African legend that the hyena was given a tree and planted it upside down, this book elegantly tells the story of the animals and their relationship to this unique tree in the African savanna.
3. ****Clever Tortoise,*** Francesca Martin. Ages 4–7. Delightful trickster tale of the tortoise and other small animals on the bank of Lake Nyasa fooling elephant and hippopotamus.
4. Nonfiction book on elephants such as ****How to Track an Elephant***, Henry Owens.
5. ****Water Hole Waiting,*** Jane and Christopher Kurtz. Ages 4–8. Dawn to dusk the animals come to drink. Interesting end notes on this true-to-life story.
6. ***Here is the African Savanna***, Madeleine Dunphy. Ages 4–8. Lyrically told realistic story with lovely illustrations of zebras, lions, giraffes, baboons, impalas, tick birds, hippos, elephants, and the grasslands.
7. Nonfiction book on savanna such as **A Home on the Savanna** (photographs), Susan Labella; **Peoples of the Savanna**, Robert Law. **African Savanna**, Claire Llewellyn (Easy Reader).
8. ***Rain,*** Manya Stojic. Ages 3–5. Descriptive story of the animals waiting for the rain—using all their senses. Great for little ones to learn animals, colors, and the five senses, as well as the rhythm of the dry and wet seasons.
9. ***This is the Tree***, Miriam Moss. Ages 5–8. Poem of life on savanna around the baobab tree.
10. ***Papa, Do You Love Me?*** Barbara Joosse. Ages 4–8. Tender story of a Maasai father's love towards his son with wonderful information about their society.
11. ***Maasai and I,*** Virginia Kroll. Ages 4–7. A modern African American girl dreams of the different life she would have if she was a Maasai in Africa.
12. ***14 Cows for America,*** Carmen Agra Deedy. Ages 5–8. True story of Maasai people in Kenya gifting precious cows to the USA after the 9/11 attacks.
13. ***Who's in Rabbit's House?*** Verna Aardema. Ages 5–10. Maasai folktale presented in the form of a play.
14. ***Kidogo,*** Anik McGrory. Ages 3–6. A little elephant searches for animals smaller than he is, and learns that his size and his home are just right. Simple and sweet introduction to several animals in East Africa.
15. ***Quick, Slow, Mango!*** Anik McGrory. Ages 3–6. Slow elephant Kidogo makes friends with fast monkey PolePole.

SUPPLIES

1. Map of Africa from last week
2. Elephant craft materials: two pieces of grey cardstock/construction paper, one piece of white cardstock/ construction paper, template available on *GO GLOBAL* Resource page

3. The rain-stick that you made when you studied South America
4. Pancake ingredients: flour, oil, cardamom or nutmeg, crushed red pepper, egg
5. OPTIONAL: dress up clothes for Maasai: red, blue, purple printed or solid cloth to wrap around child, belt, beaded necklaces, bracelets, or anklets
6. OPTIONAL: spears for lion hunt (can be a yard stick!)
7. OPTIONAL: blocks or mud and sticks to build Maasai village model

DAY 1 — SAVANNA

EVERYONE

1. Review Africa on the map. Review information you added last week and emphasize the savanna or grasslands.
2. Read **We All Went on Safari**.
    a) Find Tanzania on the globe.
    b) Find the Serengeti Plain on the globe. Trace with your finger.
    c) Find and label Mount Kilimanjaro on your map.
    d) Find and label Lake Victoria on your map.
    e) Talk about the animals mentioned in the book and add one or more to your list of African animals. Do NOT make your child add every animal mentioned in the book. There will be plenty of time to add additional animals.
3. Learn more about Mt. Kilimanjaro by reading **This is the Mountain**.
    a) Talk about how Mt. Kilimanjaro, a dormant (sleeping or inactive) volcano has three cones. Ask your child what he remembers from making a volcano when you studied Mexico.
    b) This is the highest elevation in Africa. It is so high that there is snow, glaciers, and an ice cap. Discuss what he remembers about glaciers from his studies of Canada and Antarctica.
4. OPTIONAL: Read **Over in the Grasslands: On an African Savanna**
    a) Talk about the primary animals, and find the hidden ones, too.
    b) Add to your African animal list if there are some new animals.

DAY 2 — SAVANNA AND ELEPHANTS

EVERYONE

1. Read **Bringing the Rain to Kapiti Plain**
    a) Find the Kapiti Plain in Kenya by looking at the **Beginner's World Atlas**.

b) Read the book again, slowly, and have a discussion. Possible points:
- "Sea of grass"—How is the savanna like a sea of grass? [Possible answers: It billows in the wind like the waves on the sea. It is vast like the sea; you might not see the end. You see the wide sky like when you are on the sea.]

> We will NOT introduce the term "metaphor" with this age group; but they can understand the concept of metaphor—equating different things to provide clarity or insight.

- What does the word "belated" mean? See if your child can guess from the context in the sentence.
- Ask your child if anyone can shoot an arrow into the sky to make it rain. Of course not. But it is fun to pretend. This is a folktale and a myth: a traditional story that explains a natural occurrence with a pretend (or supernatural) element. Ask your child if we have read other fanciful tales that provided make-believe explanations of natural phenomena. [Possible answers: Just So Stories, Trickster Tales.]
- Can your child remember another myth that promised to bring rain? We made it when we studied South America. And there are some people groups in Africa that also make rain-sticks. Play with your rain-stick.
- Ki-pat stood on one leg like the big stork bird. Ask your child if he can stand on one leg. How long can he last? Would adding a staff help?
- Have your child relay the story in sequence.

> This is an important prewriting skill as it will help them to sequence their own original stories.

- Have your child tell you about the animals in the book. Which is his favorite? Why?

c) Add one or more new animals to your African animal list.

2. Read *The Elephant's Child,* from the ***Just So Stories.***
3. Read some other books about elephants, including at least one that has photographs of real elephants. Dramatize elephants after reviewing some of these facts. See what your child can remember!

   a) Asian elephants live in India and Southeast Asia; African elephants live south of the Sahara Desert. Some live in the jungles and others live in savannas. We will learn the difference between Asian and African elephants when we study India. This week make sure he notices the African elephant's large ears, which are sort of shaped like Africa!

   b) Elephants are the largest land animals in the world.

   c) Elephants have two long teeth called tusks and a long trunk used for breathing, drinking (by sucking up the water and spraying into their mouths), and even picking things up.

d) Males are called bulls. Females live in a herd with other females and their calves.

e) Elephants communicate with their bodies, such as folding an ear or a curling their trunk. They also roar, scream, and trumpet. They often greet one another with a hug using their trunks.

f) They are mammals, which means the mothers produce milk to feed the babies.

g) They are herbivores, which means they eat plants.

4. Elephant Art Activity tutorial available on *GO GLOBAL* Resource page

Materials

- Cardstock/construction paper. Two sheets of gray, or any color you would like
- White cardstock/paper
- Template available on *GO GLOBAL* Resource page
- Glue

Process

a) Fold paper in half and cut out elephant body with the top of his body on the fold. A template is provided on the *GO GLOBAL* Resource page. Cut out eyes and tusks out of white paper. Cardstock is more durable, but either paper can work.

b) Use one page of construction page (not cardstock) to fold accordion style for the ears.

c) Glue on eyes and tusk.

d) Insert ears.

DAY 3   AFRICAN HOSPITALITY AND GENEROSITY

EVERYONE

1. Read **Mama Panya's Pancakes: A Village Tale from Kenya**.

    a) Talk about how to be polite when you greet your friends. Practice saying "Jambo" which is hello in Swahili when greeting family members and friends this week.

    b) What interesting plants and animals did you observe in the book?

    c) Make the pancakes per the book. These crepe-like pancakes need some modifications. Add a beaten egg to help the crepes hold together, only add 1/8 tsp. of the crushed peppers, and you can decrease the oil to ¼ cup.

    OPTIONAL: Invite another family and make it a potluck, just like in the book. Someone could bring some protein like fish, or the more American choice of bacon or ham. Someone else could bring plantains (which need to be cooked) or seasonal fruit.

2. Read **My Rows and Piles of Coins**

    a) This is another story based in Tanzania. Find it on the globe—you will be quicker this time!

b) What do you admire about this young man?

c) This book has wonderful onomatopoeia.

> Onomatopoeia is a word that imitates, resembles, or suggests the sound it describes. Common onomatopoeia is found in animal noises such as meow, moo, or ruff. Have your child repeat some of the fun sounds in this book such as: tuk-tuk-tuk and pikipiki.

3. Add any new animals to your African animal list.

4. Inspired by ***My Rows and Piles of Coins,*** go for a bike ride and talk about being grateful for your bike. Greet people that you see like they did in ***Mama Panya's Pancakes***.

ADD FOR SIX-YEAR-OLDS AND UP

5. Discuss the similarities and differences in these two books. For instance, one seems in a more distant past, or in a more remote and rural area, while the other seems to be more in our present time. Discuss the importance of family, hospitality, and hard work in each book.

DAY 4 — SAVANNA AND MAASAI

EVERYONE

1. Reread books from this week that your child particularly likes. Use the books as a springboard to talk about the savanna. Most of this information will be picked up naturally by your child as he reads the wonderful books in this unit. You can gently talk to him about these facts. If you do it in the form of questions he will demonstrate how much he has learned. Information on the savanna will be covered next week as well. At the dinner table prompt your child to tell Daddy about the things he has learned.

> As he relays what he knows, learning is solidified into long term memory. In addition, this important social skill of dinner time conversation yields the benefit of drawing Dad into your learning adventure.

Here are some things you might encourage your child to discuss.

a) There are two seasons: rainy and dry; rather than the four seasons we typically experience.

b) There are only a few trees.

c) There are plant-eating animals: giraffe, zebra, antelope. Encourage him to use the big words, herbivore, and define for Dad.

d) There are meat-eating animals known as predators: lions. Encourage him to use the big words, carnivore and predator, and define what those are for Dad.

e) There are meat-eating animals known as scavengers: jackals, vultures. Use the big words, carnivore and scavenger, define.

f) There are birds such as the ostriches and weaver birds.

ADD FOR SIX-YEAR-OLDS AND UP

2. Learn about the Maasai. Read or reread some of the books that are about Maasai. After you have read some books, ask your child what he can tell you about the Maasai people.

    a) He should be able to tell you:
    - They herd livestock. (cattle, sheep, or goats)
    - They live in circular houses made of sticks and mud. Their villages are surrounded by corrals for protection.
    - They live on the savannas or plains.

    b) He might be able to tell you:
    - They dance by jumping.
    - They wear arm and ankle bracelets.
    - They wear red or blue robes.
    - They hunt with spears and have decorated shields made from animal skins.

    c) Dance like a Maasai. To see this unique dancing follow the link to a video available on the *GO GLOBAL* Resource page. Jump and see who can jump the highest.
    - OPTIONAL: Dress like a Maasai. Use a bright colored sheet or piece of fabric to wrap around you. Add a belt and some beaded jewelry.
    - OPTIONAL: The highest jumper can lead his siblings on a lion hunt. Add a spear and shield if you desire.

    d) OPTIONAL: Do one of these activities about the Maasai.

    > This would be a great activity for the kids to do while you are cooking dinner!

    - Make a Maasai village out of blocks.
    - Make a small Maasai village outside with mud, sticks, grass.

WEEK 18
AFRICA
SAVANNA AND COASTAL BULGE

BIG PICTURE

Continuing to study the African savanna will now include a look at some of the coastal bulge countries and the jungle region. Unlike the tropical rain forest, the jungle forest does not have a dense canopy and separate layers. The floor of the Amazon rain forest is relatively easy to walk through; the floor of a jungle has thick foliage that might need to be cut down to walk. Though we will use the same forest emblem to mark these places on our maps there are differences that some children might find interesting.

Kente cloth is elaborately woven cotton/silk blend cloth used for ceremonial and festive occasions. While its origin is in the Ashanti Kingdom in Ghana, it is the best known African textile and is popular throughout Africa and other continents where Africans have settled. This very expensive material is usually not cut—but worn by men and women as a drape. You will read an origin tale about kente cloth, and design a kente pattern.

Reading books about the living conditions in less developed countries and then doing role playing can develop empathy and understanding.

You will learn about animals in the savanna and jungle with an emphasis on the honeybird/ honeyguide, honey badger, lion, and rhinoceros.

MATERIALS

Books

1. ***Honey, Honey, Lion! A Story from Africa***, Jan Brett. Ages 4–8. In this lively read-aloud based in Botswana, honeybird leads badger on a merry chase after he refuses to share with her. Each page shows an African animal spreading the news through the bush telegraph. Accurate illustrations, though the badger is much fiercer than portrayed in this book.
2. ***One Hen: How One Small Loan Made a Big Difference***, Katie Smith Milway. Ages 5–10. A young boy starts a business with a loan to purchase one hen. Inspiring story loosely based on a real event of micro-credit in Ghana.
3. ***The Spider Weaver: A Legend of Kente Cloth***, Margaret Musgrove. Ages 4–8. Ghana legend of a master spider teaching the people to weave the kente cloth from yellow, red, and blue thread. OR ***Seven Spools of Thread***, Angela Medearis. Ages 5–9. Folktale of seven bickering brothers challenged to make a pot of gold out of seven spools of thread. This delightful origin tale of the kente cloth has woodcut illustrations. These two books are very different; read both if available!
4. ***A Collection of Rudyard Kipling's Just So Stories***, Candlewick Press. This week read ***How the Rhinoceros Got His Skin.***

Secondary Books

1. ***Best Beekeeper of Lalibela**, Cristina Kessler. Ages 5–10. An Ethiopian girl perseveres and becomes a beekeeper with the encouragement of her Ethiopian Orthodox priest. Lalibela is famous for its monolithic rock-cut churches and predominant Christian population. While the book does not highlight this fact, you might want to share pictures of the churches and talk about how it is believed that the apostle Matthew preached here.
2. ***You Look Ridiculous Said the Rhinoceros to the Hippopotamus**, Bernard Waber. Ages 4–8. Delightful story of accepting yourself. It is not totally accurate as the monkeys with prehensile tails are in the New World. Have your child name the animals. They might like to draw animals with parts from other animals. A lion with wings?
3. ***Jubela**, Cristina Kessler. Ages 4–8. Based on a true story from Swaziland about an orphaned baby rhino. Lovely illustrations and heartwarming story of life on the savanna.
4. ***In the Small Small Night**, Jane Kurtz. Ages 4–8. Ghana immigrant sister tells traditional bedtime stories to her little brother. Sweet trickster tales.
5. **Rain School,** James Rumford. Ages 4–7. Children in rural Chad rebuild their school each year before they can begin their book learning.
6. **Beatrice's Goat**, Page McBrier. Ages 4–8. True story of how the gift of a goat changes an African girl's life in Uganda.
7. **Planting the Trees of Kenya: The Story of Wangari Maathai**, Clarie Nivola. Ages 5–8. Story of Nobel Peace Prize winner who started a movement to reforest Kenya. Or **Wangari's Trees of Peace**, Jeanette Winter. Ages 4–8.
8. **Anansi and the Moss-Covered Rock**, Eric Kimmel. Ages 4–8. Fable of trickster Anansi being taught a lesson.
9. **Chidi Only Likes Blue,** Ifeoma Onyefulu. Ages 4–8. Lovely photographic essay that covers colors and life in Nigeria.
10. **Chinye: A West African Folk Tale,** Obi Onyefulu. Ages 5–8. Cinderella story set in Nigeria.
11. **The Water Princess**, Susan Verde. Ages 4–8. Based on the real childhood experiences of Georgie Badiel, a young girl dreams of bringing clean drinking water to her African village in Burkina Faso.

SUPPLIES

1. Bottle/jars to carry water; basket to carry wood; garden to weed
2. Materials for kente cloth art: thick white paper, cardstock, paint, brushes, black marker, scissors
3. Rhino craft materials: any color cardstock, white cardstock, template available on *GO GLOBAL* Resource page

DAY 1 — ANIMALS ON THE SAVANNA

EVERYONE

1. Read **Honey, Honey, Lion!**

a) Locate Botswana on your globe or in the ***Beginner's World Atlas***.

b) After a first read, ask your child if this story takes place in the desert, the jungle, or the savanna.

c) Have your child point out the animals to you as you mention them: honeyguide (bird), honey badger, Guinea hens, meerkat, elephant, hippo, warthog, hyena, scarlet bird, zebra, giraffe, lion.

d) Talk about the vegetation such as the baobab tree, papyrus, bristle grass, acacia tree.

e) Talk about the water hole and remember other books that you have read about the water hole. Ask your child why she thinks this place might be so important to everyone.

f) Look at the termite mound! (These are also found in South America and Australia.)

g) Run races like the animals. Mom calls: walk, run, skip, hop, gallop, slide, jump, leap, etc.

h) Add animals to your African animal list.

i) Talk to your child about cooperation or working together. How do honeyguide and badger usually work together? Why did badger not share? What was the result? How do you work together with your sibling? How do you feel if they do not share with you? How do you think they feel when you do not share with them?

DAY 2 — LIFE IN RURAL AFRICA

EVERYONE

1. Read ***One Hen: How One Small Loan Made a Big Difference.*** Younger children can just enjoy the story. Questions and discussion are for older children—perhaps six and up.

    a) You might need to explain what a loan is to your child. What did the families buy with their loans and why did they buy these? [Answer: Fruit, a cart, a sewing machine. To be able to make money.]

    b) What did Kojo want to buy? What was his business idea? [Answer: To buy a hen so they could eat some of the eggs, and then sell the extra ones.]

    c) How was Kojo a good worker and entrepreneur? [Answer: He was a hard worker, studied hard, and saved his money to expand his business.]

    d) Did Kojo pay the loan back? How is a loan different than a gift? [Answer: Yes, Kojo paid the loan back so others could get a loan to start their businesses. A gift does not need to be paid back, though you should send a thank you note.]

2. Read or reread other books that highlight the life of a child in rural Africa. You might want to comment on how important an education is in almost all of these books. Give thanks for the abundance of books and ability to read (or the prospect of learning to read) in your home.

3. Using the books from the last few weeks, talk to your child about how life is different in the third world. What are some hard chores that many children must do in rural Africa, but most do not do in the US? Have your child simulate some of these hardships.

   a) Carry water from the stream.

   b) Carry wood to build a fire.

   c) Plant a garden. Dig up the ground, plant, water, weed. Even harvesting is work.

   d) Walk or bike to the store.

DAY 3 — KENTE CLOTH

EVERYONE

1. Read *The Spider Weaver: A Legend of Kente Cloth* or *Seven Spools of Thread*.
2. Talk about kente cloth and look at examples on the internet. Links available on the *GO GLOBAL* Resource page.

   a) Kente is a handwoven cloth originally from the Ashanti Kingdom in Ghana, west Africa.

   b) It was originally worn by the wealthy and the royalty in west Africa. Now it is worn by many people in Africa for special occasions, ceremonies, and holidays.

   c) Kente means basket and the cloth patterns seem to be woven.

   d) The Smithsonian Institute has a wonderful site full of information and visuals on the kente cloth. Link available on the *GO GLOBAL* Resource page. Of special interest for young children will be the page on "How to Wear Kente." Both men and women wear the cloth, but in different ways. The expensive cloth is usually not cut, but the men wear it as a toga, and the women wear it as a wraparound skirt or shawl.

   e) OPTIONAL: The colors and patterns have special meanings. Here are some of the meanings of the colors. Here are the basic colors mentioned in the Seven Spools of Thread:

      • black—grownups, parents, ancestors
      • white—purity, healing, festive occasions
      • blue—peace, harmony, love
      • green—plants, harvest, growth
      • red—strong feelings, blood
      • yellow—preciousness, beauty, holiness
      • orange/ gold—royalty, wealth

3. Make kente cloth patterns out of painted paper. While the Smithsonian site does have a program to design your fabric, making one out of paint and paper is more age-appropriate, and will yield a better learning experience. Art tutorial is available on the *GO GLOBAL* Resource page.

   Materials
   - Thick white paper
   - Cardstock in one or two of these colors: blue, green, red, yellow, orange
   - Blue, green, red, yellow, and orange paint, brushes, scissors
   - Black marker
   - A straight edge

   Process
   a) View image of kente cloth on the internet as well as in your books. Point out the geometric shapes, bold colors, and bold lines.

   b) Using a thick black magic marker let your child add stripes onto the colored cardstock.

   c) Mom draws black lines about two inches apart on the white paper to give the children guidelines, so their papers end up somewhat geometric. Have children paint stripes and patterns onto the large white paper.

   d) Let the paint dry overnight.

DAY 4   FINISH KENTE CLOTH AND RHINOCEROS

EVERYONE

1. Continue kente cloth activity from yesterday.

   a) Cut the colored paper long way in 1 ½–2-inch strips.

   b) Fold their white sheet in half and cut 1–2-inch slits. Don't cut all the way to the edges or you'll cut apart your base.

   c) Now weave the strips into your white painted pater.

2. Learn about the rhinoceros.

   a) Read **How the Rhinoceros Got His Skin.**

   b) Read other books about the rhinoceros.

3. Rhinoceros Art

   Materials
   - Cardstock/construction paper, one sheet of any color you would like
   - White cardstock/paper
   - Template available on *GO GLOBAL* Resource page
   - Black marker

Process

    a) Fold paper in half and cut out rhino body with the top of his body on the fold. A template is provided on the *GO GLOBAL* Resource page. Cut out ears and horn out of white paper. Cardstock is more durable, but either paper can work.

    b) Draw mouth, eyes, and mouth.

    c) Make small cuts on back to insert ears and horn.

4. Add any additional animals to your African animal list.
5. Read and reread any other books about Africa that you have. There are so many!

WEEK 19
AFRICA
JUNGLE AND SOUTH AFRICA

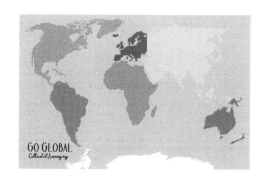

BIG PICTURE

As you finish your time in Africa review the different types of habitats and vegetation: <u>desert</u>, <u>grasslands</u> (savanna) and <u>jungle forests</u>. Africa is the warmest continent in the world. There is no polar region, though there are a few places that do get some snow every year including South Africa, Mount Kilimanjaro, and the Atlas Mountains. There is additional desert in southern Africa, though not nearly as large as the Sahara, and there are stretches of savanna and jungle in southern Africa as well.

While we do not delve deeply into the history of South Africa, two famous men will show up in our books this week: Archbishop Desmond Tutu and Nelson Mandela.

Celebrated African animals featured this week include the dassies, chameleon, lion, and leopard.

MATERIALS

Books

1. ***Why Mosquitoes Buzz in People's Ears***, Verna Aardema. Ages 4–9. Mosquito tells a story that results in a jungle disaster. An African Aesop fable that won the Caldecott Medal.
2. ***The 3 Little Dassies,*** Jan Brett. Ages 3–6. Retelling of the three little pigs with dassies (guinea pig like creatures), an agama lizard, and an eagle. Clothing and landscapes of the Kalahari Desert in southern Africa are depicted.
3. ***Desmond and the Very Mean Word***, Archbishop Desmond Tutu. Ages 6–9. Based on a true story of young Desmond learning a lesson on forgiveness. A respectful view which honors Christianity.
4. ***The Herd Boy,*** Niki Daly. Ages 6–10. A herd boy shows character in his work as he guards his herd from the dangers of the steep cliff and the hungry baboons. End notes about shepherds who have become great leaders are included.
5. ***Moja Means One: Swahili Counting Book***, Muriel Feelings. Ages 4–7. Charming charcoal illustrated Caldecott winner gives a glimpse of Africa—from Mt. Kilimanjaro to African musical instruments, animals, and clothing.
6. ***A Collection of Rudyard Kipling's Just So Stories***, Candlewick Press. This week read ***How the Leopard Got His Spots.***

Secondary Books

1. *****Chameleon, Chameleon***, Joy Cowley. Ages 4–7. Extraordinarily fabulous photographs and delightfully simple text about African chameleon. Extra information is on end pages.
2. *****Chimpanzee Children of Gombe,*** Jane Goodall. Ages 5–7. Photographic essay of taking care of families of chimpanzees.

3. ***A Color of His Own,*** Leo Lionni. Ages 3–6. Learn your colors and about the chameleon and other animals.
4. ***The Chameleon that Saved Noah's Ark,*** Yael Molchadsky. Ages 3–7. Cute story of Noah discovering what the chameleon eats.
5. ***Ivan: The Remarkable True Story of the Shopping Mall Gorilla,*** Katherine Applegate. Ages 4–7. True story of a gorilla captured in the Congo, sent to a shopping mall in Washington State, and finally delivered to his final home at the Atlanta Zoo.
6. ***A Streak of Tigers: Animal Groups in the Jungle,*** Alex Kuskowski. Easy Reader. Simple book for those nonfiction lovers in your family that includes animals from South America.
7. ***Mufaro's Beautiful Daughters: An African Tale,*** John Steptoe. Ages 4–8. A tale of two beautiful daughters in the Zimbabwe region who exhibit entirely different character.
8. ***Nabulela,*** Fiona Moodie. Ages 5–8. South Africa Nguni folk tale of village girls defeating a mythical people-eating beast. Lovely landscapes with exciting story.
9. ***Jafta,*** Hugh Lewin. Ages 5–8. Young boy expresses his feelings by comparing them to the actions of African animals.

Movies

1. **The Lion King,** Disney

SUPPLIES

1. Chameleon art supplies: wooden clothespin, white cardstock, paint, toothpicks, googly eyes
2. *GO GLOBAL* Game

DAY 1   AFRICAN ANIMALS AND CHAMELEON ART

EVERYONE

1. Read **Why Mosquitoes Buzz in People's Ears**. This charming folktale has animals from both the jungle and the savanna. An iguana is one of the chief characters of the book. BUT, iguanas live in Mexico, Central America, and some Caribbean and Polynesian islands, not in Africa. Despite this one inaccuracy, this Caldecott Award winner is a delightful book because of its elegant art, fun story, read-aloud brilliance, and great moral.

    a) What does each animal do? [Answer: They cause harm of some kind and blame another animal for their actions.] Can you think of a Bible story where someone blamed someone else for what they both did? [Answer: Adam and Eve.] Was the mosquito to blame?

    b) Read it a second time and make a list of all the animals and the sounds they make. These are such fun sounds. More onomatopoeia!

> Remember that onomatopoeia is a word that imitates, resembles, or suggests the sound it describes. These animals' sounds are fun to say out loud!

- c) Who do you think is the narrator? Who told this story? Hint: there is one animal who appears on every single page. Can your child find him?
2. Learn about chameleons. Read **Chameleon, Chameleon** or another nonfiction book about chameleons.
    - a) Ask your child to describe what the chameleons look like
        - Beaded skin
        - Colorful
        - Wobbly eye
        - Grippy hands and feet with two toes like thumbs on one side and three toes like fingers on the other
        - A long, sticky tongue
        - Can change colors
        - Curly tail
        - Eats bugs such as caterpillars, grasshoppers, flies
    - b) Read other chameleon books.
3. Chameleon Art. Art tutorial is available on the *GO GLOBAL* Resource page.

Materials

- Clothespins, the colored ones are best
- Cardstock for tail, arms, legs (similar color to body of clothes pin), and red for tongue
- Paint for body, and dots, florescent colors recommended
- Small paint brushes or toothpicks to make dots.
- Eyes: self-stick pearls, or some small roundish objects to make the eyes; You can add a dot of black magic marker for the iris.
- Glue

Process

- a) Cut the tail and the four legs out of cardstock that matches the color of the body. Cut tongue out of red cardstock.
- b) If you get plain colored clothes pins, paint them with paint close to the color of the card stock. Let dry.
- c) Make dots all over the clothespin and on both sides of the tail with various colors. Don't worry if it gets a bit smudged! Let dry. You can read a chameleon book while it dries
- d) Curl tail and tongue. Glue them and the legs to the chameleon.
- e) Glue on the eyes.

DAY 2 LIFE IN RURAL AFRICA, LEOPARDS, AND APES

EVERYONE

1. Read *Mojo Means One*. Enjoy this simple book and realize how much you have learned about Africa! Ask your children: How are the people in this book different than you and your family? How are they the same? [Possible answers: They carry food on their heads; we put it in sacks and carry in our cars. They have open air markets; we have grocery stores. We both make music, tell stories, and love our families.]

2. Read *How the Leopard Got His Spots* in *A Collection of Rudyard Kipling's Just So Stories*.

   OPTIONAL art activity: Using crayons or colored pencils draw the fur patterns of the animals in this story.

ADD FOR SIX-YEAR-OLDS AND UP

3. Learn about the apes, or primates, that reside in Africa. Read and learn some facts:
   a) These animals are tailless and differ from the New World monkeys who have prehensile tails that can grasp things and be used as a fifth appendage.
   b) Gorillas are ground dwelling, plant eating apes that live in the jungles of central Africa.
   c) Chimpanzees are also tailless and live in sub-Saharan Africa, primarily in the Congo jungle.
   d) Have a gorilla race by walking/running on your knuckles!
   e) While gorillas do NOT brachiate, chimps and many New World monkeys do. Go to the monkey bars and see if your kids can brachiate by swinging from hold to hold using alternate arms.

> As Heather Haupt discusses in depth in her book, **The Ultimate Guide to Brain Breaks**, movement is crucial for a child to learn. Movement gets the heart pumping, the oxygen flowing, and helps integrate the two halves of the brain. In addition, when you add these kinds of activities to your learning the information will go into more long-term memory.

DAY 3 SOUTH AFRICAN DESERT

EVERYONE

1. Read *The 3 Little Dassies*.

a) Find the Namib & Kalahari deserts on your globe. The first one is on the western coast, the second is in the central area of southern Africa.

b) Read the story just for the joy of the story.

c) With a second read, ask some, or all, of these questions.

- How do you know this is a desert? [Some possible answers: There are only a few trees, mostly brown ground rather than grass, a windmill, rocks, cacti, and desert animals like the tortoise and lizard.]
- What hints are there that this is Africa? [Answer: The bright kente-like cloth, the distinctive hats (flat turbans), wood carried on back, the baobab tree.]
- What story does this remind you of? [Answer: The Three Little Pigs, The Three Little Javelinas.]

    How are the pigs, javelinas, and dassies in these stories similar? How are they different? [Answers could include: There are three smaller animals that build three different kinds of homes. The homes are of grass, sticks, and stones/bricks. The bad guy destroys two of the homes but cannot destroy the last sturdy home. The bad guys blow the houses down with their breath in the first two instances, and with the power of his wings in the third story. The second two stories take place in different deserts—in the USA and in southern Africa. The javelinas and dassies wear traditional costumes from their areas. The dassies have a special friend—the agama lizard.]

    Who was the bad guy in The Three Little Pigs, the Three Little Javelinas, and in this story? [Answer: The wolf, the coyote, and the eagle.]

- See if your child can tell the story back to you.
- Make sure your children understand the last page. [Answer: This is a pretend tale that explains why the Dassise live in the rocks with the Agama lizards, and why the eagles have black feathers.] In reality, the eagles are predators and do want to eat the dassies who live in the rocks alongside the agama lizards.

2. Read *The Herd Boy*.

    a) What are the dangers the herd boy must face? [Answer: The cliff, the snake, the baboons.]

    b) Describe the good character the boy demonstrates. [Answer: He works hard taking care of his sheep and goats, making sure they do not fall into the canyons. He bravely faces the responsibilities and dangers. He collects dung to sell. He carries the hurt lamb.]

    c) What does he want to be when he grows up? [Answer: The president.]

    d) What characteristics has he learned by being a herd boy that will help him be a good leader? [Answer: Courage, hard work, compassion, responsibility, cooperation.]

    e) Can your child think of another Herd Boy (or shepherd) who grew up to be a great leader? [Answer: David in the Bible. Nelson Mandela, who makes a cameo appearance in the book, was also a herd boy!]

ADD FOR SIX-YEAR-OLDS AND UP

3. Read ***Desmond and the Very Mean Word***. Read, enjoy, and if your child wants to, discuss! Make sure your child knows this is a real story about a real man who is a famous South African social rights activist and an influential Anglican bishop.

DAY 4 — REVIEW

EVERYONE

1. Reread your favorite Africa books
2. Review your African animals by playing charades.
3. Play the *GO GLOBAL* Game. Add the African cards to the North American, South American, and Antarctica cards.
4. Watch ***The Lion King***. You and your children will be amazed by how much you all know and recognize about Africa in this movie.

WEEK 20
CATCH UP OR TAKE A BREAK

WEEK 21
EUROPE
GENERAL AND FRANCE

BIG PICTURE

Europe is the second smallest continent and is situated where it receives warm ocean currents. Because of its geographic location, it has a temperate climate of warm summers and cold winters. There are several important mountain ranges including the Alps, the Ural Mountains, the Apennines, the Pyrenees, and the Caucasus Mountains.

Most of Europe is covered by forests—both deciduous and coniferous. Europe has some unique geographic shapes that your children will like to "see" once you point them out to them: Italy is shaped like a boot and England is shaped like Woodstock (from the Peanuts cartoon) with funny hair. We will also define some major landforms—as the UK is on two islands, and Spain and Italy are on peninsulas. We will also learn what a channel and strait are as we find and discover the English Channel and the Strait of Gibraltar.

Europe has the largest percentage of coastline of all the continents. In a certain sense, Europe is like a peninsula jutting out from Asia divided from Asia by the Ural Mountains and the Caucasus Mountains. Europe is bounded on the north by the Arctic Sea, on the west by the Atlantic Ocean, on the south by the Mediterranean Sea. All this coastline and temperate climate helped Europe develop cultures that explored and settled other parts of the world.

Europe is of great interest because of the cultures and people who have lived there, who developed what is known as Western Civilization, and then spread this culture across the globe. While you will have an overview of the physical geography, you will focus these five weeks on the cultural geography of Europe. In addition to the physical characteristics of climate and coastline, Europe is the home of Western Christianity (both Catholic and Protestant), the Renaissance, the Age of Exploration, and the Industrial Revolution. The main purpose of studying the world in these early years is to give a foundational understanding of place, time, and culture so that your child can understand further study of history and natural science.

Many of America's customs originated in Europe, and most citizens of the United States consider their ethnic origins to come from one or more of the countries in Europe. Young children cannot grasp all the different and interesting European cultures in just five weeks. Rather than giving a lackluster overview of all the cultures, you will be focusing on Great Britain, France, Italy, Spain, Germany, and Holland. These countries are pivotal in the Age of Exploration and the European impact on the rest of the globe. Consider adding a week to study your country of origin, if it is not covered here.

This first week in addition to an overview of Europe, you will explore France. Your children will learn about Paris, some of the iconic locations there including the Eiffel Tower, Arc de Triomphe, the Louvre (pronounced LOOv r), the Seine River (pronounced sain), and Notre Dame Cathedral. Singing Frère Jacques and eating crêpes, croissants, macaroons, or éclairs will be a wonderful culmination.

Note: Russia and Turkey are considered in both Europe and Asia. You will study Russia for a whole week when studying Asia. And Turkey will be mentioned the week you study the Middle East.

Utilize the *GO GLOBAL* Game map as the children physically trek out from Europe to the points on the earth that these countries impacted.

MATERIALS

Books

1. *Beginner's World Atlas 3rd Edition*, National Geographic. 2011.
2. *Madeline*, Ludwig Bemelmans. Ages 3–7. Familiar story of Miss Clavel and her twelve charges including the irrepressible Madeline is a wonderful introduction to France and Paris.
3. *Adèle & Simon*, Barbara McClintock. Ages 4–8. Delightful story of a brother and sister wandering through Paris. The end pages included extra information on places they see.
4. *Dodsworth in Paris*, Tim Egan. Easy Reader. The two animals see Paris: the Eiffel Tower, sidewalk cafes, mimes, Notre Dame, Euros, Tour de France, baguettes, Mona Lisa and impressionistic paintings. Fantastic!
5. *Everybody Bonjours*, Leslie Kimmelman. Ages 3–7. Delightful tour of Paris with simple text and details about locations in the end pages.
6. *The Cat Who Walked Across France*, Kate Banks. Ages 4–8. A cat returns from the north of France to his home on the French coast of the Mediterranean Sea. The post-impressionistic illustrations in rich colors add to the French ambience.
7. *13 Buildings Children Should Know*, Annette Roeder. Ages 8–12. Used previously in Week 16 and geared towards older children, this book is a gem, and could be used with younger children as they explore many buildings studied in this curriculum, including: the Notre Dame Cathedral, and the Eiffel Tower, which we will study this week.

Secondary Books: Find *some* of these excellent books to read aloud and make available to your children for their quiet times. * means especially recommended.

1. **An Armadillo in Paris*, Julie Kraulis. Ages 5–8. Wonderful story and illustrations of Arlo's trip to Paris to find the Iron Lady. You get to visit many of the sites of Paris and experience the tastes of France.
2. *My Tour of Europe: By Teddy Roosevelt, Age 10*, Ellen Jackson. Ages 6–8. Illustrated excerpts from 10-year-old TR's journal as his family traveled through Europe shows a child's perspective to Europe.
3. An easy nonfiction book on France and/or Paris such as *France: True Books*, Elaine Landau, or *Look What Came from France*, Miles Harvey. For parent's reference, for the pictures, and for reading to older children.
4. *The Inside Outside Book of Paris*, Roxie Munro. Ages 7–12. Illustrations of sites in modern Paris.
5. An easy kid's French cookbook such as *France Food and Festivals,* Teresa Fisher. This is even a good overview of France as it has a map and discusses holidays as well.
6. *Madeline Says Merci; The Always-Be-Polite Book*, John Bemelmans Marciano. Ages 4–7. Sweet story about manners.
7. *Madeline's Rescue*, Ludwig Bemelmans. Ages 4–7. Madeline is saved by the heroic pup Geneviève.

8. ***Zarafa: The Giraffe Who Walked to the King***, Judith St. George. Ages 4–8. True story of the gift of a giraffe to the King of France in the 19th century.
9. **A Lion in Paris**, Beatrice Alemagna. Ages 4–8. Wonderful fantasy tale of a lion statue in Paris that includes a map and famous locales.
10. **Let's Go, Hugo**! Angela Dominguez. Ages 3–6. Simple book about a bird in Paris who faces his fear and flies to see the Eiffel Tower.
11. **Katie Meets the Impressionists**, James Mayhew. Ages 4–10. Katie steps into famous paintings and meets Monet, Renoir, and Degas.
12. ***Mirette on the High Wire***, Emily Arnold McCully. Ages 6–10. Late 19th century girl learns to "dance" on the wires above Paris. Lovely watercolor illustrations are in this Caldecott winner.
13. ***Chasing Degas***, Eva Montanari. Ages 5–7. A young dancer races through Paris searching for Degas. This story is inspired by the Degas' paintings.
14. ***Linnea in Monet's Garden***, Christina Björk. Ages 8–12. Story of a girl who travels to France to see Monet's garden. Wonderful mix of history and art. Parents should preview: The story of Monet's family life might be confusing to young children.

Movies

1. **Ratatouille**, G Rated Pixar film of a rat who fulfills his dream and destiny as a great chef in Paris

SUPPLIES

1. Map of Europe (available on the *GO GLOBAL* Resource page) printed on cardstock
2. Globe
3. French language tutorial available on the *GO GLOBAL* Resource page
4. Eiffel Tower materials: Legos/Duplos
5. *GO GLOBAL* Game
6. Purchase at a bakery or make your own French food: crêpes, quiche, croissants, macarons, éclairs, or chocolate mousse
7. OPTIONAL toys: links to toys that correlate with this unit are available on the *GO GLOBAL* Resource page

DAY 1 — EUROPE OVERVIEW AND FRANCE

EVERYONE

1. Find Europe on the *GO GLOBAL* Game mat and then on the globe. This continent is confusing as it seems to be part of Asia. Explain that the Ural Mountains and the Caucasus Mountains are the division between Europe and Asia. Have your child feel the Ural and Caspian mountains on the globe. This tactile activity will solidify this piece of information.

    a) Can your child name any of the bodies of water? [Answer: The Atlantic Ocean, the Mediterranean Sea, and perhaps the North Sea.]

    b) Can your child name the land mass to the south of the Mediterranean Sea? [Answer: Africa.]

c) Can she name the land mass to the east of the Mediterranean Sea? [Possible answers: Asia; the Middle East, or the small country of Israel.]

2. Read ***Beginner's World Atlas***, pages 32–37.

3. Using the map of Europe from the *GO GLOBAL* Resource page,

   a) Color the mountain symbols in Europe. Point out the different mountain chains: the Alps, the Urals, the Caucasus', the Apennines, and the Pyrenees. Label just the Alps and Ural Mountains.

   b) Color and label the oceans, and seas: the Atlantic Ocean, the Mediterranean Sea, the North Sea. Children ages seven and up can also label the Black Sea, the Caspian Sea, and the Baltic Sea.

   c) Have your child trace the coastline of Europe with her finger so she can physically feel how long it is. Ask her if she would use a boat if she was near an ocean or large river. Before there were roads (or planes for that matter), traveling on water was easier than traveling on land. Can you see that the Europeans would be good sea travelers and build good boats?

   d) Color the forest symbols. Most of Europe is covered with deciduous and coniferous forest.

   e) Color the grassland symbols located in southern Spain, Italy, Greece, and southeast Europe.

   f) There is a bit of tundra if you would like to find and color those symbols on your map as well.

4. Read ***Madeline***.

   a) Find France on your map of Europe. Label it and label Paris.

   b) Look at a guide book to Paris such as ***France: True Books*** to see some of the famous structures in Paris. Then see if your child can name some of the famous locations in Paris that are pictured in Madeline. Even a four-year-old should be able to identify the Eiffel Tower. Do NOT make this a test, or a list to memorize. See if you can make it a game. Other locations include: Paris Opera House (lady feeding the horse), Notre Dame in the rain, and the Gardens at Luxembourg on the sunny day. Do not worry about learning all these places—you will see them again, and perhaps a bit more clearly, in the other books on Paris.

DAY 2 — EIFFEL TOWER

EVERYONE

1. Read ***Adèle & Simon***.

   a) On the title page ask your child about this story. When in time does she think this story occurred? Why? What season of the year is it? Why? Have her describe the buildings and streets. Do they look like her home? Point to the bridge. Without saying it is a bridge, ask your child what she thinks it is.

   b) On the first page point out Simon's <u>knapsack</u>, since Americans call these backpacks.

    c) On each page, have your child find the children and the lost item. If your child cannot find the item, do not find it for her. She can look again on a subsequent read. And on the last page there are hints to be able to find the lost objects.

    d) In a subsequent reading, discuss the lovely locations in Paris. Ask your child where she would like to visit.

    e) Mom—read the end pages about the places pictured. Mention some of what you know about the places. Explore these exquisite, detailed pictures to see what you both can find.

2. Read *13 Buildings Children Should Know*, pages 30–31 or look at pictures of the Eiffel Tower. Then build the Eiffel Tower out of Legos or Duplos.

ADD FOR SIX-YEAR-OLDS AND UP

3. Learn some French words. Language tutorial is available on the *GO GLOBAL* Resource page.

English	French	Pronunciation
hello	bonjour	bohn JOOWR
goodbye	au revoir	ahr- VWAH
yes	oui	wee
no	non	nohn
please	s'il vous plaît	see voo PLAY
thank you	merci	mehr SEE
enjoy your meal	bon appétit	bohn a pey tee
Mrs., Ma'am	Madame	muh DAM
Mr., Sir	Monsieur	muh S'YUHR
How are you?	Ça va?	Seh VAH
very good	tres bien	tray bee-IN
have a good trip	bon voyage	bo(n) vwa YAZH

ADD FOR SEVEN-YEAR-OLDS AND UP

4. Read *13 Buildings Children Should Know*, pages 12–13 to learn about the Cathedral of Notre Dame.

DAY 3 — FRÈRE JACQUES AND FRENCH COLONIZATION

EVERYONE

1. Read ***Dodsworth in Paris***.

   Even though this is an easy reader there is a lot of great vocabulary. Try to use these words when you are talking to your children. For instance, you could ask your child to tell her dad about the hat the Frenchmen wear. Ask her if she remembers the name of the special hat.

beret	euros	Notre Dame	cobblestone
debonair	chateau	cathedral	Tour de France
café	maniac	hunchback hippo	Louvre
mime	Seine River	Eiffel Tower	City of Lights

2. Read ***Everybody Bonjours,*** another delightful book that tours Paris.

   a) Read through first for the story.

   b) Mom should read the back pages to learn information about the places. Some children will like you to read the paragraphs, but many will respond better if you talk about the places. You might even begin by asking if they know the name of the place.

   c) During subsequent readings, you can take time to talk about the places they visited. You might want to add some vocabulary: bridge, barge, scooter, beret, dining alfresco, poodle.

   d) The children will probably realize there is a mouse hiding in each scene.

3. Sing Frère Jacques in English or French. Sung on the language tutorial available on the *GO GLOBAL* Resource page.

   Frère Jacques, Frère Jacques,
   Dormez-vous? Dormez-vous?
   Sonnez les matines! Sonnez les matines!
   Ding, dang, dong. Ding, dang, dong.

   Are you sleeping? Are you sleeping?
   Brother John, Brother John,
   Morning bells are ringing! Morning bells are ringing!
   Ding, dang, dong. Ding, dang, dong.

   A more accurate translation might be, "Morning bells need ringing!" as the song is calling Brother John to his duty to ring the morning bells.

   For any preschoolers in the home, sing and do the finger play to the same tune:

   Where is thumbkin? Where is thumbkin? (with both hands behind back)
   Here I am, Here I am. (One hand at a time comes out with thumb shown)

How are you today, sir? Very well I thank you! (Have thumbs wiggle to talk to one another)
Run away, Run away (thumbs return one at a time to behind back)

Repeat with pointer, tall man, ring man, pinkie.

4. Read additional books about France.

ADD FOR SIX-YEAR-OLDS AND UP

5. Explain that European people groups discovered, traveled, and settled in various parts of the globe before long distance travel was common. Using your *GO GLOBAL* Game map have your child finger-walk from France to the various locations across the world where the French explored and settled. She can greet each area with a bright, "Bonjour!"

    a) Canada—especially Quebec/Montreal, though they also spread into the Great Lakes area and down the Mississippi in the USA.

    b) Have your child go back to France and march with your fingers to the United States—they settled and stayed in New Orleans at the mouth of the Mississippi.

    c) While the French also settled other locations such as Africa, South America, and Asia, this kind of detail is too much for this age of children. While France colonized widely, they did not settle and keep their French identity in most of these locations. Quebec and New Orleans are the only two locations that the French settled and kept their culture in a significantly sized community.

    d) If you are from Louisiana add a small French flag with the date they arrived to your time line, 1682. Do not add this if you are not from there; you do not want to clutter your timeline with information they will not remember at all. Young children are most interested in what affects them personally—which includes the place they are from!

6. Practice your French.

DAY 4 — FRENCH FOOD AND MUSIC

EVERYONE

1. Read (or re-read) more of your books about France.

2. France is famous for its food! Look at an easy cookbook, and discuss the common food of France. What would your child like to eat? The pastries, the bread, the frogs' legs, the snails? Cook (or buy) and then eat some French food. Choices are vast, including quiche, croissants, baguettes & cheese, crêpes, macarons, éclairs, or chocolate mousse. Make, or buy, some French delicacies.

3. Watch **Ratatouille**. The movie is GREAT. Caution: We made ratatouille to eat, and even the kids who normally eat everything, did not like it! Stick with macaroons, éclairs, or chocolate mousse.

ADD FOR SIX-YEAR-OLDS AND UP

4. Practice your French.

5. Listen to these well-known French songs. Links to the songs are available on the *GO GLOBAL* Resource page.

    a) La Vie En Rose

    b) La Marseillaise

    c) Au Clair De La Lune

6. France has some beautiful countryside—from the coast in the north to the Alps in the east to the Mediterranean coast in the south. To get a sense of the country of France outside of Paris read ***The Cat Who Walked Across France***.

    a) Read once through for the story.

    b) Read looking at the map of France. The story starts in the south by the Mediterranean Sea. Then the cat is moved to the north of France; find the area on the map. See if you can trace the cat's trip. Does your child recognize the pages about Paris? Can you recognize any of these locations? How about those tall, snow-covered mountains? If your child is interested, you might talk about the Roman aqueducts. We will learn more about them when we study Italy.

    c) The art style of this book is Post Impressionism, reminiscent of Paul Gauguin. Beware of just googling him in front of the children—he painted several nudes. A curated collection of his paintings is available on the *GO GLOBAL* Resource page. IF your child is interested you might ask her how the pictures are unlike photographs, [Answer: Objects are outlined in black, brush strokes of paint are visible, the forms are generalized and lack details; the windows are doors and walls and roofs are not straight, but are at odd angles; etc.]

WEEK 22
EUROPE
SPAIN

BIG PICTURE

Spain is the home of the <u>matadors</u> and <u>bulls</u> and flamenco dancing! You will trek to the countries that Spain impacted, especially those in the New World. You will review the Spanish words studied with Mexico and learn a few new ones that specifically apply to Spain.

Spain (together with Portugal) is a <u>peninsula</u>. The children will look for other peninsulas in Europe and in the United States.

In addition to sniffing the flowers with Ferdinand, you will act out being a toreador, eat flan, listen to the March of the Toreadors, and dance the flamenco!

MATERIALS

Books

1. ***Beginner's World Atlas 3rd Edition***, National Geographic. 2011.
2. ***Madeline and the Bad Hat***, Ludwig Bemelmans. Ages 4–7. The ambassador from Spain and his son move in next door to Madeline.
3. ***Ferdinand the Bull***, Munro Leaf. Ages 3–7. The Spanish bull who prefers flower sniffing to fighting. Use the edition published by Viking with its larger illustrations and more paced story, if you can find it.
4. ***Lola's Fandango***, Anna Witte. Ages 5–8. This delightful book with a CD tells of a little girl learning the flamenco dance.

Secondary Books: Find *some* of these excellent books to read aloud and make available to your children for their quiet times. * means especially recommended.

1. *****Three Golden Oranges***, Alma Flor Ada. Ages 4–8. A fairytale of three brothers who need to cooperate and obey to get their dreams fulfilled. Wonderful illustrations showing the traditional costumes and landscape transport you to Spain.
2. *****The Princess and the Painter***, Jane Johnson. Ages 5–8. Delightful story of the Infanta Margarita, princess of Spain in 1656 who was painted by Diego Velasquez. This book shows life in Spain, costumes, art history, and a realistic look at the life of a princess.
3. An easy nonfiction book on Spain such as ***Been There! Spain***, Annabel Savery, or ***Spain, A True Book***, Martin Hintz.
4. ***Let's Eat!*** Ana Zamorano. Ages 3–7. Sweet story of a three-generational family in Spain eating dinner.
5. ***Squash It!*** Eric Kimmel. Ages 5–9. A louse bites the king of Spain. Ridiculous tale from Spain that will make your kids smile… or squirm.

6. ***El Chino***, Allen Say. Ages 4–9. True story of the son of Chinese immigrants to America who becomes a matador in Spain. If you get this book, make sure to have your child trace from China to Arizona to Spain on your globe.
7. ***Anno in Spain***, Mitsumasa Anno. Wordless book with wonderful pictures to explore; best if mom can give some perspective and guidance.
8. ***Bernal and Florinda: A Spanish Tale***, Eric Kimmel. Ages 4–8. Fun and slightly ridiculous tale of Bernal making his fortune and winning the hand of fair Florinda.

SUPPLIES

1. Map of Europe from last week
2. Red silk, scarf, or fabric for bullfighting
3. Spanish language tutorial available on the *GO GLOBAL* Resource page
4. Flamenco dance tutorial available on the *GO GLOBAL* Resource page
5. Four quarters (per child) and packing tape to make tap shoes
6. OPTIONAL: costumes for flamenco dancing: full skirt, sash, fan
7. OPTIONAL: castanets or rhythm instruments (can be wooden spoons)
8. Materials to make castanets: large buttons, elastic
9. *GO GLOBAL* Game
10. Ingredients for food dish from Spain, or purchase already made dishes
11. Oranges and olives
12. Art examples available on the *GO GLOBAL* Resource page

DAY 1 — SPAIN AND FERDINAND THE BULL

EVERYONE

1. Find Spain on the map in the ***Beginner's World Atlas***, and then on your map of Europe.

    a) Ask your child to describe the shape of Spain (with Portugal). If needed point out the water to the north and west (the Atlantic Ocean), and the water to the south and east (the Mediterranean Sea). Mention that this landform is called a peninsula, a piece of land jutting out from a larger land body that is surrounded on three sides by water. The place where Spain almost touches Africa is the Strait of Gibraltar.

    b) Ask your child if he sees any other peninsulas in Europe. He might mention Italy, Greece, Turkey, Denmark or Norway/Sweden. Do not make him find all of them, but praise him for what he does find. You can mention the names of the countries, but do not expect mastery. He might also like to look for a large peninsula in the US. [Answer: Florida.]

    c) Add Madrid to your map.

2. Read ***Ferdinand the Bull***. Read it again!

    a) Discuss.

       - What did most of the young bulls like to do? [Answer: Run and butt heads.]

- What did Ferdinand like to do? [Answers: Sit and smell the flowers under the cork tree.]
- What did his mom do? [Answer: She asked him if he was lonely. Once she saw he was happy, she let him be.]
- Do you like to be by yourself more or with people more? What do you do when you want to be by yourself?
- Were the men who came to look at the bulls funny or scary or…? Look at the picture of the five men as you let your child answer. Describe each of the funny hats.
- Why wouldn't Ferdinand fight? How do you think he felt when they took him home?

b) Vocabulary to use and discuss: Toro, Matador, Cork Tree, snorting and butting, fierce.

c) Sequencing: See if your child can tell you the story back to you without looking at the pictures. If he cannot, let him do it with the pictures. Then try again without the pictures.

d) Play charades by acting out these scenes from Ferdinand and let your child guess who you are and what is happening. Then let him act it out.
- Sitting on the bee (as Ferdinand)
- Sitting on the bee (as the bee)
- Matador when Ferdinand wouldn't fight
- The other bulls—running, butting, and snorting
- Ferdinand sitting and smelling the flowers

e) Dramatize matador and toro. Using a red cape let your child take turns being the toro or the matador.

f) Listen to *March of the Toreadors*, from the opera *Carmen*, by Bizet. A link to the music is available on the *GO GLOBAL* Resource page.

DAY 2 — FLAMENCO DANCING AND SPANISH LANGUAGE

EVERYONE

1. Read **Lola's Fandango**.

    a) Do the clapping rhythms. 1-2-**3**, 1-2-**3**, 1-**2**, 1-**2**, 1-**2**. This is not only fun, but helpful as we learn syllabication and spelling. If the number rhythms are hard, try word rhythms: el-e-PHANT, el-e-PHANT, gir-AFFE, gir-AFFE, gir-AFFE.

    b) Dance Flamenco. A dance tutorial is available on the *GO GLOBAL* Resource page.

    c) Turn any shoes into tap shoes by simply securing four quarters to the bottom of their shoes with packing tape.

    d) Make castanets for the kids to play to keep the beat. Art tutorial is available on the *GO GLOBAL* Resource page.

EASY Castanets

Materials

- Four large buttons
- Elastic

Process

Thread a 2-inch length of elastic through two holes and knot. Slip in your fingers and click together.

    e) OPTIONAL: Girls can wear full skirts. (Perhaps the ones you used while studying Mexico.)

    f) OPTIONAL: Add a fan for your little girl to use during the dance. A link to inexpensive fans is available on the *GO GLOBAL* Resource page.

2. Practice your Spanish. Language tutorial available on the *GO GLOBAL* Resource page.

New for Spain

English	*Spanish word*	*Pronunciation*
bull	toro	TOH-roh
one	uno	oo-NOH
two	dos	dohs
three	tres	trehs

Review

English	*Spanish word*	*Pronunciation*
hello	hola!	OH-lah
good-bye	adios	ah-dee-OHS
party	fiesta	fee-EHS-tah
hat	sombrero	sohm-BREHR-oh
container of toys/candy for game	piñata	pee-NYAH-tah
corn tortilla with meat filling	taco	TAH-koh
hurray	olé!	o-LAY

Harder

please	por favor	pohr fah-VOR
thank you	gracias	GRAH-see-yahs
yes	si	see
no	no	no

Advanced

How are you?	Cómo está?	KOH-moh ehs-TAH
I am fine.	Estoy bien.	ehs-TOY bee-EHN
What is your name?	Cómo se llama?	KOH-moh seh YAH-mah
My name is John.	Me llamo Juan.	meh YAH-mo Wahn

DAY 3 — MADELINE IN SPAIN AND SPANISH COLONIZATION

EVERYONE

1. Read **Madeline and the Bad Hat**. While this story does not take place in Spain, it is an enjoyable tale. Explain what an ambassador is, look for hints of Spain [Answer: An ambassador is a person sent by a country to represent the country to a foreign country. Hints of Spain include the flag of Spain, the matador costume, including a red cape, the pictures of bulls.]

2. Practice your dancing again.

3. Practice your Spanish.

ADD FOR SIX-YEAR-OLDS AND UP

4. Review the fact that several European people groups discovered, traveled, and settled in various parts of the globe before long distance travel was common. Using your *GO GLOBAL* Game mat have your child finger-walk from Spain to the various locations across the world where the Spanish explored and settled. Your child can great each area with a friendly, "Hola!"

    a) Have your child march from Spain to the Caribbean islands. These islands are not visible on the map but have your child finger-walk to the Caribbean which is directly north of South America. Columbus sailed there under the Spanish flag in 1492. Add a small Spanish flag with a figure labeled Christopher Columbus and the date 1492 to your timeline.

    b) Have your child finger-march from Spain to Mexico and up into Arizona and California; Spaniards explored much of western North America.

    c) Have your child finger-march from Spain to Central America.

    d) Have your child finger-march from Spain to South America EXCEPT the area of Brazil—the Amazon River basin, which is where the Portuguese settled.

e) If you are from the southwest or Florida, Add a small Spanish flag with the date they arrived to your time line, sometime in the 1500s. You might use the exact date they arrived in your state: sometime between 1528 and 1542. Do not add this if you are not from there; you do not want to clutter your timeline with information your children will not remember at all. Young children are most interested in what affects them personally—which includes the place they are from!

The Spanish Empire left a huge cultural and architectural legacy in the Western Hemisphere. The long colonial period resulted in the Spanish language and Roman Catholic religion being dominant in Latin America. Most Hispanics in the Americas have mixed European and Native American ancestry, with a portion also having some African ancestry. Have your child again finger-walk from Spain to Mexico and all the way down South America.

DAY 4   FOOD, OLIVES, AND GIBRALTAR

EVERYONE

1. Read additional books based in Spain.
2. Eat some Spanish food. While food in Spain is not as famous as France and Italy, it is delicious. Experiment with empanadas, flan, churros, or paella.
3. Eat some oranges and olives and discuss some fine art. Spain is famous for producing much of the citrus fruit for Europe. Olive production is all along the Mediterranean border in Europe, Asia, and Africa. Much of Spain has olive groves. Spanish families love to serve and eat olives. Eat some different kinds from black, to green, to Kalamata olives.
4. Practice your dancing.
5. Practice your Spanish.

ADD FOR SIX-YEAR-OLDS AND UP

6. Using the prints available on the *GO GLOBAL* Resource page compare the Van Gogh paintings of olive trees to the photograph of olive trees in Spain.

    a) Ask your child to describe the differences between the paintings of Van Gogh and the photograph. [Possible answers: The brush strokes are visible in the grass and sky. It is obviously painted and not real. The tree trunks and branches are outlined in black.]

    b) Why does he think that Van Gogh painted the way he did? [Possible answer: To make it look like everything is moving, to emphasize the shape of the trees, to give an impression of the trees without other distracting things in the picture.]

    c) Ask your child if he prefers the painting or the photograph, and why.

ADD FOR SEVEN-YEAR-OLDS AND UP

7. Point out that there are mountains across the neck of the peninsula, separating Spain from the rest of Europe. Mention the name again: Pyrenees Mountains. (Pronunciation: PEER-uh-neez)

8. Show on a map where Spain is very close to Africa. This narrow passage of water between the Mediterranean Sea and the Atlantic Ocean is called the Strait of Gibraltar, named after the Rock of Gibraltar. Find a picture of the rock. The saying "solid as the Rock of Gibraltar" is used to describe something or someone that is very safe, steady, or stable.

WEEK 23
EUROPE
BRITISH ISLES

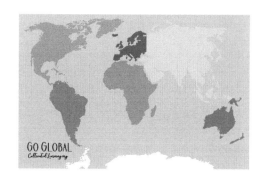

BIG PICTURE

The British Isles are the ancestral home of many people living in the United States. These islands had a disproportionate impact on the world culturally and academically. The three countries of England, Wales, and Scotland make up Great Britain. Great Britain and Northern Ireland make up the United Kingdom. The United Kingdom, the Republic of Ireland, and about 6000 small isles make up the British Isles. We will concentrate on England, Scotland, and Ireland.

The British Isles are wet and rainy and therefore very green. There are rolling hills, moors, forests, and many lakes.

The Union Jack, the U.K. flag, is a combination of three of the countries' flags. You will learn some of the symbols of each country and learn about the vast British Empire.

You will learn about the real St. Patrick and the mythical leprechauns, the Irish luck, and the Irish fortitude. You will learn about Edinburgh, clans, kilts, tartans, bagpipes, and lochs in Scotland. You will learn about London, the Thames River (Pronunciation: Timz), Parliament, Big Ben, Buckingham Palace, Tower of London, and Tower Bridge. You will listen to Scottish and Irish folk music and learn both types of folk dancing.

MATERIALS

Books

1. ***Madeline in London***, Ludwig Bemelmans. Ages 3–7. Madeline and friends visit Pepito in London and get to see the Queen's Life Guards, Trafalgar Square (pronunciation: tra FAL gar), double-decker buses, and the London Bridge.
2. ***Dodsworth in London***, Tim Egan. Easy Reader that covers it all: Double-decker buses, Buckingham Palace, Big Ben, Trafalgar Square, a pub, and the Queen.
3. ***Patrick: Patron Saint of Ireland***, Tomie dePaola. Ages 5–9. Story of St. Patrick from his noble birth in Britain, to his capture and slavery in Ireland, to his escape, and to his call to go back to Ireland to share the love of Christ.
4. ***Fiona's Lace***, Patricia Polacco. Ages 4–8. Based on the true story of young Fiona in Ireland who helps her family with her skilled lacemaking. Leprechauns, blarney, textile industry, lace making, indentured servitude, and the Chicago Fire are all in this delightful tale of a family that loves each other and trusts the Lord.
5. ***Always Room for One More***, Sorche Nic Leodhas. Ages 3–8. Scottish folk tale (and song) about the generous hero who lives in his "wee house in the heather" with his wife and "ten bairns" who takes hospitality to a new level. Intermixed Scottish words and a glossary in the back add to the wonderful feel of the Scottish Highlands. Caldecott Winner.

Secondary Books: Find *some* of these excellent books to read aloud and make available to your children for their quiet times. * means especially recommended.

United Kingdom—England

1. ***Anno's England***, Mitsumasa Anno. All ages. Wordless trip through England starting at the White Cliffs of Dover, past Stonehenge, London Bridge, Big Ben, St. Paul's, Trafalgar Square, the Tower of London, Buckingham Palace, and more.
2. A nonfiction book on England/London such as ***England: True Books***, Michael Burgan, or ***A Walk in London***, Salvatore Rubbino, or ***England (First Reports)***, Susan Gray, or ***Look What Came From England***, Kevin Davis.
3. ***Winnie-the-Pooh***, A.A. Milne. All ages. Read the original, not the retellings. This is a fabulous chapter read-aloud for young children and mixed ages. Set in an English garden, this book should be read aloud by every family!
4. ***The Tale of Peter Rabbit***, Beatrix Potter. Ages 3–7. Make sure to get the original text and art work. Delightful story of Peter set in the English garden.

Ireland

5. *****Tim O'Toole and the Wee Folk***, Gerald McDermott. Ages 5–9. Rollicking fun tale of Tim meeting some wee folk (leprechauns) who give him gifts. Cheerful illustrations capture the rich verdant Irish landscape, cottages, and mythology. Reading aloud easily brings forth the rhythm of an Irish brogue!
6. ***S is for Shamrock***, Eve Bunting. Ages 6–10. The alphabet book has large bright pictures and simple text to read in addition to more detailed text for older children.
7. A nonfiction book such as ***Ireland*** by Julie Murray.
8. ***Fiona's Luck***, Teresa Bateman. Ages 4–8. Fanciful story of how a girl got the Irish luck back from the Leprechaun king.
9. ***The Ring of Truth: An Original Irish Tale***, Teresa Bateman. Ages 6–11. Patrick O'Kelley was full of the blarney until he meets the king of the Leprechauns.
10. ***The Irish Cinderlad***, Shirley Climo. Ages 4–8. Retelling of an Irish fable where Becan rescues a princess in distress after meeting a magical bull.
11. ***Fin M'Coul, the Giant of Knockmany Hill***, Tomie de Paola. Ages 4–7. Fin's wife saves him from the most feared giant in Ireland.
12. ***Finn McCool and the Great Fish***, Eve Bunting. Ages 5–8. Kind giant is looking for and finds wisdom.

Scotland

13. *****Wee Gillis***, Munro Leaf. Ages 4–8. Orphaned Wee Gillis grows up between the lowlands and highlands and finds his calling as a bagpiper. Caldecott Honor Book.
14. *****Little Toot and the Loch Ness Monster***, Hardie Gramatky. Ages 3–6. Little Toot travels to Scotland and befriends Nessie. Very cute, and you can trace his trip from NYC to Loch Ness, Scotland on your globe.

15. ***B is for Bagpipes***, Eve Begley Kiehm. Ages 6–9. A–Z tour of Scotland. Extensive information, with large font for younger children, Additional information in small font for older kids.

SUPPLIES

1. Map of Europe used the last two weeks
2. British Isles flag printable available on the *GO GLOBAL* Resource page
3. Tea, cucumber sandwiches, scones, and jam
4. Big Ben craft materials: thin milk carton, paint and brushes, printable from *GO GLOBAL* Resource page
5. Scottish dance tutorial available on the *GO GLOBAL* Resource page
6. Irish dance tutorial available on the *GO GLOBAL* Resource page
7. *GO GLOBAL* Game

DAY 1 — UNITED KINGDOM

EVERYONE

1. Read **Madeline in London**. Find London on the map in the **Beginner's World Atlas**, and then mark on your map of Europe. Have your child trace with her finger the trip from Paris to London. Why did Madeline have to fly rather than drive? [Answer: They had to go over water.] Explain that this bit of water between the United Kingdom and the rest of Europe is called the English Channel. A channel is a body of water between two pieces of land that is wider than a strait. Ask your child if she remembers the Strait of Gibraltar. Find and compare to the English Channel. At this age, these terms are synonymous; and you do not need to differentiate the two terms.

2. The United Kingdom includes four countries: England, Scotland, Wales, and Northern Ireland. Find these on the map in the **Beginner's World Atlas**. Explain that each area has unique cultural and historical backgrounds, though they are one country. Each area has a unique culture and accent.

    Print the flags of the British Isles which are available on the *GO GLOBAL* Resource page. Learn about Scotland's cross of St. Andrew, England's cross of St. George, and Ireland's cross of St. Patrick. Color them, and then color the Union Jack (flag of UK). Discuss how it is a mixture of the three flags. Share that this flag was designed at the time of the political union of England, Scotland, and Ireland.

    Scotland's cross of St. Andrew is in honor of Andrew, the first-called of the disciples of Christ. Andrew was a fisherman from Galilee and the brother of Peter. It is reported that he was crucified on an X shaped cross by the Romans in AD 69. In AD 832 the Scots first flew a blue flag with a white x-cross in honor of St. Andrew.

    England's cross of St. George is a red cross on a white flag and can be traced back to the Middle Ages. Legend says it was adopted by Richard the Lionhearted. St George was a popular "warrior saint" immortalized in the myth where he slays the dragon. If interested, read **Saint George and the Dragon** by Margaret Hodges.

St. Patrick's symbol is a red X shaped cross on a white flag. Its origin dates from the 18th century. You will learn about St. Patrick tomorrow.

OPTIONAL to explore more: Wales had been conquered by England several centuries earlier and was considered incorporated territory of England. Color the red dragon in the Welsh flag.

OPTIONAL to explore more: The Republic of Ireland is a separate country. Older children might be interested in coloring its flag as well. The stripes represent the desire for the Protestants (represented by the orange strip) and the Roman Catholics (represented by the green stripe) to live together in peace (represented by the white stripe).

ADD FOR SIX-YEAR-OLDS AND UP

3. "The Sun Never Sets on the British Empire!" is a famous saying that refers to when the British Empire (comprised of the dominions, colonies, protectorates, and other territories) was the largest empire in history. Using your *GO GLOBAL* Game mat have your child finger-walk from the United Kingdom to the various locations across the world where the British explored and settled. Your child can greet each area with a bold, "The Sun Never Sets on the British Empire!"

    a) Have your child finger-march from the UK to the United States—to New England and to Virginia.

    b) Have your child finger-march from the UK to Canada—all of it, though she should remember that there is a significant French minority in Quebec.

    c) Have your child finger-march from the UK to Africa—especially to Egypt, down the Great Rift to South Africa.

    d) Have your child finger-march from the UK to Australia. You will need to direct her since we have not yet studied this continent.

    e) Have your child finger-march from the UK to India. You will need to direct her since we have not yet studied this country.

    The British Empire not only colonized widely, they settled and developed a British identity in many of these locations. The Commonwealth of Nations is an organization of 53 independent nations that were mostly territories of the former British Empire. Sixteen Commonwealth realms voluntarily continue to share Queen Elizabeth II of England as their monarch. Have your children again finger-walk to some of these nations:

    a) Canada

    b) Australia

4. Add a Pilgrim boy and/or girl with the date 1620 to your time line. Remind your child of the story of Thanksgiving and how the Pilgrims came to America. Thanksgiving is memorable enough that most American children will have some sense of the historicity of the Pilgrims and Plymouth.

If you are from Virginia and have already learned about Jamestown, you might want to add a small British Flag with the name Jamestown, and the date 1607 to your timeline. Young children are most interested in what affects them personally—which includes the place they are from!

DAY 2 — IRELAND

EVERYONE

1. Read **St. Patrick**.

    a) Patrick was a 5th century missionary to Ireland. Because he lived so long ago, much of his story is not entirely verified. DePaola does a good job of reconstructing the truth about Patrick's life. The last few pages are legends about St. Patrick which are probably not true.

    > A legend is an unverifiable story handed down by tradition which is based on a real person, and many times accepted as true. Myth is a story with supernatural beings and events concerning the early history of a people.

    b) The most famous symbol of Patrick and Ireland is the shamrock. The story of St. Patrick using the three-leafed plant to explain the Trinity is a recent (18th century) story, though it may have older roots. Make and use a shamrock to explain the Trinity to your child. Ask your child: Is it one leaf or three leaves? The answer is that it is both one leaf and three. And so it is with God, There is only one God, but three persons: the Father, the Son, and the Holy Spirit. While the mystery of the Trinity is complex, this simple lesson can be beneficial.

    c) Add Patrick holding a shamrock to your timeline.

2. Read **Fiona's Lace** and other books about Ireland to learn about leprechauns, the luck of the Irish, the Blarney Stone, the potato famine, and Irish immigration to America.

3. Listen to Irish music. A link to lovely Irish music is available on the *GO GLOBAL* Resource page. Notice the Irish harp.

    Watch, and dance, an Irish jig. Links to the music, and a tutorial are available on the *GO GLOBAL* Resource page.

DAY 3 — SCOTLAND

EVERYONE

1. Read **Always Room for One More** and other books about Scotland to learn about tartans, clans, bagpipes, the Highlands, and Loch Ness. Loch means lake.

2. Listen to *Scotland the Brave* on pipes and drums. Link available on the *GO GLOBAL* Resource page.

3. Watch the Scottish dance tutorial available on the *GO GLOBAL* Resource page. You can learn the steps, or just play the music and let your child improvise!

4. Ask your child to describe the difference between the Irish and the Scottish dancing.

DAY 4 — ENGLAND

EVERYONE

1. Read **Madeline in London** again. This time look for famous landmarks and icons of London: the UK flag, double decker buses, the Queen's Life Guards at Buckingham Palace, Trafalgar Square, Westminster, the Tower of London, Tower Bridge, Big Ben, the British Museum. As with Paris, this is not a test—just an exploration.

2. Read **Dodsworth in London** and other books about London and England. Make sure to point out or discuss: the rainy weather, fog, pubs, famous locales such as the ones listed above, and the Thames River, St. Paul's Cathedral, Parliament, the Globe Theater.

3. Search your books for pictures of and information on Big Ben. It is a cultural icon and is one of the most prominent symbols of the UK, often used in films and books.

    Your child may not have heard a chiming clock. Watch a video to see and hear Big Ben. Link is available on the *GO GLOBAL* Resource page. Explain that a town clock was how people knew the time before watches (and cell phones) were almost universal.

    Make a simple paper plate clock to teach your children how to tell time. Many children are not learning to tell time with a traditional clock face because of the overwhelming use of digital clocks. Tutorial available on *GO GLOBAL* Resource page.

4. Make a model of Big Ben. Art tutorial is available on the *GO GLOBAL* Resource page.

    ### Materials
    - Tall thin milk carton
    - Paint and brushes
    - Four copies of the Big Ben clock face, available on the *GO GLOBAL* Resource page

    ### Process
    a) Paint top of carton brown, Paint vertical stripes on the sides of the carton.

    b) Cut out and paste clock face on all four sides near the top.

5. Watch a movie located in England such as **Mary Poppins** or **The Great Mouse Detective.** Both movies have some of the iconic places in London, St. Paul's Cathedral and Big Ben, to name two. As you watch these movies your child will learn that education and learning make even movies more fun.

6. Celebrate tea time by drinking tea, and eating cucumber sandwiches or scones.

7. Dance all your dances and reread your favorite books.

WEEK 24
EUROPE
ITALY

BIG PICTURE

Italy is a crucial and interesting country to study. Its distinctive shape of a boot makes it fun and easy for children to locate. Italy is pivotal in understanding Western Civilization as it is the home of the Roman Republic, the Roman Empire, western Christianity, and the birthplace of the Renaissance.

This is just an introduction to a country your children will return to study many more times. You will start with some basic geography of the boot shape, the spine of mountains going down the peninsula, and the extensive coastline.

You will learn about Rome, the Eternal City, and some of its highlights with delightful children's picture books. Older children will learn about Vatican City, and some Italian words.

While Ancient Rome is too large a subject for this world overview, you will learn a bit about the grand building projects of the Romans—from the roads to the aqueducts to the Coliseum. You will also outline the far reaches of the Roman empire by finger-marching, as well as recreating the trip by Marco Polo from Italy to China and back.

Visiting the canals of Venice and the Leaning Tower of Pisa will round out the exploration of Italy. In addition, you will listen and dance to the Tarantella and sample some Italian cuisine.

MATERIALS

Books

1. ***Madeline and the Cats of Rome***, Ludwig Bemelmans. Ages 3–7. Madeline and friends cross the Alps to Italy and Rome. They visit the Sistine Chapel, the ancient ruins, and many of the fountains of Rome.
2. ***Dodsworth in Rome***, Tim Egan. Easy Reader. Our friends now visit Rome where they ride scooters, and visit Vatican City, the Sistine Chapel, the Coliseum, and the Trevi Fountain. A lot of good Italian food rounds out their visit!
3. ***13 Buildings Children Should Know***, Annette Roeder. Ages 8–12. While geared towards older children, this book is a gem, and could be used with younger children as they explore many buildings studied, including: The Leaning Tower of Pisa and St. Peter's Basilica.
4. ***Marco Polo: A Journey through China***, Fiona MacDonald. Ages 6–12. While this book might contain too much information to read it in its entirety to your child, read at least the large print paragraph on each page and then look and discuss the pictures. OR ***Animals Marco Polo Saw: An Adventure on the Silk Road***, Sandra Markle. Ages 5–10. Polo's trip to China including the exotic animals he encountered, with lovely illustrations and just the right amount of text.

Secondary Books: Find *some* of these excellent books to read aloud and make available to your children for their quiet times. * means especially recommended.

1. *****Tony's Bread**, Tomie dePaola. Ages 4–8. Tony dreams of being the most famous baker in northern Italy. He invents panettone (a rich Christmas bread) in this delightful story with Italian words and phrases cleverly woven into the text.
2. *****Anno's Italy**, Mitsumasa Anno. All ages. Wordless trip through Italy with wonderful detailed pictures of Rome and Venice. Laced through the book runs the theme of the life of Christ interwoven with the daily activities of the people in every walk of life.
3. **The Famous Nini**, Mary Nethery. Ages 4–7. Fanciful story of a historic cat in Venice who meets Verdi, the king and queen of Italy, the Pope, and a Russian Czar. After reading the book find on a map where her favorite visitors came from.
4. **Gabriella's Song**, Candace Fleming. Ages 4–8. A sweet song sweeps through the canals and streets of Venice.
5. **Papa Piccolo**, Carol Talley. Ages 4–9. A tomcat in Venice takes care of two lost kittens. Luscious pictures of Venice with canals, bridges, gondolas, and more.
6. **Orani, My Father's Village**, Claire Nivola. Ages 4–8. A beautiful and poignant memoir of the author's childhood visits to her father's ancestral village in Italy.
7. **Papa Gatto: An Italian Fairy Tale**, Ruth Sanderson. Ages 5–8. A charming retelling with an excellent modern twist on the happily-ever-after ending.
8. **Angelo**, David Macaulay. Ages 4–12. The touching story of friendship between a pigeon and an old man who is restoring Roman buildings.
9. A nonfiction book on Italy such as **Italy, A True Book**, Christine and David Petersen, or **Italy ABC's**, Sharon K. Cooper.
10. A nonfiction book such as **Ancient Rome**, Deborah Murrell.
11. A book such as **Stone Giant: Michelangelo's David and How He Came to Be**, Jane Sutcliffe. Ages 6–9, or **Michelangelo**, Darice Bailer. Ages 7–10, or **Michelangelo**, Mike Venezia. Ages 7–10.
12. A kid's Italian cookbook such as **I Can Cook! Italian Food**, Wendy Blaxland.

SUPPLIES

1. Map of Europe used the last three weeks
2. Paper, paint, and brushes
3. Italian language tutorial available on the *GO GLOBAL* Resource page
4. Tarantella dance tutorial available on the *GO GLOBAL* Resource page
5. Building materials: blocks, Legos/Duplos, cardstock and crayons
6. Materials for Leaning Tower of Pisa: cardboard tube, white paint, black paint or magic marker, white paper napkin
7. Ingredients for Italian dinner: spaghetti and meatballs, bread sticks, gelato, red checkered table cloth
8. OPTIONAL: tambourine for dancing Tarantella

DAY 1   OVERVIEW, ROME, THE VATICAN AND SISTINE CHAPEL

EVERYONE

1. Review the map of Europe and find the peninsula of Italy. Ask your child what he thinks it looks like—He will probably answer: a boot! Review the mountains to the north—known as the Alps. Add a string of mountains from north to south down the center of Italy. Review how much coastline Italy has, and how difficult it is to travel over mountains. Is it any surprise the Italians are sailors and explorers?

   Add Rome to your map.

2. Read ***Madeline and the Cats of Rome.***

3. Read ***Dodsworth in Rome.***

   a) Talk about the difference between roam and Rome.

   b) Dodsworth and the duck visit many places in Rome. Have your child tell you back all the places he can remember. Where would he like to visit?

ADD FOR SIX-YEAR-OLDS AND UP

4. Vatican City is the smallest country in the world. It is inside the city of Rome and less than ½ square mile. But it does have its own money, post office, military (the Swiss Guard), and leader (the Pope). Read **13 Buildings Children Should Know**, pages 20–23. Make sure your child sees and recognizes pictures of the Vatican, St. Peter's Square, and the Sistine Chapel.

ADD FOR SEVEN-YEAR-OLDS AND UP

5. Read about Michelangelo and look at some of his artwork. If there are not appropriate images in your books there are some available on the *GO GLOBAL* Resource page. Pick one or more of these iconic pieces to discuss.

   a) Sistine Chapel ceiling

   i. Look at the picture of the whole ceiling. Make sure your child understands that this is several paintings.

   ii. Look at this detail of the creation of Adam. Have your child point out which figure is Adam and which is God. How does he know? [Possible answers: Adam doesn't have clothes on; Adam is below God; Adam is young, while God is older.]

   iii. OPTIONAL: Tape paper to underneath a table and

WEEK 24 | 157

let your child paint their own Sistine Chapel ceiling. He will never forget Michelangelo if he does this activity!

   b) Pieta (also in **13 Buildings**, pg. 23)

      i. Look at the folds in the woman's robe. This is carved stone but looks like fabric!

      ii. Ask your child if he knows who these two people are. [Answer: Jesus and his mother Mary.] Ask your child if he knows when this event took place. If he needs a hint have him look closely at Jesus' hand. [Answer: After the crucifixion.]

      iii. Look at Mary's face. How do you think she feels? Why does she feel this way?

      iv. Talk to your child about the resurrection of Christ. The resurrection should always be included when we talk about the death of Christ.

   c) David (Read the story of David if your child is unfamiliar with the event.)

      i. This masterpiece of the Renaissance is iconic. The picture available on the resource page is only the waist up. The statue is 17 feet tall (5.17 m.) and is in Florence, Italy.

      ii. Tell your child this is a statue of David. Ask him how old David seems, and why your child thinks so. [Answer: He seems young, since he has neither facial hair nor wrinkles on his face.]

      iii. Ask your child to look at the face. What does he think David is thinking or feeling? If your child needs prompts ask him, "Is David happy, satisfied, scared, angry, determined?" [Answer: He seems serious and determined.]

      iv. Then tell your child that this carving is David right before he fought Goliath. Look for the sling in his hand, slung over his shoulder.

DAY 2 — ANCIENT ROME

EVERYONE

1. Learn some Italian words and phrases. Language tutorial available on the *GO GLOBAL* Resource page.

English	Italian	Pronunciation
hello or goodbye	ciao	CHow
thank you	grazie	GRAHTS yah
well done!	bravissimo	Brah VEE see mo
goodbye	arrivederci	ah ree veh DEHR chee
beautiful	bellissima	Bel EES ee mah
good morning	buon giorno	BWAHN ger no
gosh!	mamma mia!	MAH mah Mee ah
sorry	scusa	SKUE sah
veni, vidi, vici	I came, I saw, I conquered.	VEH nee, VEE dee, VEE cee

2. Ancient Rome is a huge subject and much of it is best covered in the older years. Today, we will emphasize the great strides the ancient Romans made as builders. Using books available, talk to your child about what the ancient Romans built.

    a) They built ROADS across their empire. Some of these roads are still in existence. Ask your child what they think the Romans used to make these roads. [Answer: 1. Some were just leveled earth. 2. Some were earth with a graveled surface. 3. Some were paved with blocks of stone, bricks, or lava.]

    b) They built AQUEDUCTS to bring water to their cities and towns. Aqueducts brought water through gravity alone by being built with a slight downward gradient.

    c) They built AMPHITHEATERS which were used for large public meetings, contests, displays, and athletic competitions. The most famous amphitheater is the Colosseum in Rome.

Using various materials outside, build roads. Have your children build a road of dirt, then one of sand and then one of pebbles to represent a cobble street. Which road works the best for them?

In the afternoon (while you are cooking dinner) they can try to build an amphitheater out of blocks or Legos.

ADD FOR SIX-YEAR-OLDS AND UP

3. Italy is the birthplace of national expansion. First the Roman Empire explored much of Europe, north Africa, and the Middle East. Then Marco Polo explored the Far East. Use the **Beginner's World Atlas** and have your child finger-walk the Italian expansion and exploration.

    a) The ancient Roman Empire extended from the southern portion of England, westward across most of Europe from the Rhine and Danube Rivers in the north to the Black Sea in the east, to the shoreline of the Mediterranean in the south. It also spread across the northern edge of Africa, including much of the Nile River, and into the Middle East. It included Turkey, Israel, and the Tigris/Euphrates River Valley all the way to the Persian Gulf. Have your child follow you as you trace the perimeter, while you both are saying: Veni, Vidi, Vici, which means I came, I saw, I conquered. Maps illustrating the extent of the Roman Empire and the Silk Road are available on the *GO GLOBAL* Resource page.

    b) Read a book such as **Marco Polo: A Journey through China**. Your child should understand that Marco Polo was an Italian explorer who traveled the Silk Road to China, and visited the Mongol Empire in the 13th century. You will revisit the Silk Road when studying Asia. Reading this book will whet your child's appetite for what will be learned in the future! Today let your child finger-march along the Silk Road, while you call out "Marco" and he responds, "Polo."

    Add a figure of Marco Polo with the dates 1269–1293 A.D. to your timeline.

    c) The Italians were not active in the Age of Exploration! While Christopher Columbus was Italian, he sailed and explored for the country of Spain. During the Age of Exploration Italy was at war with France, Spain, Austria, and had internal arguments as well. An outburst of plague claimed about 14% of the population in 1630. Because of these stresses, they not only did not explore and expand, but the trade with the far east that had been developed after Marco Polo declined. Have your child sit in Italy on the *GO GLOBAL* Game mat and bemoan, "Mama mia!" This literally means "my mother," but is used like "Gosh" or "Oh, my."

DAY 3 — VENICE, TOWER OF PISA, AND TARANTELLA DANCE

EVERYONE

1. Learn about Venice by reading one or more of the picture books based in Venice. Discuss with your child the idea of canals rather than roads and make sure he knows what a gondola is!

2. Learn about the Leaning Tower of Pisa by reading **13 Buildings Children Should Know**, pages 14–17. This bell tower was built in three stages over 200 years. The first two floors were built in the 12th century, and the building began to tilt during construction because of inadequate foundation. The construction halted because the city was at war, which allowed the soil time to solidify. About 100 years later, in the 13th century, construction resumed and they tried to compensate the tilt by building one side taller that the other. This means the tower is curved! The seventh floor and bell chamber were completed in the 14th century. The tilt gradually increased until it was stabilized in the late 20th century.

Talk about the importance of a foundation. Tell Jesus' story from the gospel of Matthew 7: 24–27. Sing, **The Wise Man Built His House**. Link to a video is on the *GO GLOBAL* Resource page.

> The wise man built his house upon the rock
> The wise man built his house upon the rock
> The wise man built his house upon the rock
> And the rain came tumbling down
>
> Oh, the rain came down
> And the floods came up
> The rain came down
> And the floods came up
> The rain came down
> And the floods came up
> And the wise man's house stood firm.
>
> The foolish man built his house upon the sand
> The foolish man built his house upon the sand
> The foolish man built his house upon the sand
> And the rain came tumbling down

Oh, the rain came down
And the floods came up
The rain came down
And the floods came up
The rain came down
And the floods came up
And the foolish man's house went "splat!" [clap hands once]

So, build your house on the Lord Jesus Christ
Build your house on the Lord Jesus Christ
Build your house on the Lord Jesus Christ
And the blessings will come down

Oh, the blessings come down
As your prayers go up
The blessings come down
As your prayers go up
The blessings come down
As your prayer go up

So build your house on the Lord Jesus Christ.

3. Make Leaning Tower of Pisa.

   ### Materials

   - Cardboard tube, such as toilet paper roll
   - White/ grey paint
   - Black magic marker
   - White paper napkin

   ### Process

   a) Trim a bit off one end of the toilet paper roll. Cut it on an angle so your tower will "lean."

   b) Paint grey or white.

   c) Draw circles around the roll to make the "floors".

   d) Add arches between the floors.

   e) Roll up a napkin and place it inside the roll to finish off the top of the tower.

4. Listen to the *Tarantella Napolitana*. Links available on the *GO GLOBAL* Resource page.

5. Dance the Tarantella, an Italian folk dance to a fast-upbeat tempo. Add a tambourine if you have one! An easy dance tutorial is available on *GO GLOBAL* Resource page.

DAY 4 — FOOD AND PARTY

EVERYONE

1. Talk about Italian food. Italian cuisine has developed through the centuries and is known to be one of the most popular in the world. Ask your children if they can name any Italian dishes. Here is a pretty complete list if you would like to discuss *some* of them with your children: pizza, spaghetti and meatballs, and lasagna, manicotti, ravioli, fettucine, tortellini, risotto, bruschetta, olives, mozzarella, parmesan, minestrone, biscotti, tiramisu, gelato.

    Eat an Italian meal—make it easy. Go to an Italian restaurant or serve spaghetti and meatballs or pizza, bread sticks, and gelato for desert. You might try making homemade pasta! If you eat at home, set the table with a red-checkered table cloth!

2. Read your books over again.
3. Speak Italian.
4. Dance the Tarantella.

WEEK 25
EUROPE
GERMANY AND HOLLAND

BIG PICTURE

In the north central portion of Europe lies Germany, which is covered with forest and is the original home of the Brothers Grimm fairytales such as Little Red Riding Hood, Snow White, and Sleeping Beauty. The Rhine and Danube rivers flow through Germany and castles spot the land. The famous Neuschwanstein (Pronunciation: Noy shwan stine) Castle inspired Walt Disney to build his Sleeping Beauty castle. You will make pretzels and learn the German clap dance.

The Netherlands, just northeast of Germany, contains the province of Holland. You will learn about tulips, dikes, and windmills by reading classic literature and viewing paintings by Rembrandt!

Wrap up the study of Europe by reviewing the books, the languages, the dances, the art, and the food you have experienced these last few weeks.

MATERIALS

Books

1. ***Little Red Riding Hood***, Trina Schart Hyman. Ages 4–8. Gorgeously illustrated retelling of the Brothers Grimm classic. Warning—the wording is a bit intense as the woodman uses an axe to kill the wolf and release the grandma; the pictures are not graphic, so you can soften as you are reading to the child.
2. ***Prayer for a Child***, Rachel Field. Ages 3–8. 1945 Caldecott winner classic with sweet, simple, and comforting illustrations melded with a lyrical child friendly prayer that encourages gratitude. Illustrations of Hummel type figurines and the little wooden chair evoke a sense of Germany.
3. ***13 Buildings Children Should Know***, Annette Roeder. Ages 8–12. While geared towards older children, this book is a gem, and could be used with younger children as they explore many buildings studied in this curriculum, including: the Neuschwanstein Castle.
4. ***The Boy Who Held Back the Sea***, Lenny Hort. Ages 4–9. Oil-painted illustrations reminiscent of the old Dutch masters grace this retelling of the traditional Dutch folktale melded with the *Boy who Cried Wolf*. A wonderful character lesson that is not heavy handed.
5. ***Hana in the Time of the Tulips***, Deborah Noyes. Ages 5–9. Tulips, history, economics, art, geography, and a tender tale of a Dutch family with art work reminiscent of Rembrandt.

Secondary Books: Find *some* of these excellent books to read aloud and make available to your children for their quiet times. * means especially recommended.

1. *****In My Pocket***, Dorrith Sim. Ages 6–10. German-Jewish family sends their young girl alone from Hamburg to Holland to England and finally to Scotland for safekeeping during World War II. Very moving story, but the separation from parents, and an ambiguous ending that does not say if she

ever sees her biological parents again might be disturbing for some children. Parents need to assess if this is a good book for their child.

2. ***From the Good Mountain: How Gutenberg Changed the World**, James Rumford. Ages 7–12. Rich illustrations inspired by 15th century illuminated manuscripts and van Eyck paintings, this book on the printing process provides insights into German life, the development of printing, and moveable type.

3. **Anno's Journey (Europe)**, Mitsumasa Anno. Wordless book travels through northern Europe showing landscapes, people, paintings, composers, and fairy tales. This is a fascinating book for a certain type of child. It is especially wonderful if the parent recognizes and knows enough about Europe to talk about the detailed pictures.

4. **The Gift**, Aliana Brodmann. Ages 5–8. With her Hanukkah money, a little girl gives a gift and receives the best gift of all. Based in Germany just pre-WWII.

5. Nonfiction book on Germany such as **Count your Way Through Germany**, James Haskins. Ages 5–9. If you use this older book you will need to explain that the two Germanys are now united. But it covers some wonderful architecture, musicians, and cultural information on Germany.

6. **Snow-White and the Seven Dwarfs**, Grimm Brothers, Nancy Burkert (illus.). Ages 4–8. Pages of beautiful rich text, alternating with full page, detailed, tapestry-like illustrations. Or **Snow White: A Tale from the Brothers Grimm**, Charles Santore (illus.). Ages 6–9. Both these books include the historic grim ending of the wicked step-mother; it does not seem to bother most children but does bother some mothers.

7. **Rose Red and the Bear Prince**, Dan Andreasen. Ages 5–9. Simple rendition of the Grimm's tale provides a unique, spirited, and quick-witted heroine with a refreshing ending that focuses on friendship instead of love at first sight.

8. **Children of the Forest**, Elsa Beskow. Ages 4–7. Magical story of a little family living deep in the forest which covers seasons as well. If possible, get the large volume that was published before 2005.

9. **Katje, the Windmill Cat**, Gretchen Woelfle. Ages 4–9. Based on a true story, a cat saves a baby during a storm that breaks a dike.

10. **Boxes for Katje**, Candace Fleming. Ages 4–8. Delightful true story of friendship between post WWII Katje in Holland and Rosie in Mayfield, Indiana.

11. **The Great Tulip Trade**, Beth Wagner Brust. Easy Reader. Cute story of a little girl trading away her tulips. Includes information on the history of tulips with cartoon-like illustrations.

12. **Rembrandt and the Boy who Drew Dogs: A Story about Rembrandt van Rijn**, Molly Blaisdell. Ages 4–8. Titus convinces his father to allow him to become an art student. Simple bright illustrations of 17th century Amsterdam juxtaposed with some of Rembrandt's own dark work make this biography shine.

Movies:

1. **The Sound of Music**, Ages 5 and up. I know it is set in Austria. But the vistas, the music, the story are a wonderful culmination to your study.

SUPPLIES

1. Map of Europe used the last four weeks
2. *GO GLOBAL* Game
3. German language tutorial available on *GO GLOBAL* Resource page
4. German dance tutorial available on *GO GLOBAL* Resource page

5. Supplies for castle craft: various sized cardboard tubes, paint, brushes, construction paper, glue, black marker, bamboo skewers
6. Ingredients for German meal, or a local German restaurant

DAY 1 — OVERVIEW, FOREST, FAIRY TALES, AND GERMAN LANGUAGE

EVERYONE

1. Find Germany in the **Beginner's World Atlas**. Now locate it on your map of Europe. It is in the north central portion of Europe. Germany has part of the Alps in the southern portion. The Rhine River flows through Germany and it has large conifer and deciduous forests, the most famous being the Black Forest. Color the forest symbol in Germany if you have not already done so. Also, Add Berlin, the capital of Germany.

2. This week we will also visit The Netherlands which is to the northwest of Germany. Find the Netherlands on your map. "The Netherlands" literally means "lower countries" and includes the region of Holland, which is famous for its windmills, and for having land that is lower than sea level protected by great dikes holding back the ocean.

3. Explore the forests of Germany and Europe by reading some classic fairy tales set in the European forest such as **Little Red Riding Hood**. The Brothers Grimm were German professors and authors who collected and published folktales in the 19th century.

4. OPTIONAL: Explore **Anno's Journey in Europe**. Does your child recognize anything?

ADD FOR SIX-YEAR-OLDS AND UP

5. Start to learn some German words. Tutorial available on the resource page.

English	German	Pronunciation
yes	ja	yah
no	nein	nine
please	bitte	BIT tuh
thank you	danke	DAHN kuh
goodbye	auf wiedersehen	Owf VEE der sane
good day/morning; hello	guten tag	GOO ten tahg
Mr.	Herr	hair
Mrs.	Frau	frow

DAY 2 — PRAYER, PRETZELS, SLAP DANCE, AND CASTLES

EVERYONE

1. Read ***Prayer for a Child***. This is such a sweet book, and though it does not mention Germany, the art has a German flair. Look at the little figurines and compare to Hummel figurines. Pictures available on the *GO GLOBAL* Resource page.

   Take this time to make a gratitude list with your child and thank the Lord for the simple and profound gifts He gives. And, like this little girl, take time to pray for the other children in the world, "Bless other children, far and near, and keep them safe and free from fear."

2. Pretzels originated in Europe where it is said a monk made them as a reward for children who have said their prayers. The strips of dough resemble arms crossed on the chest in prayer. They also have three holes representing the three persons of the Trinity: The Father, the Son, and the Holy Spirit.

   Make and eat pretzels. Fold your arms like the pretzel and recite the Lord's Prayer and thank God for His great gifts. If you prefer you can purchase frozen pretzels and bake them.

> Making the pretzels gives you an opportunity to discuss yeast, and the need of a sugar to help the yeast to leaven the bread (make it rise). Children who knead and form the dough build strength and dexterity that will help them when they are writing. Making the pretzels is fun and nutritious, but also teaches science, geography, and develops strength and dexterity for writing. This _is_ school.

Ingredients

- 1½ cups lukewarm water
- 1 packet active dry or instant yeast (2¼ teaspoons)
- 1 tsp. salt
- 1 Tbsp. granulated sugar
- 3¾–4¼ cups all-purpose flour + more for work surface
- 1 large egg, beaten
- coarse sea salt for sprinkling

Directions

1. Preheat oven to 425°F. Line baking sheet with parchment paper or silicone baking mat.
2. Dissolve yeast in warm water. Stir with a spoon about 1 minute. Add salt and sugar; stir until combined. Slowly add 3 cups of flour, 1 cup at a time. Mix with a wooden spoon until dough is thick. Add ¾ cup more flour until the dough is no longer sticky. Add up to ½ cup more if needed. Poke the dough with your finger—if it bounces back, it is ready to knead.

a) Turn the dough out onto a floured surface. Knead the dough for about 3 minutes and shape into a ball. With a sharp knife, cut the ball of dough into about 1/3 cup sections.

b) Roll the dough into a rope with an even diameter. My ropes were twenty inches long. This measurement will depend on how large you want the pretzels. Once you have your long rope, take the ends and draw them together so the dough forms a circle. Twist the ends, then bring them towards yourself and press them down into a pretzel shape.

c) **Optional:** Whisk 9 cups of water and ½ cup baking soda together in a large pot. Bring to a boil. Place a pretzel onto a large slotted spatula and dip into the boiling water for 20–30 seconds. Any more than that and your pretzels will have a metallic taste. The pretzel will float. Lift the pretzel out of the water and allow as much of the excess water to drip off as possible. Repeat with the rest of the pretzels. This will give the pretzels a nice color and a soft white interior when baked.

d) Beat the egg and pour into a shallow bowl or pie dish. Dunk the shaped pretzel into the egg wash (both sides). Place on baking sheet and sprinkle with salt.

e) Bake for 10 minutes at 425°F. Turn the oven to broil and bake for 5 more minutes to brown the tops. Watch closely to avoid burning.

f) Allow to cool and enjoy. Serve warm or at room temperature. Pretzels may be stored in an airtight container or zip top bag for up to 3 days, but they will not be as soft.

3. Learn the German clap dance. In Germany, it seems that only the boys do the slapping of their thighs and feet, while the girls just sway. But in the USA, we all like the active parts. :-) Tutorial available on the *GO GLOBAL* Resource page.

4. Germany is famous for its castles—it has more than any other country in the world. Read about the Neuschwanstein Castle, which is the inspiration for Disney's Sleeping Beauty Castle, in **13 Buildings Children Should Know**, pages 26–29.

OPTIONAL: Build the castle out of paper tubes. Paint a variety of sizes of tubes. Letting your child make it splotchy will add to the charm. Add black arched windows and doors. Fold bright colored construction paper into cones for the roofs. Add triangular flags on skewers. Art Tutorial available on *GO GLOBAL* Resource page.

ADD FOR SEVEN-YEAR-OLDS AND UP

5. Read **From the Good Mountain**.

    a) Many pages of this book have a question. Pause and let your child try to answer!

b) Find Mainz in Germany on a map or globe.

c) Let your child examine the illustrations. How is this like her home town? How is it different? Discuss both time (it is clearly a long time ago) and geography (house types, windows, shutters).

d) The gold came from Africa. Review where Africa and "the burning Sahara" are located.

DAY 3 — DUTCH DAMS, TULIPS, AND A GERMAN MEAL

EVERYONE

1. Read *Hana in the Time of the Tulips.*

    a) This is a complex and moving story. Do not overanalyze, but let it wash over your children.

    b) Look at tulip bulbs. Compare to onions. Plant if it is the right time of the year.

    c) What were Hana's gifts to her father, and what was their purposes? [Answer: Rosemary for remembering; fireflies to chase away dark thoughts; daisies to cure frowning; a painting to provide money.]

    d) Look at some of Rembrandt's paintings and compare to the art style in the book. Some examples of Rembrandt's paintings are on the *GO GLOBAL* Resource page.

    e) OPTIONAL: Paint flowers alfresco (which means outside in the fresh air), just like Hana did.

2. Read *The Boy Who Held Back the Sea*. The boy has very poor character at the beginning of the story, and deals with the consequences.

    a) How was the boy naughty? What was the consequence of his naughtiness?

    b) Read Proverbs 20:11. "Even a child makes himself known by his acts." How does this story illustrate this proverb?

    c) What happens at the end? [Answer: The boy repents and does restitution.] Do not tell your child. Let him figure it out himself. He might need time to think it through. If you simply tell him the answer you will lose much of the benefit of the story.

3. Read other books about Germany and Holland from this week.

4. Eat a German meal. Going out to eat at a German restaurant is the easiest, but making this food is not too difficult. You may want to avoid sauerkraut since it is a strong flavor and may be an unpleasant experience for your child, though my children grew up with it and love it! Add if you are feeling adventurous.

    a) **Bratwurst on a bun** or

       Wiener Schnitzel Veal is expensive—but you only need ¾ lb. for a family of 4 or 5.

Pound veal cutlets thin, dip in egg, then flour, egg again, then breadcrumbs. Lightly fry in a bit of butter.

b) **Cucumber salad** (serves 3) Fix ahead as it tastes even better if it sits.

1 cucumber sliced, 3 Tbsp. cider vinegar, 1 Tbsp. sugar, ¼ tsp. salt, ¼ tsp. pepper, 1 small red onion sliced, 3 Tbsp. chopped fresh dill/ 3 tsp. dried dill

a) **German potato salad** (serves 4 or 5)

4 C. diced peeled potatoes, 4 slices bacon, 1 small onion diced, ¼ C. vinegar, 2 Tbsp. water, 2 Tbsp. sugar, 1 tsp. salt, 1/8 tsp. pepper, 1 Tbsp. chopped parsley.

Boil potatoes 10 min, drain. Fry bacon crisp; remove. Add onion to bacon grease and cook over med heat until brown. Add vinegar, water, sugar, salt, and pepper to pan. Bring to boil, Add potatoes and parsley. Crumble in half of bacon. Transfer to serving dish and garnish with the rest of the bacon.

b) **Strudel** (from the bakery) or

German Apple Pie Cake

Ingredients

- 6–8 Granny Smith apples, peeled and sliced
- 2½ Tbsp. cinnamon-sugar (2 Tbsp. sugar + ½ Tbsp. cinnamon)
- 3 large eggs
- 1½ C. superfine white sugar (not powdered sugar. Pulse regular sugar very briefly in food processor)
- 1½ C. vegetable oil
- 3 tsp. vanilla extract
- 1½ C. flour

Directions

1. Preheat the oven to 350°F. Spray 9½ to 10-inch springform pan with nonstick spray. Line the bottom with round of parchment paper and spray again.

2. Layer apple slices in pan until they come about two thirds up the side. Sprinkle 1½ Tbsp. of cinnamon-sugar over the apples.

3. Prepare the batter by beating eggs and sugar until light and fluffy. Add the oil and vanilla. Beat well. Pour over the apples and sprinkle with extra cinnamon-sugar. Tap the pan on the counter to allow the batter to sink down and around the apples.

4. Bake for 1 hour 20 minutes, or until a toothpick inserted into the center of the cake comes out clean. Cool <u>completely</u> in the pan. Serve with ice cream.

DAY 4 — REVIEW OF EUROPE

EVERYONE

1. Review the European countries you have studied by asking your children where they would like to visit and why.
2. What have been their favorite books in this unit on Europe?
3. Dance the various dances you have learned. Which is their favorite?
4. Which has been their favorite meal from Europe?
5. Which has been the most interesting building?
6. Play the *GO GLOBAL* Game with the cards for the Continents, North America, South America, Antarctica, Africa, and Europe.
7. Watch ***The Sound of Music***.

ADD FOR SIX-YEAR-OLDS AND UP

8. Play a game with the foreign language words you have learned.
    a) Call out a word and see who can tell its meaning and its language. 1 point for each answer.
    b) Pick an English word and a foreign language and see who can say the correct word. 2 points for this.

French	Spanish	Italian	German
Page 138	Page 145	Page 158	Page 165

ADD FOR SEVEN-YEAR-OLDS AND UP

9. Review where the different countries in Europe colonized.

France	Spain	Italy	Britain
Pages 140	Page 146	Pages 159	Page 152

WEEK 26
CATCH UP OR TAKE A BREAK

WEEK 27
ASIA
OVERVIEW AND RUSSIA

BIG PICTURE

Asia is the largest continent. In addition to having all the different habitat types, it has many diverse cultures. We will have a broad overview this week and study Russia.

Russia is the largest country in the world (twice as large as the USA), and is part of what used to be an even larger country called the Soviet Union, which included countries now in Central Asia and Eastern Europe. Russia is also unique in that some of the country is west of the Ural Mountains and therefore in Europe, while the rest is east of the Urals and is in Asia. This area west of the Urals is called Siberia. Outside of Antarctica, Siberia is the least populated land in the world.

The most northern strip of Russia is the tundra. This area of very low temperatures and short growing seasons does not support trees, but there can be dwarf shrubs, grasses, mosses, and/or lichens. While few animals live in this area, ones of note include: caribou (reindeer), musk ox, Arctic hare, Arctic fox, and polar bears.

Much of Russia is coniferous forests called taiga (pronunciation: TIE gah), located south of the tundra. This forest is also found in the Scandinavian countries, and Scotland, Japan, much of Canada, and some of northern USA, where it is sometimes called "the North Woods." The taiga is very cold in the winter time but has a warmer climate during the summer. This area has the largest fluctuation in temperatures of any place on earth.

Another important area of Russia is the steppes. This is the grassland that is characterized by hot summers and cold winters. In other continents, we have called this general type of land grassland, plains, prairie, pampas, or savanna. These fertile rolling plains of central Russia provide much of the food for the rest of the country.

The Caspian Sea is the largest enclosed inland body of water. It was not called a lake because it was considered an ocean by its earliest inhabitants, probably because of its huge size and saltiness. Lake Baikal (pronunciation: BIE kahl) is the deepest and largest freshwater lake by volume in the world. It contains more water than all of the North American Great Lakes combined! The Bering Strait is the narrow sea passage between Asia and North America, connecting the Arctic Ocean and the Pacific Ocean.

Russia's political history is complex, bloody, and best studied by older students. In the primary grades, children should learn that the early rulers were called tsars rather than kings. Depending on the books you choose to read to your children this week, you might also want to discuss religious persecution, especially of the Jews.

You will learn a bit about the Russian Orthodox Church, the Matryoshka (pronunciation: ma tree AHSH kah) nesting doll, the Siberian tiger, and the brown bear. Round out your visit to Russia by listening to Peter and the Wolf.

MATERIALS

Books

1. ***Beginner's World Atlas 3rd Edition***, National Geographic. 2011.
2. ***The Littlest Matryoshka***, Corinne Demas Bliss. Ages 4–8. A doll maker in old Russia makes a set of six nesting dolls which travel to a toy shop where the littlest "sister" is lost and goes through adventures before being reunited with the others and their new owner. The dolls are authentically illustrated and a note on the history of these dolls is included.
3. ***Little Lost Tiger***, Jonathan London. Ages 3–8. Poetic story of a Siberian tigress who flees a forest fire. The end pages have extra information.
4. ***Sergei Prokofiev's Peter and the Wolf***, (pronunciation: seer GAY Pro KOE fee ev), Janet Schulman. Ages 3–8. Book and CD with narration and fully-orchestrated music. You can use another rendition if you prefer.

Secondary Books: Find *some* of these excellent books to read aloud and make available to your children for their quiet times. * means especially recommended.

1. *****The Miracle of Saint Nicolas***, Gloria Whelan. Ages 5 and up. Fictional story of a 20th century Russian boy who sees a Christmas miracle when his church has the first service in decades. Sobering, inspiring, and a wonderful glimpse of the Russian Orthodox church.
2. *****Rechenka's Eggs***, Patricia Polacco. Ages 4–8. Injured goose accidentally breaks Babushka's painted eggs and provides beautiful replacements for the Easter Festival in old Moscow.
3. *****Easter Eggs for Anya: A Ukrainian Celebration of New Life in Christ***, Virginia Kroll. Ages 4–8. Anya's family is too poor to buy eggs to decorate this year, but there is a surprise for her. Wonderful origin legend about pysanky eggs, with the Easter story clearly presented.
4. *****Molly's Pilgrim***, Barbara Cohen. Ages 6–10. Touching story of 20th century Russian immigrants.
5. *****The Tale of the Firebird***, Gennady Spirin. Ages 5–10. The Tsar's son goes on a quest for the amazing firebird, flies over mountains and woods on a talking wolf, confronts a wicked Baba Yaga, and rescues an enchanted princess. Entrancing, luminous illustrations.
6. *****The Firebird***, Demi. Ages 6–10. With the help of a magical horse, a young archer fulfills the requests of the evil Tsar and wins the hand of the princess. Extraordinary detailed illustrations that echo the culture and history of the tsars.
7. *****Another Celebrated Dancing Bear***, Gladys Scheffrin-Falk. Ages 4–8. The story of a friendship between two bears, elegant Max who teaches glum Boris how to dance. The sepia illustrations enhance the nostalgic imperial Russian setting, replete with samovars, nesting dolls, and onion domes.
8. *****Tiger Math**: Learning to Graph from a Baby Tiger*, Ann Whitehead Nagda. Ages 5–10. Photographic narrative of a true story of an orphaned Siberian tiger cub nurtured by the staff at the Denver Zoo.
9. ***A is for Asia***, Cynthia Chin-Lee. Ages 5–9. Overview of all of Asia in an ABC book with detailed, childlike, stylized illustrations.
10. ***Asia***, Allan Fowler. Easy Reader. Nice summary if you would like a reader. For the most part a repeat of information in the ***Beginner's World Atlas***.

11. Easy nonfiction book on Russia such as: ***Russia***, Kevin Blake. Ages 4–8. Just the right amount of information for early primary ages with great photographs; or ***Dropping in on Russia***, David King; or ***Moscow***, by Allan Fowler.
12. ***Shoemaker Martin***, Leo Tolstoy and Bernadette Watts. Ages 5 and up. After showing kindness to three strangers, the Russian shoemaker learns that Jesus visited him.
13. ***Luba and the Wren***, Patricia Polacco. Ages 4–8. Ukrainian retelling of *The Fisherman's Wife* where a girl saves a wren and asks for wishes from her greedy parents.
14. ***Babushka's Doll***, Patricia Polacco. Ages 3–7. Natasha learns to be less demanding because of Babushka's (Grandma's) magical doll.
15. ***Latkes, Latkes, Good to Eat: A Chanukah Story***, Naomi Howland. Ages 4–7. In an old Russian village, an old woman gives hungry children a frying pan that makes potato pancakes until it hears the magic words to stop.
16. ***The Golden Mare, the Firebird, and the Magic Ring***, Ruth Sanderson. Ages 5–10. Lovely retelling of the Firebird legend.
17. ***Vassilisa the Wise: A Tale of Medieval Russia***, Josepha Sherman. Ages 6–10. Tale set in the 12th century about the wise Vassilisa who saves her husband and herself from the legendary Prince Vladimir.
18. ***Fool of the World and the Flying Ship: A Russian Tale***, Arthur Ransome. Ages 5–8. Caldecott winner where a simple-minded, but kind-hearted son wins the princess's hand.
19. ***Little Polar Bear, Take Me Home!*** Hans de Beer. Ages 4–8. Polar bear helps a little lost tiger find his way home. Sweet pretend story set in Russia.
20. ***The Tale of Urso Brunov, Little Father of All Bears***, Brian Jacques. Ages 6–8. Tall tale from the Redwall creator introduces the Little Father who teaches manners and rescues captured animals. Russian names, clothing, and landscape.
21. ***Urso Brunov and the White Emperor***, Brian Jacques. Ages 6–8. Little Father of All Bears returns the lost polar bear cubs to their home in the far north. Russian like names, clothing, animals, and the troika sled make this a fun read.
22. ***Masha and the Bear***, Lari Don. Easy Reader. Cute story about a bear in the Russian forest.
23. A nonfiction book on brown bears.

SUPPLIES

1. Map of Asia (available on the *GO GLOBAL* Resource page) printed on cardstock
2. Matryoshka dolls craft materials: template available on *GO GLOBAL* Resource page printed onto cardstock, colored pencils or crayons. There is a link on the *GO GLOBAL* Resource page for an alternative, more difficult craft of painting an inexpensive nesting doll set.

DAY 1 — ASIA AND RUSSIA OVERVIEW

EVERYONE

1. Read ***Beginner's World Atlas***, pages 38–41.

2. Refer to the map on page 40–41 to help your child label and mark his own map of Asia found on the *GO GLOBAL* Resource page. This area is so massive we will review and learn about more locations as we visit those areas in the next five weeks.

    a) Ask your child to name the bodies of water around Asia. He should be able to name the Arctic Ocean, the Pacific Ocean, the Indian Ocean, the Mediterranean Sea, and the Red Sea. Color the water blue and label these bodies of water.

    b) Children **six-years-and-older** can be introduced to the Black Sea and the Caspian Sea that are on the border of Asia and Europe. Children **seven-years-and-older** can also learn Lake Baikal and the Bering Strait. Review what a strait is and see if he can remember the others we learned. [Answer: Strait of Gibraltar and the English Channel.] Color the water blue and label these bodies of water.

    c) Color the Ural Mountains and the Caucasus Mountains on your map. These are important boundaries to know. Label the Ural Mountains only. Color and label the Himalaya Mountains. We will learn some of the rivers as we study the specific countries. As the **Atlas** mentioned, Mt. Everest is the highest place on the earth. Locate and label.

    d) The northern edge of Asia and Europe is tundra, an area of very low temperatures and short growing seasons. While it does not support trees, there can be dwarf shrubs, grasses, mosses, and/or lichens. Color on your map.

    e) There is a large coniferous forest in the northern part of Asia. Review what a coniferous forest is and have your child color the coniferous symbol on his map. [Answer: Coniferous forest is made up of cone-bearing trees with needles or small leaves that stay green all year.]

    f) There is also a sizeable deciduous forest. Review what a deciduous forest is and have your child color the deciduous symbol on his map. [Answer: Deciduous trees lose their leaves each fall, are brown during the winter, and grow new leaves in the spring.]

    g) There is some jungle/ rainforest in China, Southeast Asia, and along the western coast of India. Have your child color this symbol on his map.

    h) Color the steppes, the grassland areas in Asia.

    i) Add strips of sandpaper for the large desert regions in Asia: the Gobi Desert and the Arabian Desert.

3. Read **Beginner's World Atlas**, pages 42–43. Talk about the size and diversity of the Asian continent. Tell your children you will take five weeks, and still only be studying *some* of the countries/areas since it is so large.

4. Introduce Russia. Start with the *GO GLOBAL* Game mat. Review the Ural Mountains that divide Asia and Europe. Then move to the globe. Point out that Russia has a large portion of land in each continent. Ask your child which continent he would designate for Russia.

ADD FOR SIX-YEAR-OLDS AND UP

5. Tradition states that the first Christian church in Russia was founded by the Apostle Andrew. The Russian Orthodox Church has several unique distinctives, including:

a) Icons—religious art work which is typically a static, flat, not lifelike portrait.

b) Church buildings with onion domes.

c) Distinctive robes and head pieces for their ministers.

The Russian Orthodox Church shares traditions with other Christian denominations, including:

a) The Bible

b) A crucifix or cross

c) An altar in the church with special altar cloths

d) Bread and wine for the Lord's supper

e) Priests (ministers) who wear distinctive clothing

Talk to your child about how your church is alike and different from the Orthodox church. Look at the picture of St. Basil's Cathedral, which is in Moscow, in the ***Beginner's World Atlas***, page 36. Look for indications (even just pictorially) of the Orthodox church in your books.

Re-read ***The Miracle of Saint Nicholas***, from Week 13 of this curriculum to get a wonderful sense of the Russian Orthodox Church. While we will not study the persecution under the communists, even a young child can appreciate this story. There are also pictures of the Orthodox church and icons in ***Rechenka's Eggs***.

DAY 2 — MATRYOSHKA DOLLS

EVERYONE

1. Review the geographic habitats in Russia. The tundra is always called the tundra. The coniferous forest is called the taiga in Russia. The Russian steppes are also called grasslands, prairies, plains, pampas, and savannas in other areas. Ask your children if they can remember what term is used on what continent? [Answer: Prairies or plains in North America; pampas in South America, savannas in Africa.]

2. Read ***The Littlest Matryoshka***. Nesting dolls are made in many countries, but the Russian ones are the best known.

    a) On a subsequent reading, see if your child can find the onion domed church on the first pages. Ask your child why it is called an onion dome. If needed, compare to a real onion.

    b) Art Activity

Materials

- Matryoshka doll template printed on card stock
- Crayons or colored pencils

Process

a) Cut dolls out.

b) Color faces and clothing.

c) Fold.

3. Learn a few Russian words.

English	Russian	Pronunciation
no	nyet	nyeht
yes	da	dah
bye	paka	pah KAH
hello	preevyt	PREH vit

4. Read one or more of the books listed in the Secondary Book list #5 to #11. Enjoy! Look for Russian terms or pictures of these Russian items.

steppes	grasslands in Russia
tundra	very cold, treeless area
taiga	forest in Russia
tsar / czar	king or emperor in Russia
babushka	old woman or a headscarf tied under the chin
Dacha (pronunciation: dah CHAH)	little house in the country
icon	religious "flat-looking" portrait
onion dome	dome resembling an onion, with a large base tapered up to a point
pysanky eggs	Ukrainian Easter egg dyed with colorful folk designs
latkes	Jewish potato pancakes

5. Read one or more of the books listed in the Secondary Book list #12 to #16. These are traditional Russian folktales/ fairytales that have been carefully chosen to represent the best moral values, artistic quality, and literary quality. Make sure to read at least one of the books recommended about the Firebird. Each book is special in its own way and there is great educational value in getting two or all three and comparing them to each other. How are they different? How are they alike? Which one do you like best?

DAY 3 — SIBERIAN TIGERS

EVERYONE

1. Read **Little Lost Tiger**. Enjoy the lovely illustrations and let the rich language and poetic structure wash over your children.

    a) On a subsequent read, look through the pictures together. Explain that this takes place in Siberia, the large portion of Russia that is west of the Ural Mountains. Ask your child if he remembers the Russian word for forest. [Answer: Taiga.]

    b) Using your world map or globe, find Russia, the Ural Mountains, and Siberia. Ask your child to describe this location. [Answer: Snowy, cold, fir/coniferous trees, etc.]

2. Read **Tiger Math** or **Little Polar Bear, Take Me Home!** or other books that you found on the Siberian tiger.

    a) Interesting facts to impart about the Siberian tiger

    - They are endangered; there are only about 500 alive in the wild.
    - They are very small when they are born—about 3 pounds, but a female can be around 250 lbs., and a male as big as 500 lbs. Have your child hold a 3-pound bag of sugar. Then compare the weight of the male tiger to his dad. [Answer: The tiger is probably more than twice as heavy!]
    - They are carnivorous—which means they eat meat.
    - They like to pounce and wrestle!
    - They shred tree bark with their claws.
    - They like the water.
    - They make a chuffing sound when greeting someone they like. Find a link to a chuffing video on the *GO GLOBAL* Resource page.

    b) Dramatize a Siberian tiger.

    c) As you read these books ask your child if the story is real or pretend. If it is pretend, ask your child to tell you what parts are true, and which are not. You can guide him in evaluating the book. Do not just instruct him, but gently and slowly guide him so the light bulb goes on in his head. For instance, the **Little Lost Tiger** is a fictional story with beautiful drawings. Ask your child if he thinks animals have names they call each other, like 'Striped One" or "Amba." Smile and let him know it is fun to pretend that they do, but we human beings give names to our animal friends. The rest of this book is relaying true information about tigers. **Tiger Math** is nonfiction—a completely true story. The tigers have names—but these are what human beings call them, not what the tigers call each other. **Little Polar Bear, Take Me Home** is a fictional story with cartoon like drawings. It has a lot of untrue aspects:

- Tigers, polar bears, and the other animals in the story do not talk in real life.
- These animals are not friendly to each other.
- They could not have traveled all the way to the desert and back in one day.

But the book has some true aspects as well:

- Polar bears and tigers do live in the northern portion of Russia.
- There are railroads in Russia (with Russian writing on them).
- Camels do live in the desert and owls do live in those forests.
- There are polar research stations in the Arctic area.

Each of these books is delightful and children love them—there is much to enjoy! If you get more than one of these books, it is interesting to compare what is real and pretend between each of them.

ADD FOR SIX-YEAR-OLDS AND UP

3. Another famous animal in Russia is the Eurasian brown bear which became a symbol of this country. At first this symbol was used by people who did not like Russia. Ask your child why people would use this bear as a negative symbol of Russia. [Answers could include: The bear is big, brutal, and mean. Russia is huge and the tsarist rulers, and later the communist rulers, were brutal.] But in the late 20th century, Russia embraced the bear as their emblem, and have embraced the positive qualities of the bear. Ask your children what these might be. [Answer: The bear is powerful, cunning, and smart.] Ask your child to tell you the animal symbol of the United States of America and the United Kingdom. [Answers: An eagle and a lion.]

4. Read one or more of the bear books listed.

DAY 4 — PETER AND THE WOLF

EVERYONE

1. Listen to **Peter and the Wolf** while following along with the picture book.

2. Ask your child to name the characters in the story and tell what instrument represents each one. [Answer: Peter—strings; Bird—flute; Duck—oboe; Cat—clarinet; Grandfather—bassoon; Wolf—French horns; Hunters shots—drums; Hunter's theme—woodwind.] Ask your child why he thinks these specific instruments were chosen for the characters.

3. Discuss the plot of the story. See if they can tell the events in the correct order.

    OPTIONAL: Printable is available on the *GO GLOBAL* Resource page to let your child mix and then put the story in order.

    i. Peter didn't listen to his Grandfather and went into the meadow where he met a bird.

    ii. Peter and the bird met a duck.

    iii. A cat tried to eat the bird.

    iv. The wolf came out of the woods and ate the duck.

    v. Peter caught the wolf and tied him up.

    vi. Peter and the hunters took the wolf to the zoo.

4. What are the feelings of each of the characters? Angry, happy, scared, sad, excited, tender? There is not one correct answer, and do not make your children come up with all the ones listed. Ask your child to describe a feeling of one of the characters, and WHY he thinks the character feels that way. [Possible answers: Peter—bold, fearless, confident, sympathetic, happy, proud; Bird—happy, excited; Duck—flustered, scared, angry; Cat—sly; Grandfather—angry, annoyed, sleepy; Wolf—angry, mean, scared at the end; Hunters—excited, perhaps afraid.]

5. Pantomime the characters or create a dance for each character using the music.

6. Read and reread your favorite Russian books.

WEEK 28
ASIA
MIDDLE EAST

BIG PICTURE

The Middle East includes the area bordered by the Mediterranean Sea, the Red Sea, the Black Sea, the Caucasus Mountains, and east to include Iran. Though you do not need to include this information to your children, sometimes Egypt is included in the term Middle East. Most of the Middle East is desert, most notably the Arabian Desert, and includes some mountain ranges and some grasslands/forests in Turkey. Major bodies of water you will explore include the Dead Sea and the Jordan, Tigris, and Euphrates rivers.

The Middle East is important historically as it is the crossroads of Asia, Africa, and Europe. You will start the week reviewing the Silk Road that Marco Polo traveled upon and the various cultures along that path. You will learn about a few ancient cultures through the famous Biblical stories of Jonah (Nineveh/Assyria), Daniel (Babylon), and Esther (Persia). Take some time to learn about Persian rugs and some of the folktales from Persia. Older children will be introduced to the Fertile Crescent in the context of Abraham.

You will take a day to learn about the land, the founding, and the flag of Israel. Then you will celebrate the Shabbat (Sabbath) by making challah bread and eating olives.

MATERIALS

Books

1. ***A Single Pebble: A Story of the Silk Road***, Bonnie Christensen. Ages 4–8. A ninth century Chinese girl sends a jade pebble west to a boy in Italy.
2. ***The Book of Jonah***, Peter Spier. Ages 3–9. Retold story with lovely illustrations that capture life in Israel, life on a boat in the Mediterranean, and life in Nineveh. End notes and map make this a great addition to your family library. OR use a Bible story book of your choice.
3. ***The Story of Daniel in the Lion's Den***, Michael McCarthy. Ages 5–8. Retelling of the Biblical story of the writing on the wall and the lions' den in rhyme. Various kings, Babylon, and Persia are mentioned by name. Illustrations capture the culture, dress, and architecture of the time and place. OR use a Bible story book of your choice.
4. ***Queen Esther***, Tomie DePaola. Ages 4–8. (Out-of-print) Simple and clear retelling with notes on Purim OR use a Bible story book of your choice. Caution: Pre-read any other books about Esther as many have age-inappropriate, sexualized material.
5. ***The Legend of the Persian Carpet***, Tomie DePaola. Ages 4–8. Tale of how the first jewel-patterned Persian carpet was created to replace a lost treasure.
6. ***Harvest of Light***, Allison Ofanansky. Ages 4–8. Photo essay of Israeli family raising olives and making oil for their Hanukkah menorah.

Secondary Books: Find *some* of these excellent books to read aloud and make available to your children for their quiet times. * means especially recommended.

1. ****Fatima the Spinner and the Tent***, Idries Shah. Ages 5–11. A young woman suffers three disasters but survives and learns from each experience. Lovely story, pictures, and a map of Fatima's trip from Morocco to Istanbul to China. A Sufi tale.
2. ***Azad's Camel***, Erika Pal. Ages 5–8. An orphan boy is forced to work as a camel jockey until a magical escape with his friendly camel. A sensitive introduction to a serious modern problem.
3. ***The Red Lion: A Tale of Ancient Persia***, Diane Wolkstein. Ages 5–12. To be crowned, the prince of Persia must prove his courage by fighting the red lion. A Sufi tale.
4. ***A Gift for the King: A Persian Tale***, Christopher Manson. Ages 5–9. Persian King Artaxerxes is unsatisfied with all gifts until he gets a simple gift from a shepherd boy.
5. ***The King and the Three Thieves: A Persian Tale***, Kristen Balouch. Ages 4–8. The disguised king slips out to meet his subjects and wisely helps them in this magical tale from Old Persia.
6. ***Hosni the Dreamer: An Arabian Tale***, Ehud Ben-Ezer. Ages 4–8. Hosni the shepherd travels to the city and spends his money to buy wisdom, which changes his life. A Sufi tale.
7. ***The Persian Cinderella***, Shirley Climo. Ages 4–8. Retelling of the traditional Persian tale of a kind young woman who outsmarts her stepsisters with help from a magical pot.
8. ***A Donkey Reads, Adapted from a Turkish Folktale***, Muriel Mandell. Ages 5–8. A Mongol ruler is outwitted by the local leader teaching a donkey to read. Fun cartoon-like illustrations of life in a Turkish village.
9. ***The Three Princes: A Tale from the Middle East***, Eric Kimmel. Ages 5–9. Saudi Arabian folktale about a princess sending three suitors on a quest and then choosing the right prince.
10. ***The Silk Route: 7,000 Miles of History***, John S. Major. Ages 6–10. Lavish illustrations and highly informative text traces the silk route from China to Byzantium exploring the geography, the people, and the products that moved along this path.

Israel

11. ****It's Challah Time!*** Latifa Berry Kropf. Ages 3–6. A photo essay of preschoolers making Challah bread for the celebration of the Seder.
12. ***Everybody Says Shalom***, Leslie Kimmelman. Ages 3–7. A trip through Israel!
13. ***First Rain***, Charlotte Herman. Ages 4–8. Abbey moves from the US to Israel and writes letters to her grandmother describing her new home.
14. ***The Chameleon That Saved Noah's Ark***, Yael Molchadsky. Ages 3–7. Cute story of Noah discovering what the chameleon eats.

SUPPLIES

1. Map of Asia that you used last week
2. Additional Middle East maps, available on the *GO GLOBAL* Resource page
3. Whichever you have on hand to examine: silk, jade, sandalwood, a wooden flute, and/or a cinnamon stick
4. Timeline figures: Jonah, Daniel, Abraham, Esther, Noah, small Israeli flag, small US flag, available on the *GO GLOBAL* Resource page
5. Scepter supplies: wooden spoon and chenille wire
6. White and blue paper to make the flag of Israel

7. Olives, olive oil, hummus, and pita to eat
8. Challah bread ingredients (from **It's Challah Time**): 2 Tbsp. yeast, 1 C. honey, 4 C. whole wheat flour, 3 C. white flour, ½ C. oil, 2 eggs, 2 tsp. salt, 1 Tbsp. cinnamon, 1 Tbsp. vanilla; toppings: poppy seeds, sesame seeds, or cinnamon sugar

DAY 1   THE MIDDLE EAST AND THE SILK ROAD

EVERYONE

1. Review Asia on the map. Point out the area that is referred to as the Middle East. This includes the area bordered by the Mediterranean Sea, the Red Sea, the Black Sea, the Caucasus Mountains, and east to include Iran. Though you do not need to include this information to your children, sometimes Egypt is included in the term Middle East.

   Point out the Arabian Peninsula. Review the definition of a peninsula. [Answer: A land that is bordered on three sides by water and attached on one side to a larger land mass.] What are the names of the water around the Arabian Peninsula? [Answer: The Red Sea, the Arabian Sea (or the Indian Ocean), and the Persian Gulf.]

   Now point out the peninsula of Turkey. What are the names of the water around the Turkey Peninsula? [Answer: The Black Sea and the Mediterranean Sea.]

   Ask your child if she can remember other peninsulas she has studied. [Answer: Spain and Portugal, Italy, Florida.]

   Ask your child what kind of habitats are in the Middle East. [Answer: Mostly desert, with some mountains east of the Persian Gulf, and some grasslands and forests in Turkey.]

   Color and label these water bodies on your map: The Jordan River, the Dead Sea, the Tigris River, and the Euphrates River. Make sure to review the information about the Dead Sea found in the **Beginner's World Atlas**.

2. Read **A Single Pebble** or **The Silk Route**.

   The Middle East lies at the intersection of Europe, Asia, and Africa. It was an area where travelers from the Far East and Europe met and traded. Both of these books follow travelers along the Silk Road from China east towards Europe. Track the trip on the map in the book, and perhaps on your globe. Tell your child that we will study more about China, the Mongolians, and India in the coming weeks.

   On a subsequent reading, have your child describe each place and group of people. You can ask about the clothing, the buildings, the landscape.

   Examine as many of the products traded on the Silk Road that you have available: silk, jade, sandalwood, a wooden flute, a cinnamon stick, frankincense, and/or myrrh.

DAY 2 ANCIENT MIDDLE EASTERN CULTURES MENTIONED IN THE BIBLE

EVERYONE

Explain to your child that many ancient cultures lived in the area.

> These ancient civilizations are more appropriately studied when students are much older. At this stage, you will touch on a few stories that are age-appropriate and within the context of the Judeo-Christian culture. The ancient Hebrews whose lives were chronicled in the Old Testament occurred entirely in the Middle East and Egypt.

1. Ask your child if she remembers which Hebrew led the Israelites into Egypt and which one led them out. [Answer: Joseph led them in, Moses led them out.] Discuss what they remember. Find the figures on the timeline. Trace Moses' 40-year journey in the wilderness. Find where Mt. Sinai is and add to your map.

2. Jonah goes to Nineveh (Assyria) in the 8th century B.C. Read the story of Jonah.

    a) Look at a map and find Jerusalem, Joppa, Tarshish, and Nineveh. What is the name of the river next to Nineveh? [Answer: The Tigris River.] What is the name of the sea between Jerusalem and Tarshish? [Answer: The Mediterranean Sea.]

    b) Which direction did Jonah go first? Have your child trace with her finger. After Jonah was expelled from the fish, which direction did he go? [Answer: To the west towards the Mediterranean Sea and away from Nineveh; after the fish to the east towards Nineveh.]

    c) The distance from Israel to Nineveh is 565 miles. Tell your child something or someone she would know that is about that distance from your home. How would she like to walk that distance? What does the land look like between Israel and Nineveh? [Answer: Desert.]

d) After looking at the pictures in the book, have your child describe the land and city of Israel and Jonah's home there. [Possible answers: He lives near the city of Jerusalem, that has a wall, gates, and a few towers. The people have simple clothing. They work in the fields and have donkeys.]

e) Now, have your child describe Nineveh. How is it different from Jerusalem? [Possible answers: A HUGE city with many decorative walls, gates, and elaborate art work unlike the smaller and simpler Jerusalem with just one wall. There were many fancy, large, multi-storied buildings and beautiful gardens. Some people are dressed in swankier clothes.]

f) What did the people of Nineveh do after Jonah gave them the message from God? [Answer: They repented and asked for God to forgive them.]

g) Why did Jonah not want to go to Nineveh? Why did Jonah change his mind? Why was he angry after God forgave the people of Nineveh? What happened at the end? [Answer: Jonah thought God might change His mind and forgive them. The incident with the whale made Jonah change his mind. And God did forgive these wicked people, which made Jonah mad. At the end God provided shade for Jonah, and then took it away. He taught Jonah that the people are more important than a vine, and that Jonah should rejoice for the people of Nineveh.]

h) Put a figure of Jonah on your timeline.

i) Dramatize the story of Jonah. Encourage your children to find objects you have in the home for props.

While still including the more familiar big fish part of the story, emphasize the part of the story that takes place in Nineveh. Assign someone to be Jonah, other(s) to be the sailors, who can later be the people of Nineveh. Mom can be the narrator and the voice of God.

Make sure to let the people of Nineveh be bad, hear the preaching of Jonah, and then repent. Don't leave out the part about the vine.

3. OPTIONAL: Assyrian Art. One of the famous art figures in Nineveh is the human headed, winged bull or lion. You might see this in your picture book of Jonah. A picture of this figure is available on the *GO GLOBAL* Resource page. Many children find a "mixed-up" animal interesting and might want to draw their own mixed-up animal.

ADD FOR SIX-YEAR-OLDS AND UP

4. Daniel in Babylon in the 6th century B.C. Read the story of Daniel. Discuss the points that are covered in the story you use.

    a) Look at a map and to find Jerusalem and Babylon. What is the name of the river next to Babylon? [Answer: The Euphrates River.]

    b) Why did Daniel go to Babylon? About how old was he? [Answer: Jerusalem was conquered, and Daniel was sent to Babylon as a slave. He was a teenager.]

    c) The distance from Israel to Babylon is about 700 miles. Tell your child something or someone she would know that is about that distance from your home.

d) Babylon conquered Jerusalem in 587 B.C. and so Daniel's home was probably in ruins. If using an illustrated story, have your child describe the city of Babylon. How is it different from Jerusalem? [Possible answers: Like Nineveh, it was A HUGE city with many decorative walls, gates, and elaborate art work unlike Jerusalem with just one wall. There were many fancy, large, multi-storied buildings and beautiful gardens. Some people are dressed in swankier clothes.]

e) Was Daniel afraid in Babylon? Why or why not? [Answer: No, he had immense faith in God to take care of him.]

f) Why was Daniel respected by some people in Babylon? [Answer: He was a man of conviction and honor, and was very respectful of others.]

g) Why was Daniel hated by some people in Babylon? [Answer: He was true to God, and would not compromise his faith.]

h) What happened to Daniel in Babylon? How did God protect him? [Answer: He publicly honored and prayed to God every day. Because that was against the law, some evil men had him thrown into a lion's den. But God preserved him.]

i) Put a figure of Daniel on your timeline.

j) OPTIONAL: Act out the story of Daniel.

5. OPTIONAL: Babylonian Art. Pictures are available on the *GO GLOBAL* Resource page.

   a) The Hanging Gardens of Babylon are one of the seven wonders of the world and were built around 600 B.C. The ruins have not been found, but people saw them and wrote about them in the distant past. There were multiple terraces with trees, shrubs, and flower from all over the empire. The gardens were next to the river and watered by slaves on a treadmill.

   b) The Ishtar Gate was reconstructed. The blue marble gate is decorated with bulls, dragons and lions. Ask your child why she thinks the Babylonians decorated with these animals? [Answer: They superstitiously thought the animals would protect them. The animals are fierce and would produce fear and respect to those who entered the city.]

6. Dramatize the story of Jonah or Daniel for Dad tonight!

ADD FOR SEVEN-YEAR-OLDS AND UP

7. The earliest civilizations developed in the Fertile Crescent and Mesopotamia. Find these areas on the map provided on the *GO GLOBAL* Resource page. Explain the crescent shape and talk about how the moon looks like a crescent at times. With your finger trace the "crescent" from the Persian Gulf up the Tigris and Euphrates rivers, over to Lebanon, and down the area of modern day Israel.

God directed Abraham to leave Ur of the Chaldees to go to the promised land in the 18th century B.C. Read the story of Abraham. Discuss the points that are covered in the story you use, emphasizing the travel from Ur to the Promised Land.

    a) Find the cities of Ur and Haran. Trace the path Abraham probably took to the Promised land. [Answer: Biblical Ur might be the major city south of Babylon on the Euphrates River, or it might be a smaller city north east of Haran.]

    b) Who told Abraham to move? Why did Abraham move? Who did Abraham take with him? [Answer: God told him; Abraham obeyed God; He took his wife, his nephew Lot, his workers, and his animals with him.]

    c) What kind of land did Lot choose? What kind of land did Abraham take? [Answer: Lot chose the green grasslands by the river; Abraham went to the mountain pastures.]

    d) Put the figure of Abraham on your timeline.

DAY 3 — PERSIA AND MORE

EVERYONE

1. Esther lived in Persia in the 5th century B.C. Read the story of Queen Esther. Discuss the points that are covered in the story you use.

    a) Find the city of Susa (also called Shushan), where Esther lived. This is east of Babylonia, and of the Tigris River. It is next to a river that runs into the Persian Gulf.

    b) Queen Esther was afraid to go to the king because he had not called her. What did she do to calm her fears and prepare to do the right thing? [Answer: She prayed and asked others to pray for her.]

    c) Queen Esther could have been executed when she went to see the king unbidden, unless he held out the scepter to her. Make a scepter out of chenille wire and a wooden spoon. Let Dad use the scepter at dinner tonight to allow children to speak!

    > Providing a few props (such as a scepter and crown), dress up clothes (play silks), and unscheduled time will enable your children to replay these stories on their own in their free time.

2. Learn about Persian Carpets. If possible, read the ***Legend of the Persian Carpet***.

Historians know that Persia was known for its high-quality, expensive rugs during the time of Esther. These rugs had lovely intricate patterns and bright colors. The Pzyrk carpet is dated from 400 B.C. It was preserved by being frozen in an ice block. In his painting of the Virgin and Child, Jan Van Eyck includes a Persian rug with a pattern tracing back to late Roman origins. Pictures of ancient Persian carpets and the Van Eck painting are available on the *GO GLOBAL* Resource page.

OPTIONAL: Visit a rug store to see Persian rugs.

3. Read one or more of the Persian tales listed in the secondary books, Books #2–8. Look for Persian rugs, mosaic tile work on walls and floors, gardens, turbans, Persian architecture, people sitting on cushions on the floor, beards on men, corsair pants.

DAY 4 — ISRAEL

EVERYONE

1. Tell your children that Israel is also called the Holy Land and is a very special place to Jews and Christians, as this is where both faiths were founded. Look at the globe to find Israel. Can your child name some important bodies of water in or next to Israel? [Answer: The Mediterranean Sea, the Red Sea, the Jordan River, and the Dead Sea. She might also remember the Sea of Galilee since Jesus spent so much time there.] Can your child name some cities in Israel? [Answer: Various; she should include Jerusalem.]

2. The flag of Israel is a blue star of David with blue horizontal stripes. Make a large replica of the flag by using a standard piece of white paper, two long blue strips ½" by 11", and six blue strips ½" by 5". Glue long strips 1" from top and 1' from bottom of white paper. Make two triangles out of the shorter strips of blue paper glued together to form the Star of David. Make sure your children understand the six-pointed star is made from two triangles.

    The modern State of Israel became a nation in 1948. Most countries of the world are much older. Tell your children which family members were alive at the time Israel became a nation. It might be their great grandparents. Put a small replica of the Israeli flag on 1948 on your timeline. Add a small replica of the US flag on 1776, when we became a nation.

3. Israel is famous for its olive trees. Ask your child if she remembers the other country we learned about that had olive trees. [Answer: Spain.] Read ***The Harvest of Light*** to see real pictures of modern Israel and to learn about olive harvesting.

    Eat olives again! Dip flatbread into hummus drizzled with olive oil for a delicious snack.

    OPTIONAL: Use an oil lamp at dinner tonight.

4. Discuss the Sabbath. The Jews celebrate a day of rest called the Sabbath. Most Christians go to church on Sunday because that is the day that Jesus rose from the dead. The original Sabbath was on Saturday.

Make challah bread with your child to celebrate the Sabbath meal. If possible find *It's Challah Time!* which includes an easy recipe for braided challah bread that you can make without a bread machine or mixer. Plan ahead, as this project will take some time to let the bread rise.

    a) Start by activating the yeast. Talk to your child about the yeast, and how the yeast needs warm water and something sweet to eat in order to grow!

    b) Let your child help you measure, mix, and knead the bread dough. Give each child a small amount of dough to knead. At the end add their dough to yours, knead it all together and put it in an oiled bowl, cover with a damp cloth to rise for an hour.

    c) Now read the book—the kids will be excited to see the children in the book doing what they just did, and then learn what they will do next. You can do other school work or chores while you are waiting for the dough to rise.

    d) Punch down the dough, and have your children help roll pieces into "snakes" or "ropes". Then let your children help to braid the bread. It may not look as pretty—but they will love doing the real work.

    e) Bake; cool; enjoy! There are some lovely prayers in the back of the book you can say before you eat.

> This activity is full of educational benefit—measuring, telling time, building hand strength and dexterity, the science of yeast, and understanding the Bible and cultural aspects of the Sabbath.

5. OPTIONAL: Re-read *The Chameleon That Saved Noah's Ark* (from Africa, week 17). Find Mt. Ararat on your map, put a figure for Noah on your timeline.

WEEK 29
ASIA
INDIA

BIG PICTURE

India is the seventh largest country in the world by area, and is second only to China in population, with over a billion people. It is a very diverse country with vast differences in geography, climate, culture, language, and people groups.

From the snowcapped Himalayas in the north, through the plains that are dry much of the year, and green when the seasonal monsoons arrive, to the jungle on the western coast, India is home to a variety of interesting animals such as the Indian elephant, the Bengal tiger, the mongoose, the cobra, and the national animal: the Indian peacock.

You will read classic literature such as *Rikki-Tikki-Tavi* and the poem about the Blind Men and the Elephant.

You will learn about the architecture such as the Taj Majal and the clothing, such as the sari. You will experience some of the spices and cuisine on your last day.

Some books about India include information and pictures expressing the religions of Hinduism and Buddhism. We have read all the books suggested and have noted when religious topics arise. There is a paragraph in the introduction about discussing world religions with your child. While there are magical beings in many of the legends and folklore stories, we have mostly excluded the ones that include the Hindu deities. Parents need to be careful what they expose their children to while focusing on the world's cultures so intensely.

MATERIALS

Books

1. **Beginner's World Atlas 3rd Edition**, National Geographic. 2011.
2. **The Story of Little Babaji**, Helen Bannerman. Ages 4–8. In this classic tale now correctly placed in India with fanciful illustrations, Little Babaji loses his fine clothes to tigers, who bicker, chase each other, and turn into "ghee"—clarified butter that originated in ancient India.
3. **13 Buildings Children Should Know**, Annette Roeder. Ages 8–12. While geared towards older children, this book is a gem, and could be used with younger children as they explore many buildings studied in this curriculum, including: The Taj Majal.
4. **Rikki-Tikki-Tavi**, Rudyard Kipling, adapted by Jerry Pinkney. Ages 5–8. Rikki is a fearless mongoose who protects a boy and his family from two enormous cobras who live in the family garden in India.

Secondary Books: Find *some* of these excellent books to read aloud and make available to your children for their quiet times. * means especially recommended.

1. ****Moon Bear***, Brenda Guiberson. Ages 4–8. With lyrical text and charming illustrations follow one Moon Bear in the Himalayas, the bamboo forests, and the lowlands as she eats, plays, hibernates, and wakes in the spring. Photographs and extra information on the moon bear in the end pages.
2. ****My Dadima Wears a Sari***, Kashmira Sheth. Ages 5–10. Dadima shares the wonders of wearing a sari with her granddaughters. Beautiful watercolors, information on saris, and a story of the bond of love across the generations. Instructions on wrapping a sari are included.
3. ***Monsoon Afternoon***, Kashmira Sheth. Ages 4–8. A boy and his grandfather play in the rain during the monsoon. Sweet story with illustrations that capture India. Parental warning: There is a girl praying at a shrine in one illustration and there are pictures of Indian gods in the background in another illustration. Both are understated, and while you need to be ready to explain if your child asks, we do not recommend pointing it out to your children. The end notes are delightful memories of a childhood in India.
4. ***Monsoon***, Uma Krishnawan. Ages 4–8. A child delightfully describes waiting for the monsoon rains to arrive. Illustrations add to the sense of waiting, dryness, and growing storm. Parental warning: On the last page, the family gives a coin to an idol. If you choose to use this book you should discuss the Ten Commandments and the prohibition of idols/idolatry. The end pages in this book explain more about the Indian monsoons.
5. ***Mount Everest***, Sarah De Capua. Early Reader. Short sentences and great photographs.
6. ***Bengal Tigers Are Awesome***, Megan Cooley Peterson. Ages 4–8. Nonfiction book with great photographs and just the right amount of information for this age.
7. ***Grandma and the Great Gourd: A Bengali Folktale***, Chitra Banerjee Divakaruni. Ages 5–8. Grandma outwits a fox, bear, and tiger on her trip through the jungle.
8. ***The Monkey and the Crocodile: A Jataka Tale from India***, Paul Galdone. Ages 3–7. A monkey tricks a hungry crocodile and gets to the mangos.
9. ***Elephants Never Forget***, Anushka Ravishankar. Ages 3–8. An elephant baby stays with a herd of buffaloes until he meets some other small-eared Indian elephants like him.
10. ***I'm the Scariest Thing in the Jungle***, David Derrick, Jr. Ages 3–6. Animals in the jungles of India watch Little Crocodile and Little Tiger argue over who is the scariest.
11. ***Mama's Saris***, Pooja Makhijani. Ages 3–6. A loving mother responds to her young daughter who wants to dress up in one of her mama's saris.
12. ***Same, Same, but Different***, Jenny Sue Kostecki-Shaw. Ages 4–8. Pen pals discover that though they live in different countries—America and India—they are similar.
13. ***The Rajah's Rice: A Mathematical Folktale from India,*** David Barry. Ages 5–12. Chandra saves the Rajah's elephants and earns a reward costlier than expected by the ruler. While the mathematics is difficult for young children to fully grasp, they will love the story.
    Or ***One Grain of Rice***, Demi. Ages 4–8. A village girl outwits a selfish rajah in this mathematical folktale with the exquisite art of Demi.
14. ***Elephant Dance: Memories of India***, Theresa Heine. Ages 4–7. Grandfather tells stories of India including information about the open-air markets, food, the Himalayas, and colorful folklore about the heat and the rain. Parental Warning: Disregard the end pages because the information is inaccurate and unsuitable.

15. ***Baya, Baya, Lulla-by-a***, Megan McDonald. Ages 3–6. Melodious words and artful pictures of the love of an Indian mother for her child. Animals and clothing from India!

SUPPLIES

1. Globe
2. Map of Asia used the last two weeks
3. Elephant drawing: art paper and colored pencils
4. Spices from your cabinet: cinnamon, cumin, turmeric, coriander, garam masala, saffron, cloves, and/or chili powder
5. Ingredients for the Indian meal: Naan bread (or pita if naan is unavailable), chicken breasts, onion, carrot, zucchini, tomatoes, cilantro, cucumber, bananas, mango, garlic, frozen peas, plain yogurt, milk, eggs, rice, sugar, white flour, vegetable stock, oil, dried coconut, raisins, chopped nuts, garam masala, ground coriander, turmeric, cinnamon, nutmeg; Optional: chili powder, saffron, mint, cardamom

   OR a local Indian restaurant

DAY 1 · HIMALAYAS AND MONSOONS

EVERYONE

1. Find India on your *GO GLOBAL* mat, then your map of Asia. Look at pages 40–44 in the ***Beginner's World Atlas.*** What are the major habitats in India? [Answer: Grasslands in the middle, deciduous forests in the east, desert in the north west, and jungle along the western coast.]

   Ask your child if he remembers the name of the ocean around India. [Answer: The Indian Ocean.] Add the major river in India: the Ganges.

   Tell your children that India is the second-most populous country in the world! Three of the largest cities in India are: New Delhi, Calcutta, and Mumbai (Bombay). Add these cities to your map.

2. Ask your child if he remembers the name of the mountains on the northern border of India. Ask him if he remembers the name of the tallest mountain in the world. [Answer: The Himalayan Mountains, Mt. Everest.] Mt. Everest is covered with snow and glaciers all year long. Read ***Moon Bear*** now if you have the book.

3. Monsoons are a seasonal reversal of winds which brings periodic rains. These rains turn large portions of India from a semi-desert into green lands. Read one of the picture books about monsoons or look for them mentioned in other books you have. The grasslands in much of India are brown and dusty much of the year. Look for the dusty land in your picture books.

DAY 2 — ELEPHANTS AND TIGERS

EVERYONE

1. Discuss Indian elephants with your child. Compare the pictures of an Indian elephant with an African elephant that are available on the *GO GLOBAL* Resource page. Ask your child to tell you how they are different. Some differences are obvious, others you may need to share.

    a) The Indian elephant has much smaller ears. A fun way to remember which elephant goes with which area is to notice the African elephant has large ears shaped like the large continent of Africa. The Indian elephant has small ears shaped like the smaller country of India.

    b) The Indian elephant is smaller and weighs less.

2. Read the poem of the Blind Men and the Elephant.

The Blind Men and the Elephant

John Godfrey Saxe (1816–1887)

It was six men of Indostan
To learning much inclined,
Who went to see the Elephant
Though all of them were blind,
That each by observation
Might satisfy his mind.

The *First* approached the Elephant,
And happening to fall
Against his broad and sturdy side,
At once began to bawl:
"God bless me, but the Elephant
Is very like a WALL!"

The *Second*, feeling the tusk,
Cried, "Ho, what have we here,
So very round and smooth and sharp?
To me 'tis very clear
This wonder of an Elephant
Is very like a SPEAR!"

The *Third* approached the animal,
And happening to take
The squirming trunk within his hands,
Thus boldly up and spake:
"I see," quoth he, "The Elephant
Is very like a SNAKE!"

The *Fourth* reached out an eager hand,
And felt about the knee:
"What most this wondrous beast is like
Is mighty plain," quoth he:
"'Tis clear enough the Elephant
Is very like a TREE!"

The *Fifth*, who chanced to touch the ear,
Said: "Even the blindest man
Can tell what this resembles most;
Deny the fact who can,
This marvel of an Elephant
Is very like a FAN!"

The *Sixth* no sooner had begun
About the beast to grope,
Than seizing on the swinging tail
That fell within his scope,
"I see," quoth he, "the Elephant
Is very like a ROPE!"

And so these men of Indostan
Disputed loud and long,
Each in his own opinion
Exceeding stiff and strong,
Though each was partly in the right,
And all were in the wrong!

    a) Ask your child what the six men found and how they each are correct, and are also all wrong.

    b) Draw a picture of the elephant. The *GO GLOBAL* Resource page has a tutorial if you would like more structure for this art activity.

    c) Could you be an elephant? Use only one arm and tape the fingers (but not thumb) together. What are you still able to do? What can you no longer do?

3. Read ***The Story of Little Babaji***. This is a story placed in the jungles of India, and features one of the most beautiful big cats in the world: the Bengal tiger. Enjoy reading the book out loud. On subsequent readings point out that Mama wears a sari and Papa wears a turban and Nehru jacket. The boy wears short harem pants and shoes turned up at the toes.

    Put on a dramatic play of Little Babaji.

4. OPTIONAL: Read other books about animals in India from the Secondary Book list #4–8.

DAY 3 — MONGOOSE, COBRAS, BRITISH INFLUENCE, AND DAILY LIFE

EVERYONE

1. Read **Rikki-Tikki-Tavi**.

    a) Remind your child that the British came to India and had a strong presence there. English is one of the two official languages of India. India peacefully gained its independence from England in 1947.

    b) Rudyard Kipling was born in 1865 in Bombay, British India. After being educated in England he returned to India at age 17. He was one of the most popular writers in the UK, and his poems and books are still standard pieces of literature! You read the Just So Stories while studying Africa. Unlike the Disney movies/books, the unabridged Jungle Book by Kipling is a series of short stories geared more for 11-years-old and up. This picture book about Rikki-Tikki-Tavi is wonderful for the younger children.

    c) Discuss with your children. How would you describe Rikki? How would the father in the story describe Rikki? How would his wife describe Rikki? How would Teddy describe Rikki? Would their description have changed from the beginning of the story to the end of the story? Understanding emotions and thoughts of people can be difficult for young children. Use the book and illustrations to help your child. Point out the mother's face when she saw Rikki in her son's bed. Perhaps reread that page. Then, have your child explain the mom's thoughts and feelings. [Answer: The man knew what a mongoose was like and described him accurately. A creature that will respond well to humans, run about, and keep Teddy safe. The wife was kind and wanted to save Rikki's life, but thought Rikki might hurt Teddy. Teddy thought Rikki was dead at first, and then thought he was friendly and playful. After Rikki killed the snakes, everyone considered Rikki brave, strong, fearless, and a protector of their lives.]

    d) Was Rikki afraid? Why? How did he overcome his fear? [Yes, he was afraid because the cobra was so big. He realized that he needed to break the cobra's back on the first jump. He killed the smaller snake first which gave him confidence. He closed his jaws and locked them so that even if he was banged to death, he would not let go of the cobra.]

2. Read other books about life in India from the secondary list of books #7–13. Look for saris, bindis (the little jewel Indian women wear between their eyebrows), Indian architecture (like the Taj Majal), peacocks (the national bird of India), camels, elephants (with small ears), monkeys, cobras, rickshaws, palm trees, the Himalaya mountains, turbans, rice, rajahs (king-like rulers).

DAY 4 — TAJ MAJAL AND INDIAN FOOD

EVERYONE

1. Start your day with an Indian smoothie called **Sweet Lassi.**

    Ingredients
    - 6 ice cubes
    - 1 mango
    - ¾ C. plain yogurt
    - 2 tsp. sugar
    - Optional: mint, saffron, or cardamom

    Directions
    1. Crush ice.
    2. Puree peeled, pitted, chopped mango and sugar.
    3. Add crushed ice and yogurt. Blend.
    4. Pour over additional ice.
    5. Optional: garnish with mint, or a pinch of saffron or cardamom.

2. Learn about the Taj Majal by reading **13 Buildings Children Should Know**, pages 24–25. Read and enjoy the lovely building. If possible show your child some marble stone. Does he remember where we saw onion domes before? [Answer: Russian Orthodox churches.]

3. The food in southern India includes very spicy dishes balanced with cool, refreshing ones. Coconut milk and flakes, fresh garlic, and fresh ginger are used in many dishes. Popular fruits include mangos, raisins, dates, and bananas.

    Spices are used widely and essential for many dishes. The most common are cinnamon, cumin, turmeric, coriander, garam masala, saffron, cloves, and chili powder.

    Have your child learn about the various Indian spices that you have on hand, by noticing their color, smelling their fragrance, and taking a bit of a taste. (Don't taste the chili powder—it would be too hot!) Which fragrances and flavors are his favorites? Later in the day see if he can name any of the spices by just a sniff.

4. Fix an Indian meal for dinner or go out to an Indian restaurant for a new experience. There is a great variety of regional and traditional cuisines in India, and India has been influenced by other nations since it was on the route between the east and the west. As mentioned above India includes very spicy dishes balanced with cool, refreshing ones. Rice and lentils are in many of their dishes. Indian people often eat using a piece of bread as a scoop. Purchase and use Naan Bread (or pita bread) instead of utensils.

    Encourage your children to take a bite of each dish and to expand their palate. Have them imagine what it would be like to be an Indian child. Would they eat on the floor?

Raita (Serves 4) Make this first and refrigerate until ready to serve.

Ingredients

- 1 C. plain yogurt
- 2 Tbsp. fresh cilantro
- ½ tsp. nutmeg
- 2 Tbsp. golden raisins

Directions

1. Finely chop cilantro and add it with the nutmeg to the yogurt.
2. Add the raisins and refrigerate until ready to serve.

Chicken Bhuna (Serves 4)

Ingredients

- 2 boneless, skinless chicken breasts
- 1 onion
- 1 clove garlic
- 3 tomatoes
- 1 Tbsp. oil
- ½ tsp. each: garam masala, ground coriander, turmeric
- ¼ tsp. chili powder (optional, as it will make it spicy-hot)
- 1 oz. dried coconut

Directions

1. Cut chicken into bite sized pieces.
2. Peel and finely chop onion and garlic.
3. Chop tomatoes in small pieces.
4. Heat oil over medium heat. Add onion, garlic, and spices. Fry for 5 minutes.
5. Add chicken pieces and tomatoes. Cook for 20 minutes.

Vegetable Biryani (Serves 4)

Ingredients

- ½ medium onion
- 1 clove garlic
- ½ carrot
- 1 medium zucchini
- 2 C. of vegetable stock, or 1 vegetable bouillon cube dissolved in 2 C. water
- 1 Tbsp. oil
- 1 tsp. ground cinnamon
- ½ tsp. each turmeric, garam masala
- ½ C. rice
- ½ C. frozen peas, thawed
- ½ C. chopped mixed nuts
- ½ C. raisins

Directions

1. Peel and finely chop onion and garlic.
2. Wash and cut carrot and zucchini in small pieces; set aside.
3. Heat oil over medium heat. Add onion, garlic, and spices. Fry for 3 minutes.
4. Add rice and fry for another 5 minutes, stirring constantly.
5. Add stock. Stir well, reduce heat to low, and cover. Simmer for about 10 minutes.
6. Add chopped vegetables and peas. Simmer an additional 10 minutes, stirring occasionally, until all the liquid has been soaked up and the rice is soft.
7. Stir in chopped nuts and raisins.

For dessert serve **fresh fruit**, or if you are ambitious make: **Banana Fritters**

Ingredients

- 2 eggs
- 1 Tbsp. sugar
- 2 Tbsp. white flour
- 2/3 cup milk
- 3 bananas
- 1 Tbsp. oil

Directions

1. Beat eggs until well mixed. Add sugar, flour, and milk. Mix well.
2. Add peeled and sliced bananas to the egg mixture.
3. Heat oil over medium heat. Spoon mixture into frying pan and gently fry for 5 minutes. Turn it over and cook the other side for about 5 minutes.
4. Slide onto plate and cut into four pieces.

WEEK 30
ASIA
CHINA

BIG PICTURE

China is the most populous country in the world and the second largest country by land area. China has diverse landscape from the Gobi Desert in the west, to the Himalaya Mountains in the southwest, to warm humid forests in the southeast, to the Yangtze River and Yellow River. You will visit these and other areas of China through the book **Adèle and Simon in China.**

As one of the world's earliest civilizations, China is rich in history and culture. You will learn about the Great Wall, and some very important inventions, discoveries, and developments that emerged in Ancient China, such as silk, drinking tea, gunpowder (and firecrackers), paper making, printing, the paint brush, porcelain, terraced fields for farming, the umbrella, and the kite.

You will learn about both of China's two national symbols: the dragon and the giant panda.

MATERIALS

Books

1. **Lost and Found: Adèle and Simon in China**, Barbara McClintock. Ages 4–8. The siblings tour China, while Simon loses his possessions and Adèle sends postcards to their mom. Endnotes include information about each location. This is a spine book—it introduces silk, pandas, the Great Wall, Peking/Beijing, the Forbidden City, and more!
2. **The Story about Ping**, Marjorie Flack. Ages 4–8. The classic tale of a little duck alone on the Yangtze River is sweet, funny, and endearing.
3. **Mrs. Harkness and the Panda**, Alicia Potter. Ages 5–8. True story of the brave woman who travels to China in 1934 to find and bring back a panda bear to the USA. Lovely illustrations, story, maps, and message.

Secondary Books: Find *some* of these excellent books to read aloud and make available to your children for their quiet times. * means especially recommended.

1. *****The Silk Princess**, Charles Santore. Ages 4–8. After a cocoon falls into her teacup and unravels to form a long, delicate thread, a princess in ancient China learns how to transform the cocoons into silk. This lovely legend is beautifully illustrated.
2. *****The Nian Monster**, Andrea Wang. Ages 4–8. Legendary dragon returns for the Chinese New Year and is defeated by a little girl with traditions of the holiday.
3. *****The Paper Dragon**, Marguerite W. Davol. Ages 5–8. The humble artist agrees to face a dragon to save his village. Wonderful theme that peacefully conquers the dragon and fabulous illustrations by Robert Sabuda. Parental Advisory: mentions "heroes and gods" which is easily shortened to just heroes.

4. ***Panda Kindergarten***, Joanne Ryder. Ages 4–8. Photo essay of pandas being raised in a Chinese nature reserve.
5. ***The Magic Horse of Han Gan***, Chen Jiang Hong. Ages 4–8. An extraordinary Chinese artist from the 11th century whose paintings became real, according to legend. Wonderful illustrations!
6. ***The Empty Pot***, Demi. Ages 4–8. Ping tries to grow flowers for the Emperor but ends up with an empty pot in this tale of honesty rewarded.
7. ***Daisy Comes Home***, Jan Brett. Ages 5–8. An unhappy hen accidentally floats away from home, meets various inhabitants, is captured by a fisherman, and learns courage before being found by her owner Mei Mei. Ms. Brett was inspired by The Story of Ping.
8. ***Seven Chinese Brothers***, Margaret Mahy. Ages 4–8. Tall tale of seven brothers who look alike, have unique abilities, and outwit the Emperor who built the Great Wall of China.
9. **My Little Round House**, Helen Mixter and Bolormaa Baasansuren. Ages 4–7. Baby Jilu recounts his first year in a nomadic Mongolian community.
10. **Adventures of the Treasure Fleet: China Discovers the World**, Ann Martin Bowler. Ages 7–12. Eighty-five years before Columbus, Chinese ships longer that a football field traveled all the way to Africa and visited more than 30 nations. This fast-paced story will delight children and impart a lot of information, too.
11. **Bitter Dumplings**, Jeanne Lee. Ages 5–8. After her father dies, a young woman struggles to survive with the help of an old woman. The Treasure Fleet is part of the story.
12. **The Greatest Power**, Demi. Ages 6–8. Emperor Ping challenges the children of his kingdom to show him the greatest power in the world. Spoiler: The answer is not power, nor beauty, nor technology, nor money. The answer is the force of Life which a girl found in the lotus seed. Parental Warning: Evil spirit masks scaring away the enemy are mentioned and pictured. A statue of the money god, Guan Yu, is mentioned and portrayed. The book states that eternal life is in the seed. Renewing life is in the seed, but eternal life is only found in Jesus. If you use this book, have this crucial conversation.
13. **The Emperor and the Kite**, Jane Yolen. Ages 4–8. Youngest and smallest princess is ignored by all, but saves the emperor with her love, loyalty, courage, and kite.
14. **The Legend of the Kite: A Story of China**, Chen Jiang Hong. Ages 4–8. A boy builds and flies a kite with his grandfather and learns the legend behind the making of the first kite.
15. **The Story of Chopsticks**, Ying Chang Compestine. Ages 3–8. Wanting to eat more, the youngest brother uses sticks to grab food quickly while it is still too hot for the others to touch. Funny fictional story of the origin of chopsticks. If you like this one, find the others in the series about the energetic and slightly naughty Chinese brothers fancifully inventing Chinese items: **The Story of Noodles**, **The Story of Paper**, and **The Story of Kites**.
16. **Ma Jiang and the Orange Ants,** Barbara Ann Porte. Ages 5–8. When her father and brothers are taken to be in the army, Ma Jiang finds a way to trap the orange ants and continue to provide for her mother and little brother.
17. **Liang and the Magic Paintbrush**, Demi. Ages 4–8. A poor boy is given a magical paintbrush that brings to life whatever he paints.
18. **Red is a Dragon: A Book of Colors**, Roseanne Thong. Ages 3–6. Rhyming book of Chinese objects arranged by color.
19. **Lanterns and Firecrackers: A Chinese New Year Story,** Jonny Zucker. Ages 2–5. Simple introduction to the Chinese New Year celebration.
20. **The Treasure Chest, A Chinese Tale**, Rosalind Wang. Ages 4–8. A rainbow hued magic fish helps a peasant boy protect his bride-to-be.

SUPPLIES

1. Globe
2. Map of Asia used the last three weeks
3. 30 small cards with "100 million people" printed on them; Printable available on the *GO GLOBAL* Resource page
4. Clock that audibly ticks the seconds
5. *GO GLOBAL* Game
6. A silk scarf, or another piece of fine silk
7. Supplies to build the Great Wall
8. Panda art: red (or other brightly colored) card stock, white paint, fork, white and black construction paper, black marker
9. Mrs. Harkness and panda timeline figure available on the *GO GLOBAL* Resource page.
10. Materials for your choice of activity on Day 4

DAY 1   GEOGRAPHY, SILK, AND POPULATION

EVERYONE

1. China is the third largest country in the world, after Russia and Canada. Look at the shape of China on the globe or your Asia map. Ask your child if she can see the shape of an animal in the outline of China. Perhaps the western portion is the tail, and the northeastern portion in the head. Many people see the shape of a rooster!

   Review the habitats in China by looking in the **Beginner's World Atlas**. About 1/3 of China is covered with mountains, including the Himalayas on its southwestern border. The Gobi Desert, some grasslands in the north, the forests in the northeast, and the rainforest in the southeast round out the vast variety of land types in China. Add the Yangtze River and the Yellow River to your map.

2. Read **Lost and Found: Adèle and Simon in China**. On the first read through your child will probably just want to hunt for the items that Simon has lost. Read multiple times so your child starts to see more: how the people are dressed, the architecture, the city, the countryside, the animals, et.al. Mark Hong Kong on your map.

3. Simon and Adèle visit a silk farm on their first day. Look at that page spread again. Remind your children about learning about the Silk Road when we studied Italy and again when we studied the Middle East. We are finally at the home of the silk industry!

   Chinese tradition is that sometime around 3000 BC a silk worm's cocoon fell into the tea cup of the Empress Leizu, and she unrolled the thread, saw how beautiful and strong it was, and had it woven into fabric. Tell your child the story (details are in the end pages of Adèle and Simon) or read the **Silk Princess**. Let your child handle some silk to see how light, lovely, and shimmery it is.

ADD FOR SIX-YEAR-OLDS AND UP

4. China has the largest population in the world: about 1.4 billion people! India is second with about with 1.25 billion. The United States' population is a distant third with only 335 million. These numbers are so huge, they are incomprehensible even to adults. Print cards (available on the *GO GLOBAL* Resource page) that read "100 million people." On your *GO GLOBAL* game map put 14 cards on China, 12½ cards on India, and only 3 cards on the US.

   Older children might be interested in understanding how big a million is. Let them listen to the ticking of a clock. They might even count the seconds. After they count for a while, let them know they would need to count continually for TWELVE days to reach just one million.

DAY 2   THE STORY OF PING, PEKING/BEIJING, AND THE GREAT WALL

EVERYONE

1. Read **The Story of Ping.** Enjoy the story first. Afterwards and on subsequent reads, discuss.

   a) Ask your child if she can remember the name of the river Ping lives on. [Answer: Yangtze.] Can she remember how Ping described the boat he lived on? [Answer: Boat with two wise eyes or the wise-eyed boat.]

   b) Why did Ping not get on the wise-eyed boat that one evening? [Answer: Because he was going to be last and did not want to be last and get a swat.] You might need to ask your child a series of questions. If she says, "because he did not want a swat," follow up with. "why would he get a swat?" It would be good to remember all the way back to the fact that Ping was swimming upside down and did not hear the call to come home.

   c) Ask to see if your child understands that people lived on their boats. Look in **Adèle and Simon** for pictures of families living on boats. [Answer: Pages 14–15, which is also on the Yangtze River. The boats are bringing produce to market, but also have wives and children on board. Pages 30–31 show fishing boats and a tourist boat.] Your child might want to discuss cormorant fishing which is in both books. More details are in the end pages of **Adèle and Simon**.

   d) How did Ping get caught by the boy? Why did the boy have a barrel on his back? [Answer: He was eating the trail of rice cakes and finally grabbed the rice cake from the boy's hand. The boy had a barrel on his back so he would float and not drown.]

   e) Why was Ping willing to take a spank to get back on the wise-eyed boat at the end of the story? [Answer: To be safe and, most of all, to be with his family. Ping had acquired wisdom.]

   f) OPTIONAL: Read **Daisy Come Home**, which was inspired by Ping. Daisy meets a water buffalo, red tailed monkeys, cormorants, goes to market, and learns a lesson of her own—to be courageous and confident. This book is a visual delight of life in China!

2. The capital of China is Beijing, which was known as Peking in 1905 when Adèle and Simon visited. Look at pages 16–17 which show Peking in the early part of the 20th century. Have your child find the musicians and acrobats. Have her describe the instruments and the performances. [Answer: There are instruments that look like a flute, a recorder, drums, a guitar, a fiddle. The performers are jugglers, acrobats, and plate twirlers.] Ask her to name some of the things being sold in this picture. [Answer: Cooked food, fresh vegetables and fruit, kites, clothing, fans.] Mark Beijing on your map.

3. Learn about the Great Wall of China by looking first at pages 18–19 in **Adèle and Simon**. The Great Wall of China is the longest man-made structure on earth, comprised of 4,000 miles of stone walls and towers. Portions of the wall were built from the 8th to 5th centuries BC. Earlier walls continually eroded and were repaired and expanded. The Great Wall was greatly restored and expanded using bricks and stones in the 15th century AD. The Great Wall is built on the crest of mountains, making it an effective barrier and watchtower, but also making it very difficult to build and maintain.

   Build a model of the Great Wall. Make a "mountain chain" out of boxes and cover with a sheet. Have the child build a wall along the crest of the mountain using any combination of blocks, Duplos, Legos, etc. You may need to give her some tape to hold the blocks together over the uneven terrain. That would be a good time to tell her that the Chinese usually used a traditional cement, but at times used sticky rice to hold the blocks together. Challenge her to build a wall that can have a small car(t) wheel across. If your child is young make the mountain top be more even to minimize frustration as she builds.

ADD FOR SIX-YEAR-OLDS AND UP

4. Read an additional book or two on China. Look for Chinese architecture, especially the pagoda with its turned-up roofs. A pagoda is a tiered tower with multiple eaves found mostly in Nepal, China, Japan, India, and southeast Asia. Photographs are available on the *GO GLOBAL* Resource page.

DAY 3   PANDAS AND MONGOLIA

EVERYONE

1. Giant pandas capture the imagination of children and adults alike for their unusual coloring and engaging personalities. Re-read pages 26–27 in **Adèle and Simon** and an additional book on pandas such as **Panda Kindergarten**. Discuss these facts with your child.

    a) Pandas are herbivores; they eat bamboo almost exclusively. One panda eats between 26–84 pounds of bamboo per day! Because of the loss of the bamboo forests, pandas now live in just a few areas of central China and are an endangered species.

    b) A newborn panda is the size of a stick of butter, and an adult can weigh as much as 200 pounds. Have your child hold a stick of butter, then name a man whom they know who weighs about 200 pounds.

c) Pandas make many sounds and are so cute! You can find links to some short videos on the *GO GLOBAL* Resource page.

2. Read **Mrs. Harkness and the Panda**. This sweetly illustrated true story of bringing the first panda to America is a delightful read for all ages. Make sure to look at the maps and trace her voyage. Perhaps your child can finger-walk her voyage on the *GO GLOBAL* Game mat. Add Mrs. Harkness figure to your timeline.

3. Paint a portrait of a panda bear. Tutorial available on the *GO GLOBAL* Resource page.

Materials

- Fork
- White paint
- Red card stock
- Black and white paper
- Scissors and glue

Process

a) Dip forks into white paint and starting in the middle of the paper, pull away towards the edge. You will end up making a round face shape.

b) Cut ears, eyes, nose and mouth. Glue to make a panda face.

4. The nomadic tribes of Mongolia lived in portable round tents to be able to follow their grazing herds. Re-read pages 20–21 in **Adèle and Simon** and drink some hot milk tea.

HOT MILK TEA (3–4 servings)

The Mongolians did not use sweetener, Adding salt instead. Most children will prefer this recipe.

Ingredients

- 12 oz. water
- 4 tea bags or 4–6 oz. loose-leaf tea, oolong is recommended
- 8 oz. whole or 2% milk
- 2–4 tsp. sugar or honey

Directions

1. Boil water.
2. Pour water over tea in teapot. Cover and steep for 3 to 5 minutes. Gradually add the milk as the tea steeps, stirring gently after each addition. Do not add the milk all at once.
3. Remove the tea bag, or strain if using loose leaf. Pour into cups.
4. Add sweetener and enjoy.

   Parents and older students might be struck with the resemblance of Star Wars' Queen Amidala to this culture.

5. OPTIONAL: Read *My Little Round House*, if you have it, to understand more about the Mongolian culture.

DAY 4   CHINESE TECHNOLOGY AND INVENTIONS

EVERYONE

1. Some very important inventions emerged in Ancient China, as are listed in the Big Picture for this week. Look at a few more of them in the spine book. Pick *one or two* to study, and do *one* hands-on activity.

    a) Tell your child that the Ancient Chinese invented paper and paint brushes. Look for examples of these in **Adèle and Simon**. [Answer: On pages 8–9 there is a store with brushes, paper, and ink; On pages 24–25 a monk is teaching Simon how to write Chinese calligraphy.]

    Hope

    OPTIONAL: Read **The Paper Dragon**, **The Story of Paper**, **The Magic Horse of Han Gan**, and/or **Liang and the Magic Paintbrush** to learn more about the paper and art of China.

    Paint some Chinese symbols.

    b) The ancient Chinese were the first to develop kites usually made of paper. Learn about Chinese kites by reading **The Emperor and the Kite** and/or **The Legend of the Kite**.

    Faith

    Fly a kite.

    c) The ancient Chinese were the first to develop the fan, made from paper, feathers, or silk. Earliest examples are dated to over 3000 years ago, and the Chinese folding fan is made from paper or silk and painted. Ask your child to find fans and umbrellas in **Adèle and Simon**. [Answer: On pages 8–9 there is a store with different kinds of fans; on pages 16–17 there are several fans.] Read **The Paper Dragon** to see the important role a fan played. Can your child find fans in other books about China?

    Love

    Make a Chinese fan or paint a purchased fan. Tutorial and links to purchase fans available on the *GO GLOBAL* Resource page.

    d) The ancient Chinese developed terrace fields so they could grow crops on their hilly and mountainous countryside. The Longheng terraces pictured on page 32–33 of **Adèle and Simon** were started in the 11th century AD. Discuss the information in the back pages of the book, making mention that their primary crop is rice. Are there pictures of terraced farming in your other books? If weather permits, find a slope and make terraces to see the difference it makes when it is watered.

Make sticky rice and try to eat with chopsticks after reading *The Story of Chopsticks*.

e) The Chinese invented a rudimentary gunpowder as early as 142 AD. though it was not perfected for many centuries. Your children will find firecrackers or fireworks the most interesting use of gun powder.

Make a fireworks painting using a wax-coated black paper plate, glue, salt, and water color paint. Tutorial available on the *GO GLOBAL* Resource page.

2. If your children are into dragons… and who isn't?... look at the dragon in **Adèle and Simon** on the page before the title page. How is the Chinese dragon different from a "European" dragon? If needed, look at the picture of a typical western dragon available on the *GO GLOBAL* Resource page. [Answer: The European dragon is a reptile-like animal with four legs and a separate set of wings. Chinese dragons are skinny, snake-like creatures, with four legs and typically no wings.] Read any other books that feature Chinese dragons that you got from the secondary list of books.

WEEK 31
ASIA
JAPAN

BIG PICTURE

Japan is an island nation which lies off the east coast of the Asian mainland. It is made up of over 6,800 islands, though the four main islands have 97% of the population. Most of Japan is mountainous and forested. The population is densely located in coastal areas. Tokyo, the capital of Japan, is the most populous metropolitan area in the world, with over 37.8 million people.

Japan is a volcanic zone on the "Pacific Ring of Fire" and has 108 active volcanoes! It is an area of many major earthquakes and tsunamis. Mount Fuji is the highest mountain in Japan with an exceptionally symmetrical cone which is snowcapped several months a year and is a well-known symbol of Japan.

This week you and your children will discover Japanese gardens with bonsai trees, lotus blossoms, cherry trees, and koi ponds. You will learn about the art of Japan including calligraphy, brush paintings, flower arrangements, and origami. You will see and experience some Japanese customs such as removing shoes when entering a home, greeting one another with a bow, kneeling on pillows at low tables, the tea ceremony, and the traditional clothing of kimonos, geta sandals, and obi sashes.

Japan is well known for its customs, manners, and order. All week you will practice Japanese etiquette culminating with a tea ceremony.

MATERIALS

Books

1. ***Dodsworth in Tokyo***, Tim Egan. Easy Reader. Screwball comedy of a trip to Tokyo!
2. ***How My Parents Learned to Eat***, Ina Friedman. Ages 4–8. American sailor courts a Japanese woman, and each learn the other's way of eating.

Secondary Books: Find *some* of these excellent books to read aloud and make available to your children for their quiet times. * means especially recommended.

1. *****Grass Sandals: The Travels of Basho***, Dawnine Spivak. Ages 6–9. Illustrated by Demi. Beautiful story of Basho traveling through Japan and writing haiku poems. Book includes maps and Japanese characters that represent words from the verses.
2. *****Turtle Bay***, Saviour Pirotta. Ages 4–8. Friendship tale of an old man and a boy observing the sea turtles lay their eggs.
3. *****The Invisible Seam***, Andy W. Frew. Ages 6–10. A wise and compassionate young girl is an apprentice to a kimono seamstress and finds her calling, a new family, and friends.

4. ***Manjiro: The Boy Who Risked His Life for Two Countries,*** Emily Arnold McCully. Ages 6–10. Picture book biography of a 14-year-old Japanese boy who is lost at sea in 1841, rescued by an American whaler, and eventually returned to Japan. Book includes maps and end notes.
5. ***Basho and the River Stones***, Tim Myers. Ages 5–9. A fox tricks the haiku master Basho into giving him all the cherries from his tree. But all turns out well in the end.
6. ***Jiro's Pearl***, Daniel Powers. Ages 4–8. A boy's courageous adventure discovering the rewards of duty, trust, and generosity.
7. *Erika-San*, Allen Say. Ages 4–9. An American girl seeks adventure in Japan. Sweet fairytale with Japanese landscape, dress, and tea ceremony.
8. *The Kamishibai Man*, Allen Say. Ages 4–9. Moving tale of an elderly storyteller who returns to his neighborhood to tell his story one more time.
9. **One Leaf Rides the Wind**, Celeste Mannis. Ages 4–8. Enchanting counting book using haiku poems follows a Japanese girl as she explores a garden and discovers Japanese culture.
10. *The Origami Master*, Nathaniel Lachenmeyer. Ages 4–8. An origami master finds exquisite origami animals on his desk. Can he find the amazing artist?
11. ***A Pair of Red Clogs***, Masako Matsuno. Ages 5–8. Japanese girl cracks her new red clogs and almost does a dishonest thing.
12. *Suki's Kimono*, Chieri Uegaki. Ages 4–8. Modern story of a Japanese-American girl who wears a kimono and geta (traditional wooden clogs) to school.
13. *The Sea Maidens of Japan*, Lili Bell. Ages 6–11. A young girl struggles to follow her mother as a sea diver.
14. *The Stonecutter: a Japanese Folk Tale*, Gerald McDermott. Ages 5–9. Story of a man who wants more and more. Cautionary tale of ambition gone wrong.
15. *Three Samurai Cats: A Story from Japan*, Eric Kimmel. Ages 5–9. Samurai cats attempt to vanquish the rat that invades the castle.
16. *Yoko's Paper Cranes*, Rosemary Wells. Ages 3–6. Yoko misses her home and family in Japan and makes origami for her grandmother's birthday.
17. *Yoshi's Feast*, Kimiko Kajikawa. Ages 4–8. The fan maker and eel broiler become friends in this fanciful tale.
18. *The Way We Do It in Japan*, Geneva C. Iijima. Ages 4–8. Gregory moves to his father's homeland, Japan, and learns about the culture while attending school.
19. Nonfiction book on Japan such as: ***Japan: Rookie Read-About Geography***, David F. Marx, Easy Reader; or ***Look What Came From Japan***, Miles Harvey. Ages 7–10.

SUPPLIES

1. Globe
2. Map of Asia used the last four weeks
3. *GO GLOBAL* Game
4. Japanese flag: white and red construction paper
5. Windsock supplies: koi fish template (available on *GO GLOBAL* Resource page) printed on cardstock, crayons/colored pencils/paint, orange tissue paper or streamer, string
6. Chopsticks
7. Tea ceremony—green tea, tea cups, whisk, sweetener, Optional: Tea cakes
8. Origami: 4"x 4" pieces of brightly colored thin paper, or 21"x 21" thin paper such as newsprint or wrapping paper

DAY 1   GEOGRAPHY AND OVERVIEW

EVERYONE

1. Find Japan on your map of Asia. Tell your child that Japan is made up of many islands. Have him point out the four large ones. Mention that there are hundreds of smaller islands that are also part of Japan.

    Ask him to name the ocean to the east of Japan. [Answer: Pacific Ocean.] Mention that the water between Japan and the rest of Asia is called the Sea of Japan.

    Mark Tokyo on your map. This capital city is the most populous metropolitan area in the world with over 13.84 million people (2018). Compare that with the largest metropolitan area in your state. For instance, NYC has a population of over 8.7 million and Phoenix metropolitan has a population of over 4.1 million.

2. Mount Fuji is one of the most famous mountains in the world, having an exceptionally symmetrical, often snowcapped cone. It is the highest mountain in Japan and is a well-known symbol of Japan frequently depicted in art and photographs. See the *GO GLOBAL* Resource page for some images of Mt. Fuji and look for images of Mt. Fuji in your books.

3. China and Japan can seem to be similar, but they are different countries, cultures, and languages. Encourage your child to notice how they are different and similar during this week.

4. Read **Dodsworth in Tokyo** to see our old friends visiting a new country. The Japanese like customs, manners, and order.

    a) This week greet one another with a bow. Practice right now, since your child has probably not done this.

    b) Say sayonara (goodbye) and bow whenever you leave—even if you just leave the room. Practice now!

    c) Take off your shoes whenever you enter a home.

    d) Tell your child that at the end of the week we are going to have a Japanese tea ceremony. Talk about Dodsworth's tea ceremony. This is a day dreaming day!

    Discuss with your child what you would like to add to your ceremony. Shall you have costumes? Does he have any ideas on what you could use for the costumes? Where could you have the tea ceremony? Encourage answers that talk about sitting on the floor or cushions.

    Make some tea now (without the ceremony) and read some of the Japan books to your children. They might look for examples and details about the Tea Ceremony.

ADD FOR SIX-YEAR-OLDS AND UP

5. Make a Japanese flag. It is a white background with a large red circle. Ask your child to guess what the circle represents. [Answer: The rising sun. Japan is called the Land of the Rising Sun because it is east of the continent of Asia and the people on the continent would see the sun rising over Japan.]

DAY 2   CLOTHING, FOOD, ART

EVERYONE

1. Read several of the secondary books to enjoy the stories. On additional readings, point out, or have your children find *some* of the following. This is an activity that should be spread out over the week.

    a) The unique clothing and hairstyles. See if they remember the names: kimono, obi, geta (sandals). Are there any umbrellas or fans? Japanese typically have straight black hair—which both men and women many times wear in buns.

    b) The food and manner of eating. Is there tea in every book? Look for and discuss sushi, sukiyaki, rice, soy sauce, fish/ tempura, wagashi, chop sticks, sitting on your knees on pillows with a low table.

    c) The buildings and the outdoors. Pagodas with their distinctive roofs, paper walls, mats on the floors, leaving their shoes outside or just inside the door. The lovely Japanese lanterns, the gardens, the lotus blossoms, the koi fish, the beautiful shape of Mt. Fuji, and the cherry blossoms are in several of the books.

    d) The arts. Japanese calligraphy and letters, the brush painting, origami, floral arrangements, bonsai trees, kites, and taiko drums. Sports such as sumo wrestling and the martial arts such as judo and karate.

2. Make koi windsock kite. Template available on the *GO GLOBAL* Resource page.

    ### Materials

    - Template printed on cardstock
    - Crayons
    - Orange tissue paper or streamer
    - String

    ### Procedure

    a) Color the template.
    b) Glue on streamers.
    c) Add string.

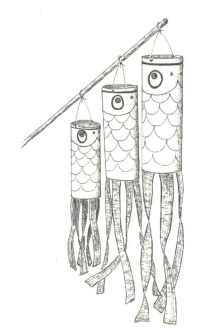

3. Discuss the food and manner of eating in one of your books, such as **How My Parents Learned to Eat.** If possible, go out for Japanese food or make some. Be sure to try eating with chopsticks!

DAY 3 ORIGAMI, SAMURAI, AND TEA CEREMONY

EVERYONE

1. Continue to read the books featuring Japan while looking for some of the cultural aspects listed above.

2. Celebrate the Japanese tea ceremony.

    a) Prepare a "tea room" by having mats on the floor. Optional: Add any Japanese decorations such as a simple floral arrangement, a bonsai tree, etc.

    b) Dress up in some way. Wear a kimono tied with an obi. This can be a silky bath robe, or even one of dad's dress shirts, with a wide cloth wrapped around as a belt!

    c) Have children bow, remove their shoes, and wash their hands as they enter the tea room.

    d) Sit in "sieza" style on knees with bottoms touching heels in a circle. The host should sit near the tea equipment. Use a low coffee table if available.

    e) Prepare the tea. Parents should describe verbally what they are doing. Clean the equipment with a "special" cloth. Scoop the green-tea powder into the bowl, Add hot water, whisk to create tea with light foam. Japanese do not add sweetener, but you might want to do so for your children. Green-tea powder may not be available in your area. Feel free to brew green tea if that is what you have available. Still pour it into a bowl and whisk.

    f) Drink the tea. After exchanging bows, the host serves the bowl of tea to the guest of honor who is seated next to the host. This guest then bows to the next guest, takes two or three sips from the bowl, wipes the rim, and passes the bowl to the next guess while bowing. This continues around the circle until each participant has tasted the tea. Then the host cleans the bowl again. The guests pass around the cleaned bowl before it is put away.

    g) OPTIONAL: Serve tea cookies or wagashi, the Japanese sweets mentioned in the Dodsworth book.

    h) As everyone leaves the tea room, they bow again to symbolize the end of the ceremony.

ADD FOR SIX-YEAR-OLDS AND UP

3. Origami is the art of folding paper and is associated with the Japanese culture. This art form is made just by folding paper without cuts, glue, or markings, though young children might like to add some features to their origami. If available, learn about origami by reading **The Origami Master**, or **Yoko's Crane**.

    Easy Origami: Make a dog. Art tutorial available on *GO GLOBAL* Resource page.

    Materials

    - One 4" x 4" square of colorful paper

Process

  a) Fold paper in half diagonally. Have the fold on top and the point close to you.

  b) Fold each corner down to form dog's ears.

  c) Fold bottom corner up and forward to form dog's chin.

Harder Origami: Make a Samurai Helmet (after learning about the Samurai—see below) Art tutorial is on the *GO GLOBAL* Resource page.

Materials

- One 21" x 21" square of newspaper (or thick wrapping paper)

Process

  a) Fold paper in half diagonally. Have the fold on top and the point close to you.

  b) Fold right corner to center corner nearest you. Fold left corner to same center corner. Paper will now have a diamond shape.

  c) Take just the top portion of each of these triangles and fold in half so that the tip will now touch the top part.

  d) Take the right side of the top layer and fold it forward about half way to form the "horn" of the helmet. Repeat with the left side.

  e) Fold one layer of the lower triangle up leaving about an inch for the hat band. Fold the one-inch hat band up.

  f) Tuck in the remaining lower section to form the hat.

4. Learn about Samurai, the military officers in medieval and early modern Japan. Much of the Samurai culture has religious elements (Buddhism and Zen) which we need to be careful with. But your boys especially will be fascinated with the strategy, martial arts, weapons, and armor of the Samurai. Pictures are on the *GO GLOBAL* Resource page. If available, read **Three Samurai Cats**.

DAY 4 — REVIEW JAPAN AND ASIA

EVERYONE

1. Review the Asian countries you have studied by asking your children where they would like to visit and why.

2. What have been their favorite books in this unit on Asia? Reread if you still have the book.

3. Review the foods you have eaten. Which has been their favorite meal from Asia?

4. Which has been the most interesting building?

5. Play the *GO GLOBAL* Game. Add the Asian cards to the North American, South American, Antarctica, African, and European cards.

WEEK 32
CATCH UP OR TAKE A BREAK

WEEK 33
AUSTRALIA
ANIMALS

BIG PICTURE

The continent of Australia includes the Australian mainland, Tasmania, New Guinea, and many small islands to the north of Australia. Most adults don't know this about the continent, but we wanted to provide you this information. You and your children will just emphasize the land and the animals of the country of Australia in this curriculum. Australia is nicknamed the "land down under" because it is the only inhabited continent totally south of the equator.

Australia is just slightly smaller than the continental United States. It is made up mostly of desert and grasslands, with some mountains and strips of forests. The sparsely inhabited interior of the country is known as the outback. The native aborigines would take a journey in this wilderness as a rite of passage called a walkabout.

This first week we will emphasize the many unique animals that inhabit Australia which have delighted children for ages. We will learn about marsupials (mammals that carry their young in pouches) such as the kangaroo and wallaby, the koala, and the wombat. The bizarre platypus almost defies belief, and the emu and kookaburra are odd and amusing birds only found in Australia.

MATERIALS

Books

1. ***Beginner's World Atlas 3rd Edition***, National Geographic. 2011.
2. ***Over in Australia: Amazing Animals Down Under***, Marianne Berkes. Ages 4–9. Ten animals in their habitats are highlighted. An additional ten animals are hidden on the pages. End notes are full of information on the animals and habitats of Australia, with art work, and activities to extend the learning.
3. At least one book with photographs of Australian animals such as: ***Australian Animals***, Caroline Arnold, or ***Destination: Australia***, Jonathan Grupper, National Geography.

Secondary Books: Find *some* of these excellent books to read aloud and make available to your children for their quiet times. * means especially recommended. Please note that while the cartoonish books about the Australian animals are numerous and entertaining, you need to include books that demonstrate these are real creatures.

1. *****About Marsupials***, Cathryn Sill. Ages 4–8. Beautiful realistic illustrations with additional text in the back of the book. This book covers 14 Australian marsupials and two marsupials from North America and South America.
2. *****A Platypus, Probably***, Sneed Collard III. Ages 5–8. Fabulous information presented in a kid friendly way. Some evolution that the parent may want to skip or explain.

3. Nonfiction book with photographs of kangaroos such as ***A Kangaroo Joey Grows Up,*** Joan Hewett. Easy Reader. Or ***Red Kangaroo***, Anita Ganeri. Ages 5–7. Photographic tale of a day in the life of a red kangaroo.
4. ***Jimmy the Joey: The True Story of an Amazing Koala Rescue***, Deborah Lee Rose. Ages 4–8. Inspirational photographic true story of a baby koala being rescued after its mother's death.
5. ***National Geographic Readers: Koalas***. Ages 4–7. Fabulous photography and clear simple text.
6. ***A Koala is Not a Bear***, Hannelore Sotzek. Ages 6–8. Clear information and lovely photographs and art work.
7. ***Koala Country: A Story of an Australian Eucalyptus Forest***, Deborah Dennard. Ages 5–9. A story with natural, detailed illustrations following a number of animals for one night.
8. ***Wombat Goes Walkabout***, Michael Morpurgo. Ages 4–7. Naturalistic art transports us to the outback as a baby wombat encounters various animals while looking for his mum. Sweet story with a lovely ending.
9. ***Wombat Walkabout***, Carol Diggory Shields. Ages 3–5. Whimsical counting poem about six little wombats who trick the dingo who is hunting them. Includes simple Australian terms, animals, and plants.
10. ***Diary of a Wombat***, Jackie French. Ages 4–7. Silly diary of a wombat who gets some "human pets."
11. ***Platypus***, Joan Short. Ages 7–12. Information on the animal and his habitat with helpful drawn illustrations and photographs.
12. ***Platypus: A Century-Long Mystery***, William Caper. Ages 7–12. Includes information on the discovery of the platypus as well as detailed information on the animal and conservation.
13. ***Echidnas (World's Weirdest Animals)***, Marcia Zappa. Ages 5–10. Basic information simply laid out with wonderful photographs.
14. ***Can You Tell an Ostrich from an Emu?*** Buffy Silverman. Ages 6–9. Vivid photography and a lively design make this a fun nonfiction read!
15. **Sand Swimmers: The Secret Life of Australia's Desert Wilderness**, Narelle Oliver. Ages 7–12. Riveting story of exploring the strange desert wilderness of Australia. Includes historical explorations and weird animals. Some evolution references.
16. ***Survival at 120 Above***, Debbie Miller. Ages 6–12. One day in the life of the Australian animals surviving in the Australian Simpson desert. Including camels is a bit disconcerting as they are feral animals introduced to Australia in the 19th century.
17. ***Possum Magic***, Mem Fox. Ages 4–7. Grandma Possum helps Hush to become visible again by traveling around Australia eating local delicacies.
18. Non-fiction book on Australia such as ***Spotlight on Australia***, Xavier Niz, or ***Australia***, Katie Bagley.

Music

1. *"Kookaburra Sits in the Old Gum Tree,"* link available on *GO GLOBAL* Resource page

SUPPLIES

1. Map of Australia (available on the *GO GLOBAL* Resource page) printed on cardstock
2. Multiple pages printed of Australian animal chart, available on *GO GLOBAL* Resource page
3. A "pouch" such as a draw string bag and baby doll or stuffed animal to carry around like a marsupial
4. Platypus art: two different colors of playdough, two beads
5. Echidna art: playdough, toothpicks or wooden skewers, red paint or marker, two beads

6. Australian Concentration Game, link for purchase available on *GO GLOBAL* Resource page

DAY 1 — OVERVIEW AND ANIMALS

EVERYONE

1. Read ***Beginner's World Atlas***, Pages 50–55.

2. Find Australia first on your *GO GLOBAL* Game mat and then on your globe. Tell your children that the Europeans who settled there started calling it Down Under. Ask your children if they can guess why. [Answer: The continent/country is entirely in the southern hemisphere, i.e. "under" the equator.]

3. Color and mark the map of Australia, available on the *GO GLOBAL* Resource page.

    a) Ask your child to name the bodies of water around Australia. She should be able to name the Pacific Ocean and the Indian Ocean. The Southern Ocean is quite a bit south, but do not correct her if she says it is there as well. Color the water blue and label these bodies of water. Label the island and province of Australia: Tasmania.

    b) The convex southern portion of the continent is called the Great Australian Bight. This is an oceanic bight—or open bay. But some have joked it looks like a great monster took a bite out of Australia! Older children might be interested in these homophones—words that are pronounced the same, but have different meanings, and can be spelled differently. Do not mark this on the map. This is just a fun conversation piece of trivia.

    c) Color the mountains called the Great Dividing Range and label. You can color the other mountain ranges, but do not label.

    d) Color the small strip of deciduous forests in the southeast portion and in Tasmania.

    e) Add strips of sandpaper to indicate the desert in the majority of the portion.

    f) Color the very small part of the northeast coast as rainforest.

    g) Color grasslands.

    h) Color the Darling and Murray rivers.

    i) Color the coral reef and label it The Great Barrier Reef. You might mention that this is under the water, and that we will learn more about it next week.

4. Have your child start to make a chart of animals from Australia. DO NOT fill it all out for her. You may do the writing, but let her do the dictating. The first column should be "Animal", the second column is "Location" and the third column is for your child to draw a picture. You will want to discuss the behavior of the animals. Add a few animals every day! Printable for this list of Australian animals is available on the *GO GLOBAL* Resource page.

    a) Location is where the animal lives: desert, grasslands, forest, or coral reef.

    b) Behavior to discuss can include anything interesting about the animal that your child mentions; this could include what the animal likes to eat (Is he an herbivore, carnivore or omnivore?), its color, if it is solitary or lives in community, etc. Include if the animal is a marsupial and has a pouch! I have included some suggestions below, but do NOT just instruct. You want to let your child have an opportunity to be creative and to tell you what she knows and thinks! Make sure to add how you would dramatize this animal. Pick a verb that the specific animal does. (kangaroo—hops, kookaburra—laughs, sugar glider—glides, wombat—burrows, etc.)

c) Slowly add to this list by asking your child what animal she would like to add. Then you can learn more about this animal. Or you can slowly add to this list in the next two weeks as you learn about the animals.

d) I have added the animal class, but do NOT introduce this if it is overwhelming to your child. OLDER children *might* like to start to categorize animals into: mammals, birds, reptiles, fish, amphibians, and invertebrates (which means no backbone—and is the catchall at this age for all animals that are not vertebrates.)

AUSTRALIAN ANIMAL CHART

(You should not do *all* of these animals as that will overwhelm most children. Try to do all the double starred, some of the single starred, and others that especially interest your child. This list is not comprehensive.)

	Animal	*Animal class, Pouch?*	*Location*
	Barking (or thick-tailed) Gecko	reptile	desert
*	Bilby	mammal—pouch	desert
	Blue-Tongue Skink	reptile	forests, grasslands
	Brolga	bird	wetlands
	Cockatoo	bird	forests
*	Dingo	mammal	desert, grassland
*	Echidna	mammal	forests, deserts
*	Emu	bird	desert, grassland
	Frilled Neck Lizard	reptile	desert, grassland
**	Kangaroo	mammal—pouch	desert, grassland
**	Koala	mammal—pouch	forests/eucalyptus
*	Kookaburra	bird	forest
**	Platypus	mammal	rivers
	Possum	mammal—pouch	forest
	Rainbow Lorikeet	bird	forest
**	Saltwater Crocodile	reptile	marshy rivers
	Sugar Glider	mammal—pouch	forest
	Tasmanian Devil	mammal—pouch	forest
	Tiger Quoll	mammal—pouch	forest
*	Wallaby	mammal—pouch	desert, grassland
*	Wombat	mammal—pouch	grassland, forests
**	Coral	invertebrate	coral reef

	Animal	Animal class, Pouch?	Location
*	Clownfish	fish	coral reef
	Octopus	invertebrate	coral reef
*	Parrotfish	fish	coral reef
*	Ray (manta ray)	fish	coral reef
	Seahorse	fish	coral reef
*	Sea snake (moray eel)	fish	coral reef
*	Shark (black-tipped reef or great white)	fish	coral reef
	Turtle (hawksbill or green sea)	reptile	coral reef

** Everybody learns

* Add if you can

DAY 2   MARSUPIALS, KANGAROO, AND WALLABY

EVERYONE

1. Read **Over in Australia**. Re-read it this week as many times as your child wants!

2. Marsupials are mammals with pouches. Ask your child if he knows what a mammal is. [Answer: A mammal is an animal that has a backbone and hair, usually gives birth to babies, and feeds their babies with their milk.] Explain that a marsupial is a mammal that keeps their young in a pouch. While most marsupials live in Australia there are some in other continents. Read **About Marsupials** if you have it.

   Strap a pouch on your child and let her carry a baby stuffed animal around all day today.

3. Read about kangaroos and wallabies in the books you have. A wallaby is in the same family as a kangaroo, but is much smaller. There are many species of kangaroos and wallabies. All have powerful hind legs which they use for bounding at high speeds, jumping great heights, and kicking to fend off predators. They also have powerful tails that are used for balance and support. The kangaroos will thump the ground with their large feet to warn others of the danger of nearby dingoes.

   A baby kangaroo is called a joey and is the size of a pea when it is born. He lives in his mother's pouch where he drinks milk. He starts eating grass at about 10 months old, and no longer fits in his mother's pouch at just over a year, though he still drinks her milk.

A kangaroo can hop (with both feet together) 15 feet. If they are hopping at their fastest speed they can jump as far as 40 feet! Measure 15 feet, which is their standing jump average, and then see how far your child can hop.

Dramatize being kangaroos by carrying your baby, hopping, running, kicking, etc.

4. Add the animals you learned about today to your list of Australian animals.

DAY 3 — KOALA, WOMBAT, AND DINGO

EVERYONE

1. Read about the koala in the books you have. Make sure your child learns to recognize the koala, and a few of these interesting facts:

    a) They only live in Australia.

    b) Koala are marsupials and the mothers carry their baby (also called a joey) in a pouch. The mama koala can close her pouch, so the baby does not fall out.

    c) Koalas have two "thumbs" and three fingers to be able to grip the branches as they climb in a tree.

    d) The thick fur keeps them warm and dry.

    e) Koalas eat eucalyptus leaves.

    f) Koalas are nocturnal—which means they are most active at night.

    Pretend to be koalas by climbing a tree and munching on some leaves (celery) and don't forget to carry your baby in your pouch, closing it to keep your baby safe as you climb.

2. Learn about wombats by rereading your books that talk about them (***Over in Australia***, ***Destination: Australia***, ***Australian Animals***, or ***About Marsupials***) or an additional book specific about the wombat. Make sure to read at least some books that show the wombat as a real animal, rather than as an anthromorphized cartoon creature. While some pretend stories are fine, we want to make sure the child realizes these are real animals. Ask your child to describe a wombat to you and to tell you some of their characteristics.

    a) They only live in Australia.

    b) Wombats are marsupials and the mothers carry the baby (also called a joey) in a pouch. She can close her pouch so the baby does not fall out or get dirty as she digs.

    c) They burrow, or dig long holes, to live in. They dig with their front paws and kick out the soil with their back feet. The burrow can be 90 feet long. Measure this distance!

    d) They have plump, furry bodies.

    e) Wombats are herbivores—they eat plants.

    f) They are nocturnal—which means they are most active at night.

Pretend to be a wombat by digging in the dirt, carrying your baby in a drawstring pouch, and eating plants for a snack.

3. Add the animals you learned about today to your list of Australian animals.

ADD FOR SIX-YEAR-OLDS AND UP

4. Learn about the dingo, the wild dog of Australia. It is the main predator for many of the animals that we have studied. Dingoes do not bark much, but do like to howl like wolves. But unlike wolves they react to gestures and social cues from humans. Add to your list of animals.

   Dramatize a dog or a dingo meeting. This is a great activity for two children. Then mom can see if she can tell which is the dog and which is the dingo!

ADD FOR SEVEN-YEAR-OLDS AND UP

5. Learn about and discuss the bilby and sugar glider and add to your list of animals.

DAY 4   PLATYPUS, ECHIDNA, EMU, KOOKABURRA

1. Learn about the platypus by rereading your books that talk about them (***Over in Australia***, ***Destination: Australia***, ***Australian Animals***) and/ or an additional book specific about the platypus.

   a) Look at a photograph of a platypus and ask your child what the different parts of the animal are like.

   - What is the bill like? [Answer: A duck.]

   - What does the tail look like? [Answer: It is flat and rounded like a beaver and furry like an otter.]

   - Look at and describe its feet. What animals have similar feet? [Answer: They are webbed feet, that is they have skin stretched between the fingers/toes. Ducks, beavers, and otters also have webbed feet. Beavers and otters also have claws.]

   - It lays eggs; what kind of animals lay eggs? [Answer: Birds, reptiles, amphibians.]

   - The platypus has fur; what kind of animals have fur? [Answer: Mammals.]

   - The platypus feeds its babies milk; what kind of animals feed their babies milk? [Answer: Mammals.]

   b) When Europeans first saw the platypus, they thought it was a hoax. Explain to your child what a hoax is, and discuss why the Europeans thought this animal was not real.

   c) OPTIONAL—Make a platypus out of playdough. Art tutorial available on the *GO GLOBAL* Resource page.

Materials
- Playdough, two colors
- Beads for eyes

Process
- a) Form body of platypus with playdough. Make sure to add a flat tail and short legs.
- b) Add duck bill and webbed claw feet.
- c) Add beady eyes and nostrils on the bill.

2. Learn about emu, the large land bird in Australia by rereading portions of your books that talk about them. (***Over in Australia***, ***Destination: Australia***, ***Australian Animals***)

   a) The emu is the world's second largest bird. Ask your child if she knows the largest bird. [Answer: The ostrich which lives in Africa.] The emu can run over 30 miles per hour. They will run a zig-zag pattern to elude predators. Very fast humans can run about 20 miles per hour—but only for short distances. Dramatize being an emu and try to elude a predator (dad?) by running zig-zag.

   b) Compare and contrast the emu and ostrich. Picture of an ostrich and emu available on the *GO GLOBAL* Resource page.
   - They are both large, both run rather than fly, both have long necks and large eyes.
   - An ostrich's head and neck are bare pink skin with just some fuzzy feathers, while the emu has more feathers.
   - An ostrich has two toes on each foot, while the emu has three toes on each foot.
   - Ostriches have large wings they use for balance, to shade their babies, and to show off. Emus have tiny wings they spread to be able to cool down.
   - Ostrich females sit on their nest of eggs, while the emu males sit on their eggs. The father emu watches the young birds for six months after they hatch!
   - Ostriches live in the dry sandy deserts of Africa, while emus wander through the forests, shrubs, grasslands, and only go to the deserts after a rainstorm.

3. Listen and sing *Kookaburra Sits in the Old Gum Tree*. Listen to a real kookaburra laugh. Links to videos are available on the *GO GLOBAL* Resource page.

ADD FOR SIX-YEAR-OLDS AND UP

4. Learn about the echidna (pronounced eh KID nah) by reading your books. Here are some interesting facts to discuss.

   a) Have your child describe the echidna. She should include:
   - It has a round body covered with fur and spines.
   - It has short legs with claws.

- It has beady little eyes.
- Its thin, long beak-like snout has a nose and mouth at the end with a long sticky tongue.

b) The echidna is a mammal that lays eggs, which it incubates in a pouch it develops just for the egg. The hatched echidna, called a puggle, stays in the pouch for four months after it hatches.

c) The echidna is also called a spiny anteater, though it is NOT like an anteater at all—other than that it eats insects with its sticky tongue.

d) Talk about how the echidna defends itself—by burrowing and then rolling up so the only part showing is his spines!

e) Make an echidna out of playdough and toothpicks. Art tutorial available on the *GO GLOBAL* Resource page.

Materials
- Playdough
- Wooden toothpicks, one painted red for tongue
- Beads for eyes

Process

a) Form body of echidna with playdough. Make sure to add a long skinny snout and four stubby legs under the body.

b) Stick in the toothpicks, except on the snout.

c) Add beady eyes, nose, and tongue.

5. Add the animals you learned about today to your list of Australian animals.
6. Play Australia Concentration.

WEEK 34
AUSTRALIA
CORAL REEF AND CULTURE

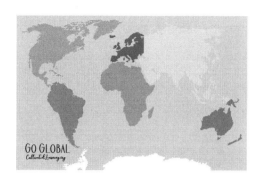

BIG PICTURE

As you continue your visit in Australia you will learn about the ferocious saltwater crocodile and the Great Barrier Reef, which is the largest reef in the world and home to many colorful animals.

You will briefly explore historical and modern Australia, including Captain Cook and the Sydney Opera House. The aboriginal people's art and music will be touched upon.

This week includes a day to go to the zoo to see the wonderful and weird Australian animals. If you do not have access to a zoo, we have provided a virtual zoo tour you can take through carefully chosen on-line videos.

MATERIALS

Books

(Keep books from last week as well.)

1. ***Here is the Coral Reef***, Madeleine Dunphy. Ages 4–8. Brightly colored illustrations and a cumulative rhyme introduce the relationship between the plants and animals in the coral reef.
2. ***13 Buildings Children Should Know***, Annette Roeder. Ages 8–12. You turn to this book again to explore Australia's Sydney Opera House.

Secondary Books: Find *some* of these excellent books to read aloud and make available to your children for their quiet times. * means especially recommended.

1. ****Meet Captain Cook***, Rae Murdie. Ages 5–8. Picture book about the first European to discover and explore the eastern coast of Australia. A great world map is included!
2. ****Sailing the Unknown: Around the World with Captain Cook***, Michael J. Rosen. Ages 6–9. This "journal of an 11-year old sailor" is enhanced with breathtaking illustrations. If the parent wants to tell the story and discuss the pictures even a four-year-old will like finding Nick in his Waldo-like striped shirt and learning about Cook's expeditions.
3. ****Are We There Yet? A Journey Around Australia***, Alison Lester. Ages 5–9. An enchanting story of a family traveling abound Australia for three months provides a fabulous overview of the diverse land, people, landforms, landmarks, towns and cities. It includes a map!
4. ***Saltwater Crocodiles***, Katie Marsico. Ages 7–10. Nonfiction with great photographs.
5. ***Do You Really Want to Meet a Crocodile?*** Cari Meister. Ages 4–9. A child travels to Australia to meet the largest croc in the world. Cartoon illustrations with brief, informative, and interesting text.
6. ***Over in the Ocean: In a Coral Reef***, Marianne Berkes, Ages 4–8. Polymer clay illustrations and text about 10 coral reef animals. End notes and motions for the song.

7. ***Ernie Dances to the Didgeridoo***, Alison Lester. Ages 4–7. Ernie moves to Australia with his family for a year while his father is a doctor in the outback. He writes letters back to his classmates telling them about the seasons, animals, activities, and friends in Australia.
8. ***Outback Adventure: Australian Vacation***, Kate McLeod. DK Reader. A family trip from Perth to Broome captured with photographs.

Music

1. *"Tie Me Kangaroo Down, Sport"* link available on the *GO GLOBAL* Resource page
2. *"Waltzing Matilda"* link available on *GO GLOBAL* Resource page

Movies

1. ***Finding Nemo.*** Disney/ Pixar movie about a father and his friends going to the Australian Great Barrier Reef to rescue the young clownfish, Nemo

SUPPLIES

1. Coral reef art: Two cardboard egg cartons, paint, brushes, chenille wire, craft foam, printed sea animal figures template available on *GO GLOBAL* Resource page, wooden skewers, small sea shells (optional), beads (optional)
2. Aboriginal Art: cardboard for boomerang; red, brown, yellow, and white paint; cotton swabs to apply paint
3. Captain Cook figure for timeline
4. Australian Concentration Game, link for purchase available on *GO GLOBAL* Resource page
5. *GO GLOBAL* Game

DAY 1 — SALTWATER CROCODILE AND GREAT BARRIER REEF

EVERYONE

1. Learn about saltwater crocodiles by rereading your books that talk about them (***Over in Australia***, ***Destination: Australia***) or an additional book specific about the crocs.

    a) These crocs, known as salties, live in the shallow water (salty, brackish, and fresh) in northern Australian and southeast Asia.

    b) They can be up 20 feet long—which is more than three grown men, lying on the ground. They have 60 sharp teeth! Have your child count his own teeth, and then see if he can count all the way to 60. He might want to draw a croc with his mouth open showing all his teeth. The crocs teeth are up to three inches long and the top teeth lock together with the bottom teeth like a steel trap!

    c) Salties lay eggs, and the mother carries the newly hatched crocklets to the water. Would you rather be carried in a pouch like the kangaroos or a mouth, like a croc?

2. Read *Here is the Coral Reef*. On a subsequent read talk to your child about each page in the book. This might need to be spread out over more than one session. You do not have to cover all this material. Gauge your child's interest and proceed accordingly.

   a) Ask him if he thinks coral is a plant or animal. [Answer: He might think it is a plant, but it is an animal.] Tell him that corals have exoskeletons—the hard part of them are outside of their bodies, unlike animals that have backbones and bones inside their bodies. Does he know other animals that have exoskeletons [Answer: Beetles, crabs, etc.] Corals are stationary which means they do not move around much.

   b) As you look at the parrotfish page, ask your child if he remembers what a parrot is. Then ask him to describe the parrot. We are looking for the detail about the beak. Why was the parrotfish named parrotfish? Hint: look at their mouths. [Answer: Parrot fish have tightly jam-packed teeth that look like a parrot-like beak. These teeth can crunch the hard sponges.]

   c) Ask your child if he knows animals that live on land and clean up after others like the wrasses do. Hint: they like to come to picnics and eat the crumbs. [Answer: Ants.] Does he like how the wrassies help the parrotfish and the cod? Do you have a dog that cleans up under your dinner table?

   d) Is the sea anemone a plant or an animal? [Answer: An animal that was named after a flower. Most anemones are stationary and stay affixed to the floor of the ocean.]

   e) The clownfish has a special symbiotic relationship with the sea anemone. After introducing the term symbiotic, see if your child can define it. [Answer: Symbiotic means two different species that live near and help each other.] Ask your child why he thinks the clownfish (and most coral reef fish) are brightly colored. [Answer: To blend in with the brightly colored coral, to help other fish recognize them, to warn predators that they are poisonous. Do not expect your child to know these. Praise him for whichever (reasonably correct) answer he comes up with.] There is a 1.5-minute educational video about the clownfish and anemone relationship linked on the *GO GLOBAL* Resource page.

   f) Is the sponge a plant or an animal? [Answer: An animal. Many young sponges drift with the ocean current, while most adults are stationary.] Sponges are difficult to understand. There is a 9-minute video linked on the *GO GLOBAL* Resource pages that includes the history of collecting and selling sponges.

   g) Some turtles live in the sea, and other on land. The land turtles are called tortoises. How are land turtles different and like sea turtles? [Answer could include: The sea turtle has fins/flippers while the tortoise has feet and claws. The sea turtles have flatter shells, tortoises can stick their head inside their shells. Sea turtles eat fish and other animals. Most tortoises eat plants. Both lay many eggs, live long lives, breathe air, and are reptiles. Do NOT expect your child to learn all this. Let him tell you what he knows without you overwhelming him with information.]

   h) Rays are sometimes called the "birds" of the sea. Why? [Answer: They seem to have wings and fly through the water.] Have your child get up and fly like a bird, then have him swim like a ray. Should be the same motion!

i) The remora has a symbiotic relationship with sharks. Remind your child that this means the two animals live close to one another and help each other. How does your child think they help each other? [Answer: The shark gets cleaned up and the remora get a meal and a ride.] Point out to your child the weird oval disk on the top (dorsal) of the remora's head. It is a sucker that helps him to attach to the shark or other large animals. Let your child play with a suction cup. There is an interesting 2-minute video about remoras, sharks and rays linked on the *GO GLOBAL* Resource page.

j) Blacktip reef sharks can grow up to six feet long. The great white shark is usually about 11 to 16 feet long, but the largest one recorded was 20 feet long! While there are great whites in Australian waters, the smaller reef sharks can navigate in the coral reef. Ask your child if he knows someone about the same size as a reef shark. Ask your child if the shark's teeth are the same shape as his teeth. [Answer: No, the shark's teeth are triangular.] Ask him if he notices anything strange about the shark's teeth as he tries to count them. [Answer: There are two rows of teeth.]

k) Is an eel a snake or a fish? Your child probably knows this is a trick question by now. How do you know? [Answer: It is a fish. It has a backbone, lives and breathes under water, and has a fin.] Where is his fin? [Answer: A long skinny ventral (that means on the top) fin.]

Now dramatize the animals of the coral reef. See if you can guess which animal the other one is dramatizing.

3. Make a Great Barrier Reef underwater scene. Art tutorial available on the *GO GLOBAL* Resource page.

   ### Materials
   - Two cardboard egg cartons for base
   - Paint and brushes
   - Chenille wire
   - Craft foam for plate coral
   - Small sea animal figures—printable available on *GO GLOBAL* Resource page
   - Wooden skewers
   - Small sea shells (optional)
   - Beads (optional)

   ### Process
   a) Paint one egg carton blue with white swirls to represent the water.

   b) Paint second egg carton green to represent the coral.

   c) Form the chenille wires in various shapes to represent the coral. You can add beads to some of them if you would like.

   d) Spiral wrap chenille wire around a large magic marker to make the sponges.

   e) Cut the craft foam in various shapes to make the plate coral.

   f) Make holes in your coral reef and water bases to attach your corals and sponges.

g) Color fish and animal figurines and attach to skewers. Stick into base.

h) Stick skewers with animals into base. Add sea shells and any other decorations you want.

DAY 2   HISTORY AND MODERN-DAY AUSTRALIA

EVERYONE

1. The indigenous native people in Australia are called Aboriginal Australians. Aboriginal people were semi-nomadic and lived mainly as foragers and hunter-gatherers. Music was an integral part of their culture and a traditional Australian instrument is the didgeridoo. Find the pictures of the Aboriginal Australians in the ***Beginner's World Atlas***. You can find a link to a performance of the instrument on the *GO GLOBAL* Resource page.

   The Aboriginal art tradition is thousands of years old and the best-known examples are rock art, bark painting, and body art. Dot paintings are created by making several small dots of paint to create an image. Often, the Aboriginal Australians would include concentric circles and arcs and geometric shapes. The dots can slightly obscure the pattern to make it "dream-like" or hidden. Use the traditional colors red, brown, yellow and white to decorate your cardboard boomerang. Art tutorial is on the *GO GLOBAL* Resource page.

   Materials
   - Cardboard to cut out boomerang shape
   - Red, brown, yellow, and white paint
   - Cotton swabs to apply paint

   Procedure
   - Show your children examples of dot art. Examples are on the *GO GLOBAL* Resource page.
   - Let them paint by making dots. Let dry.
   - Play with the boomerang!

2. Ask your children what language is spoken in Australia? The answer is English since the British settled there. Australians have a distinctive accent and have come up with some unique words. You have already heard most of these in the books you are reading. Add some to your vocabulary for the rest of the week!

Aussie	Australian
Barbie	barbeque
Billabong	water hole formed when a u-shaped bend in a river is cut off
Bloke	man
Bush	outback; not in a town
Down under	Australia
G'day	hello
Mate	friend

Outback	the interior of Australia
Stations	large ranches or farms in the outback
Swag (bag)	a vagabond's bedroll and sack
Walkabout	a long walk in the outback

3. Europeans discovered and explored Australia in the 18th century. Retrace the "march" from England to Australia using your *GO GLOBAL* Game mat. Read **Meet Captain Cook** or **Sailing the Unknown** if either book is available. Add Captain Cook to your time line.

4. As the British settled in Australia they developed huge ranches or farms. The cowboys were called jackaroos. Listen to *Tie Me Kangaroo Down Sport*. Link available on the *GO GLOBAL* Resource page.

5. Read **Are We There Yet? A Journey Around Australia** or one of the other books about children in Australia. Look for animals, words, and other things you have learned these last two weeks.

6. Play Australia Concentration.

ADD FOR SIX-YEAR-OLDS AND UP

7. Read about the Sydney Opera House in **13 Buildings Children Should Know**, pages 38–41. Can you find this iconic building in any of your books on Australia? What does your child think the roof resembles? [Traditional answer: Sails. But don't correct your child if he imagines something else.]

DAY 3 — REAL OR VIRTUAL FIELD TRIP

If possible, go to a REAL zoo to visit REAL animals. It you are unable to go to a real zoo, take a virtual zoo trip. The links are available on the *GO GLOBAL* Resource page. Many of the videos will roll onto another one that I did not list, so be prepared to close the individual videos down. These are too many to watch in one sitting. Perhaps spread the trips out over the weekend.

1. **Field Trip A** (30-minute) includes an overview and videos on the kangaroo, wombat, echidna, dingo, saltwater crocodile, possum, Tasmanian devil, and cockatoo.

2. **Field Trip B** (30-minute) includes an Australian zoo tour and videos on the koala, bilby, sugar glider, platypus, emu, frilled lizard, kangaroo, and possum.

3. **Field Trip C** (30-minute) includes videos on the barking gecko, lyrebird, rainbow lorikeet, blue tongue skink, rock wallaby, and saltwater crocodile.

4. **Field Trip D** (30-minute) includes overviews of the coral reef and videos of the sea anemone, pufferfish, leafy sea dragon, pygmy seahorse, stonefish, and sharks.

DAY 4 — REVIEW

EVERYONE

1. Finish up your projects for Australia.

2. Review the animals of Australia by playing charades.

3. Listen to the iconic song *Waltzing Matilda*. This classic Australian bush ballad tells the story of traveling on foot (waltzing) with one's belongings wrapped in a matilda/ swag (bundle wrapped in cloth) slung over one's back. This swagman (hobo) drinks billy tea and captures a stray jumbuck (sheep) while sitting by a billabong (watering hole). The swagman comes to a bad end. Talk about the various words that are used, enjoying the unique Australian lingo. Link available on the *GO GLOBAL* Resource page.

4. Re-read any of your favorite Australian books.

5. Play Australia Concentration.

6. Play *GO GLOBAL* Game with Australian cards added in.

7. Watch **Finding Nemo** this weekend. Even if you have seen it before, your children are going to be delighted with how much more they understand!

WEEK 35
WRAP UP
PART I

BIG PICTURE

You have made it! You and your children have Gone Global! This week is a time to celebrate by reading books that span the globe and by putting together a memory book.

Pick several books from this huge list. There are some that are more science oriented and some are more people or cultural oriented. Make sure to get some of both, but perhaps you could emphasize what you know your child specifically likes.

Read, play, reminisce, and assemble a book to be able to look back at this year of exploring *GO GLOBAL*.

The parent will need to do some advance preparation for assembling the notebook. Take some time to collect materials and photographs. You might want to make the pages yourself and then just read and discuss with the child.

MATERIALS—REMEMBER JUST GET A FEW OF THESE BOOKS!

Books—Atlas type books

1. *The Alphabet Atlas*, Arthur Yorinks. Ages 4–8. Vibrant quilt illustrations and brief text about 26 countries of the world.
2. *Panorama: A Foldout Book of World Scenes*, Fani Marceau. Ages 4–8. Stunning, stylized black and white pictures of various locales from across the world joined together in this accordion paged book. The reverse pages show the same locations at night.
3. *Maps*, Aleksandra Mizielinska. Ages 6–12. An atlas of continents and some countries with a plethora of stylized small cartoons of historical and cultural places, animals, plants, and people of interest. A reference book that children will pore over. Parental warning: A few small cartoon illustrations of nudity, mostly topless indigenous women.

Books—Global science books

1. **I See a Kookaburra! Discovering Animal Habitats Around the World*, Steve Jenkins. Ages 4–8. Six habitats and the animals that live there. North American desert, Amazon jungle, Australian forest, African savanna, English tide pool, North American pond.
2. **A Moon of My Own*, Jennifer Rustgi. Ages 4–8. Beautiful silhouette illustrations of a girl traveling around the world. You will visit all seven continents and many things that we studied.
3. *Somewhere in the World Right Now*, Stacey Schuett. Ages 5–10. This book listed in the first week of the curriculum was too difficult for most of your children. But NOW that you have learned about the world, almost all of them will enjoy this story, and many will understand the concept of time around the globe.

4. *The Ever-Living Tree: The Life and Times of a Coast Redwood*, Linda Vieira, Ages 5–9. The 2000-year lifespan of a sequoia which ties together time and space. While mostly US-centric, there are several world events.
5. *Going Home: The Mystery of Animal Migration*, Marianne Berkes. Ages 4–10. Wonderful story of the migration of penguins, moose, gray whales, and other animals. These migrations are in, or between, the different continents. This is a great review of animals and continents. Extra information and activities in the last pages.
6. *The Long, Long Journey: The Godwit's Amazing Migration*, Sandra Markle. Ages 4–10. Lovely story of the 7000-mile migration from Alaska to New Zealand. Map included.
7. *Jump into Science: Volcano!* Ellen J. Prager. Ages 4–8. While about volcanoes, this book ends with a map of the world indicating the names and locations of well-known (and not so well-known) volcanoes.

Books—How people around the world are different, and yet the same

1. **The Colors of Us, Karen Katz. Ages 3–6. Different skin shades from around the world are described in this delightful book using food comparisons such as caramel, ginger, chocolate, peaches, peanut butter.
2. ***One World, One Day*, Barbara Kerley. Ages 4–8. Exquisite, moving photographs and brief text convey a day in the life of children across the world. Map and pages in the back indicating where all the photographs were taken.
3. ***A Cool Drink of Water*, Barbara Kerley. Ages 4–8. National Geographic pictorial essay of people around the world seeking and drinking water. Great pictures, poetic verbiage, and a map on the back to find where all the pictures were taken!
4. **You and Me Together: Moms, Dads, and Kids Around the World*, Barbara Kerley. Ages 4–8. Parents and children across the world experiencing life and love together.
5. *The World Turns Round and Round*, Nicki Weiss. Ages 4–8. Children receive gifts from relatives from around the world. Last page includes a glossary and pronunciation guide for the relatives and gifts.
6. *To Be a Kid*, Maya Ajmera and John D. Ivanko. Ages 4–8. Sparse text and bright photographs from countries around the world illustrate how all these children have much in common.
7. *What We Wear: Dressing Up Around the World*, Maya Ajmera. Ages 4–8. Photographs of children around the world.

Books—How cultures are different, and yet the same

1. **Market, Ted Lewin. Ages 4–9. Exquisite pictures and stories about markets around the world, including in Chile, Ireland, Uganda, NYC, Morocco.
2. ***If You Lived Here: Houses of the World*, Giles Laroche. Ages 6–9. Wonderful papercutting illustrations of and information about homes around the world. Map included.
3. *Architecture According to Pigeons*, Speck Lee Tailfeather. Ages 7–12. Renderings of famous buildings around the world from a pigeon's perspective. Amusing and lots of great mixed medium illustrations, with a map. Younger children will enjoy the pictures.
4. The Everybody Cooks series by Norah Dooley features a multicultural neighborhood where they all eat the same food, but different. A wonderful look at cultures and foods that immigrants bring to a community. Each book can stand alone. Recipes are included. Ages 5–9. ***Everybody Cooks Rice, Everybody Bakes Bread, Everybody Serves Soup.***

Books—People travel the world

1. **How I Learned Geography**, Uri Shulevitz. Ages 4–9. Having fled their homeland, a boy's father brings home a map instead of bread for supper. As the boy studies the map, he is transported to exotic places without ever leaving his room. Based on true story.
2. *Because You Are My Teacher*, Sherry North. Ages 3–6. Children travel the world with their teacher, visiting all seven continents and many different habitats.
3. *Madlenka*, Peter Sis. Ages 5–10. A NYC girl travels around her block visiting her neighbors from around the world. Intricate illustrations, much like NYC! Parental warning: There are some religious and potentially frightening images.
4. **Born in the Breezes: The Voyages of Joshua Slocum**, Kathryn Lasky. Ages 6–10. Beautiful paintings illustrate this biography of the first solo circumnavigator of the world. His earlier years as a ship's captain, taking his wife and children on board with him make for an interesting read. Parental warning: There is a phantom/ghost of one of Columbus's sailors who helps the captain on his solo voyage.

Books—Imaginary friends travel the world

1. *How the Queen Found the Perfect Cup of Tea*, Kate Hosford. Ages 4–8. A spoiled queen goes looking for a cup of tea in Turkey, India, and Japan. She meets children there, and learns about their tea…. and the importance of home and friends.
2. *From Kalamazoo to Timbuktu!* Harriet Ziefert. Ages 4–8. A brother and sister take a trip around the world. Read once for fun. Then read and trace their path on the globe. Which places do you remember learning about?
3. *Toot & Puddle*, Hollie Hobbie. Ages 4–7. Toot sends his best friend Puddle postcards as he travels around the world.
4. **Toot & Puddle: Top of the World**, Hollie Hobbie. Ages 4–7. Puddle tracks down Toot as he travels abroad.
5. **First Dog**, J. Patrick Lewis and Beth Zappitello. Ages 4–8. A dog travels the world looking for the perfect home. He meets various dogs in other countries (including a Newfoundland, a bulldog, a poodle, a dingo, etc.) and ends up back in the USA.
6. **Emma's Turtle**, Eve Bunting. Ages 3–6. After hearing stories about the faraway world, turtle ventures out to see these exotic countries and animals.

Movies

1. **The Great Race** movie

SUPPLIES

1. *GO GLOBAL* Game
2. Notebook and dividers for the continents
3. Materials created this past year in *GO GLOBAL*
4. Pictures of projects and activities from this past year in *GO GLOBAL*

DAY 1 — REVIEW NORTH AMERICA

EVERYONE

1. Read some world books and discuss.
2. Review and remember the two introductory weeks.
    a) Add materials (including their map book) and pictures from the introductory weeks. Discuss and reminisce with your child.
    b) Add a list of books you read in these weeks.
3. Review and remember North America.
    a) Look at your map and discuss what you remember learning. Talk about the habitats you have learned about: grassland, desert, coniferous forest, deciduous forest, mountains, tundra. Add the map to your notebook.
    b) Talk about the cultures you learned about. What was your child's favorite activity?
    c) Add materials and pictures from these weeks. Discuss and reminisce with your child.
    d) Practice the Spanish you learned.
    e) Add the list of books you read and enjoyed.
4. Play the *GO GLOBAL* Game.

DAY 2 — REVIEW SOUTH AMERICA

EVERYONE

1. Read more books and discuss.
2. Review and remember South America.
    a) Look at your map and discuss what you remember learning. Talk about the habitats you have learned about: grassland (pampas), desert, rainforest, mountains. Add the map to your notebook.
    b) Talk about the animals of South America. Make sure to add the list you made to your notebook.
    c) Talk about the cultures you learned about.
    d) What was your child's favorite activity?
    e) Add materials and pictures from these weeks. Discuss and reminisce with your child.
    f) Add the list of books you read and enjoyed.
3. Play the *GO GLOBAL* Game.

DAY 3 — REVIEW ANTARCTICA

EVERYONE

1. Read more books and discuss.
2. Review and remember Antarctica.
   a) Look at your map and discuss what you remember learning. Talk about the habitats and landforms you have learned about: icecap, ocean. Add the map to your notebook.
   b) Talk about the exploration of Antarctica.
   c) Talk about the animals of Antarctica.
   d) Which was your child's favorite activity?
   e) Add materials and pictures from these weeks. Discuss and reminisce with your child.
   f) Add the list of books you read and enjoyed.
3. Play Penguin Bingo.
4. Play the *GO GLOBAL* Game.

DAY 4 — REVIEW AFRICA

EVERYONE

1. Read some books and discuss.
2. Review and remember Africa.
   a) Look at your map and discuss what you remember learning. Talk about the habitats you have learned about: grassland (savanna), desert, rainforest/jungle, mountains. Add the map to your notebook.
   b) Talk about the animals of Africa. Make sure to add the list you made to your notebook.
   c) Talk about the cultures and history you learned about.
   d) What was your child's favorite activity?
   e) Add materials and pictures from these weeks. Discuss and reminisce with your child.
   f) Add the list of books you read and enjoyed.
3. Play the *GO GLOBAL* Game.

WEEK 36
WRAP UP
PART II

BIG PICTURE

Finish well!

MATERIALS

Books and supplies from last week.

DAY 1 — REVIEW EUROPE

EVERYONE

1. Read some world books and discuss.
2. Review and remember Europe
   a) Look at your map and discuss what you remember learning. Talk about the habitats you have learned about: grassland, desert, coniferous forest, deciduous forest, mountains, tundra. Add the map to your notebook.
   b) Talk about the cultures and history you learned about.
   c) What was your child's favorite activity?
   d) Add materials and pictures from these weeks. Discuss and reminisce with your child.
   e) Practice some of the French, Spanish, Italian, and German that you learned.
   f) Add the list of books you read and enjoyed.
3. Play the *GO GLOBAL* Game.

DAY 2 — REVIEW ASIA

EVERYONE

1. Read more world books and discuss.
2. Review and remember Asia.
   a) Look at your map and discuss what you remember learning. Talk about the habitats you

have learned about: grassland (taiga), desert, rainforest, taiga forests, mountains, tundra. Add the map to your notebook.

    b) Talk about the animals of Asia.

    c) Talk about the cultures and history you learned about.

    d) What was your child's favorite activity?

    e) Add materials and pictures from these weeks. Discuss and reminisce with your child.

    f) Add the list of books you read and enjoyed.

3. Play the *GO GLOBAL* Game.

DAY 3 — REVIEW AUSTRALIA

EVERYONE

1. Read more world books and discuss.
2. Review and remember Australia.

    a) Look at your map and discuss what you remember learning. Talk about the habitats you have learned about: grassland, desert, rainforest/jungle, mountains, coral reef. Add the map to your notebook.

    b) Talk about the animals of Australia. Make sure to add the list you made to your notebook.

    c) Talk about the cultures and history you learned about.

    d) What was your child's favorite activity?

    e) Add materials and pictures from these weeks. Discuss and reminisce with your child.

    f) Add the list of books you read and enjoyed.

3. Play the *GO GLOBAL* Game.

DAY 4 — REVIEW DANCES AND ANIMALS

EVERYONE

1. Read some more world books and discuss.
2. Dance any of the dances that you particularly enjoyed.
3. After looking at your lists of animals, play animal charades or 20 questions with all the animals you have studied.
4. Play the *GO GLOBAL* Game.

APPENDIX

HOW TO START A CO-OP WITH *GO GLOBAL*

Homeschooling is such an amazing journey and there are so many ways to travel this road. *GO GLOBAL* was written for parents to do with their own children, but it can be easily adapted to work in a co-operative setting as well.

Doing *GO GLOBAL* in a co-op environment can be twice the fun with half the work! A co-op can provide friends for you and your children and a richer learning experience for all. It provides accountability and incentive to stay the course. You get to split the teaching responsibilities and even split the mess! If you want to join up with another family or two (or more), here is the low-down on how to make that happen.

FIND YOUR PARTNERS

Look for other homeschoolers who have children that are similar in age where both the adults and the children enjoy one another. When exploring the idea of coming together to do some of the learning as a co-op it is helpful to discuss your educational goals for the co-op. Is it primarily for social interaction? Is it going to be more academically rigorous or somewhere in between? Will you meet to do some activities to intro a section or meet at the end of the week on the assumption that everyone is familiar with the topic already?

Think about the ideal number of families. When co-oping with only one or two other families there is plenty of room for flexibility and personalization. Crowd control is less of a concern and children tend to learn more in smaller groups. While you lose some of that flexibility when the group is larger, some prefer to co-op with several families to increase social interaction and reduce an individual mom's preparation time. If the group is larger, however, you will want to consider breaking up into smaller groups—perhaps a younger and an older group. Remember to be flexible with one another and communicate regularly as you figure out what will work best for your group!

PLAN THE CO-OP

You will want to meet together and discuss how often you want to meet. Weekly, twice a week, every other week? Does a morning or afternoon time work best?

You can just assign one day's worth of activities to co-op day, such as day 4 if you are meeting on a Thursday or Friday. If you are wanting to consolidate all of the mess, you can just forgo any craft projects for co-op day. Dramatization activities also lend themselves well to doing as a group! When you get together, lay out a schedule of your year, including who will teach what and where you will meet. You might even want to schedule some fun field trips for the "Take a Break" weeks!

HAVE FUN

Meeting together with other homeschool families can be such a rewarding experience. We have found that not only do the kids benefit from interaction with other kids, but that as a mother and teacher, you will learn so much from watching other moms in action.

ACKNOWLEDGEMENTS

Thank you to our children who led us into this teaching and curriculum development adventure. Learning with our own children is enjoyable and enriching intellectually, emotionally, and spiritually. Heather, Bethany, and Evie this work is dedicated to you! Alexander, Keegan, Trey, and Greta, this work is dedicated to you!

Thank you to the kids: Alexander, Keegan, Trey, Greta, Josias, Elisha, Evangeline, Keith, Abraham, and the babes Joy and Isaiah for being our practice children for many of the books and activities in this curriculum. Their reactions and enthusiasm kept us going.

Thanks to our husbands who believe in us and don't think we are wasting our time spending hours, and days, and weeks, and months reading children's books and talking about education, children and learning.

Thanks to the sisters: Evie for the input and encouragement while putting this all together. Bethany for the brilliant editing, photography, and academic challenges.

Thanks to our friends who helped: Katie Kruger for your amazing illustrations; Cindy Duell for your editing expertise; Melanie Young and Israel Wayne for your gracious and generous counsel; Rachel McInturff, Aubrey Lyts Celaya, Mark Converti, and Tyler Ardiles for your foreign language support; Melinda Martin for your publishing and design guidance; Sam Pagel for your brilliant video skills; Savanna Kutz for your photography, and Dennis and Chris Miller and ArtMil for your lovely design and layout of the GO GLOBAL game.

Thanks be to God and His Son, Jesus Christ, from whom all blessings flow.

Made in the USA
Middletown, DE
18 June 2023

32318585R00146